ADVANCE PRA

Gothic Perspectives on the American Experience

"*Gothic Perspectives on the American Experience* is a brilliant and highly individual work of cultural criticism seen through the lens of the Gothic imagination.... It is a timely and absorbing historical narrative for those who would pursue the American dream in turbulent and troubling times."

John F. Strauss, Professor, Luther College, Iowa

"In reading this book, I was reminded of issues, personalities, and ideas that I had not thought about for many years. Gregory G. Pepetone's book not only made me think about them again, it convinced me of their contemporary relevance. As one who teaches a college-level course in politics and the arts, I found this book insightful as well as fascinating—an informative and scholarly resource that promises to be an effective teaching tool."

Alan Weinberg, Professor, Columbia College, North Carolina

"At my initial reading of *Gothic Perspectives on the American Experience*, I found that I could not put the book down. I was drawn into Gregory G. Pepetone's compelling and thought-provoking treatment of events and experiences that have shaped our country as well as my own personal life and thoughts. I heartily recommend this book to anyone interested in exploring their own perspective on the American experience."

Michael Rhodes, Producer and Director

"In this book, Gregory G. Pepetone has offered a fresh lens through which to view late-twentieth-century national life in the United States. Combining intuitive and intriguing observations on past events with a challenging glimpse into the shadow side of our country, Pepetone has managed to create the ideal history book—one that enlightens while simultaneously leading to deeper exploration. This book is well worth reading not simply once, but many times over."

C. K. Robertson, Author and Consultant

"Gregory G. Pepetone is providing interrelated scholarly, pedagogical, and artistic contributions to interdisciplinary studies that are of national significance."

William H. Newell, Director, Institute of Integrative Studies, Miami University

GOTHIC PERSPECTIVES
ON THE AMERICAN EXPERIENCE

PETER LANG
New York • Washington, D.C./Baltimore • Bern
Frankfurt am Main • Berlin • Brussels • Vienna • Oxford

Gregory G. Pepetone

GOTHIC PERSPECTIVES
ON THE AMERICAN EXPERIENCE

PETER LANG
New York • Washington, D.C./Baltimore • Bern
Frankfurt am Main • Berlin • Brussels • Vienna • Oxford

LIBRARY OF CONGRESS CATALOGING-IN-PUBLICATION DATA

Pepetone, Gregory G.
Gothic perspectives on the American experience / Gregory G. Pepetone.
p. cm.
Includes bibliographical references and index.
1. American literature—History and criticism. 2. Gothic revival (Literature)—
United States. 3. National characteristics, American, in literature.
4. Subversive activities—United States. 5. Popular culture—
United States. 6. United States—Civilization.
7. Conspiracies—United States. I. Title.
PS374.G68 P47   810.9′11—dc21   2001050396
ISBN 0-8204-5763-9

DIE DEUTSCHE BIBLIOTHEK-CIP-EINHEITSAUFNAHME

Pepetone, Gregory G.:
Gothic perspectives on the American experience / Gregory G. Pepetone.
–New York; Washington, D.C./Baltimore; Bern;
Frankfurt am Main; Berlin; Brussels; Vienna; Oxford: Lang.
ISBN 0-8204-5763-9

Cover photo by Justin Kasulka
Cover design by Joni Holst

The paper in this book meets the guidelines for permanence and durability
of the Committee on Production Guidelines for Book Longevity
of the Council of Library Resources.

© 2003 Peter Lang Publishing, Inc., New York
275 Seventh Avenue, 28th Floor, New York, NY 10001
www.peterlangusa.com

Printed in the United States of America

✧ TABLE OF CONTENTS

✧ ACKNOWLEDGMENTS

I would like to begin by thanking my family, whose patience, assistance, and willingness to serve as a sounding board are greatly appreciated. Over the years, I have collaborated closely with Professor Robert Viau in developing a team-taught course dealing with the Gothic imagination. Inevitably, many of the ideas expressed in this book arose in connection with that valued collaboration. I also owe a special debt of gratitude to the Rev. Dr. C. K. Robertson whose generosity of spirit and practical help made this project possible in the first place. Michael Rhodes, gifted Hollywood producer of *Romero* and the *Spirit of America* educational film clips series, took the time and trouble to read my work and offer encouragement to a virtual stranger, an act of kindness for which I am sincerely grateful. I would also like to express my appreciation to my primary editor, Ms. Heidi Burns, for her professional expertise and to Dr. Richard Green, Chair of the Music Department and Dr. Anne Gormly, Vice President of Georgia College and State University, for granting the necessary release time from routine teaching assignments to accomplish my task. A special "thank you" goes to friends and colleagues such as Mark Porter, John Strauss, Bob Wilson, and Alan Weinberg for taking the time to read my work and respond to it. Finally, I wish to thank my mother, Edith Corry, for having communicated her abiding faith in the authentic American dream.

Preface

This book deals with the shadow side of American history as expressed in Gothic arts, especially literature and film. Our nation's Gothic artists offer a countercultural perspective on the American experience, an alternative to consensus understandings that are dangerously one-sided and self-congratulatory. Ultimately, however, they offer a positive definition of a nation that too often defines itself negatively, i.e., according to what it stands *against* rather than *for*—a nation that sees itself in relation to its enemies rather than its ideals. Consequently, this book explores ways in which the Gothic imagination seeks to achieve a more balanced perspective by subverting historically and philosophically inauthentic versions of the American dream. In the process, it will seek to remind us of the authentic standard that serves as our guidepost.

A brief word concerning the editorial, at times frankly subjective, tone of this text: According to Sebastian Haffner, "Historical events have varying degrees of intensity. Some may fail to impinge on the central, most personal part of a person's life. Others can wreak such havoc there is nothing left standing. The usual way in which history is written fails to reveal this....I believe history is misunderstood if this [subjective] aspect is forgotten (and it usually is forgotten)" (Haffner 7). A fundamental tenet of the Gothic mind-set holds that valid history draws upon personal insight as well as seasoned scholarship. According to this tenet, the carefully cultivated tone of intellectual and emotional neutrality characteristic of standard academic prose, i.e., its alleged objectivity, is neither a touchstone of sound reasoning nor a guarantee of impartiality. On the contrary, a passionate, if provisional commitment to a well defined point of view is, in part, what distinguishes the Gothic imagination from alternative modes of perception. It follows that any textbook on this particular subject that seeks to avoid the onus of subjectivity by shirking such a commitment is inconsistent with its own fundamental tenets. *Gothic Perspectives on the American Experience* is both a history of how and why the political Gothic evolved in our culture and a platform for my own passionately, but provisionally, held views as to its contemporary significance.

This textbook is suitable for a variety of personal and academic purposes. First, it is a self-study program, an introduction to American Gothic arts for leisure reading and viewing. Second, it is serviceable as a supplemental text in connection with a wide range of humanities courses such as The Fine Arts in Civilization, American Cultural and Political History, American Literature, Pop Culture Studies, and Special Interdisciplinary Topics (e.g., Utopias and Dystopias, Sociology of the Arts, Psychology of the Creative Process, Civics, Current Events, The 1960s in America, and so forth). Finally, *Gothic Perspectives on the American Experience* is designed as a primary text for a one-semester undergraduate level course dealing with the Gothic imagination as it applies to America's political history.

Essentially, this book is organized around a small cluster of historical, mythological, psychological, and literary concepts: Chapter 1 defines the Gothic imagination and discusses its significance in relation to other models of reality that have shaped our political and cultural identity. Chapter 2 explores the republicanism, i.e., the democratic idealism, of Thomas Jefferson as definitive of the American experience and considers the Gothic subversion of Jefferson's agenda as expressed in the writings of Gothic novelist Charles Brockden Brown. Chapter 3 examines the dystopian-utopian dialectic in nineteenth-century literature and relates that dialectic to previous and subsequent political developments, especially the devastation and upheaval of the Civil War. Chapter 4 considers America's emergence upon the stage of international affairs in the first half of the twentieth century and how demographic and other cultural changes influenced the dialectic between utopianism and dystopianism. Chapter 5 examines the Gothic imagination in relation to the Cold War era from the end of WWII through the 1960s and its relevance to America's present Gothic dilemmas.

1 Introduction: Preliminary Issues

Twentieth-century film has furnished a small number of mythological concepts and Gothic icons that are symbolic types of the social and political pathologies to which powerful nation states are prone: The werewolf, for instance, a graphic representation of the primitive beast within, is an obvious symbol of aggression and predation. Similarly, the vampire, the zombie, the robot, and the mummy are pop culture types of T.S. Eliot's straw man, alive to outward appearance but dead within (though some modern versions of the automaton, as in Spielberg's film *A.I.*, are noticeably more human than the humans they are designed to serve). The Frankenstein monster, itself a subset of Faustian man, is an enduring symbol of science and technology run amok. Jekyll and Hyde are *doppelgangers,* or mirror images, of the discarded self, the shadow side of a collective national psyche that we vainly seek to deny. Throughout this study, each of these archetypes from Gothic mythology will be invoked as a shorthand for social and political forces that are unleashed when the individualistic and civic ideals that constitute the authentic American dream are sacrificed to other agendas.

Along with this Gothic typology, the close historical connection between political strife and the emergence of the Gothic is another unifying concept that will govern much of this discussion. In our two hundred year plus history, American culture has been profoundly influenced by three revolutionary upheavals and two international conflicts: the War of Independence, the Civil War, the Cold War, and the two world wars with Germany, and in the case of World War II, Italy and later Japan, that punctuated the first half of the previous century. Each of these conflicts served as a catalyst for the Gothic imagination because each provoked the kind of national identity crisis, pervasive social anxiety, and deep psychological denial for which Gothic arts have always provided a cultural outlet.

A third unifying concept is the discrepancy between official, or consensus, versions of American history and alternative interpretations. Sophocles' *Oedipus Rex,* Shakespeare's *Hamlet,* Walpole's *The Castle of Otranto,* and Oliver Stone's cinematic conspiracy narratives *JFK* and

Nixon are all broad Gothic explorations of hidden history. As Hamlet says at the conclusion of Act I, Scene two "Foul deeds will rise, though all the earth o'erwhelm them to men's eyes." The issue at hand is not historical revision in the commonly accepted sense. From the standpoint of the Gothic imagination, it is the official lies and cover stories with which Gothic villains seek to cloak their foul deeds that are revisionist, not the narratives that expose their deceptions.

Gothic perspectives on the American experience fit into a wider cultural context that is best understood as an ongoing conversation, or *dialectical process.* An examination of this process comprises a fourth unifying concept. The participants in this cultural conversation represent two distinctly different orientations to life that may be broadly categorized as classicism and romanticism. These all-encompassing categories of thought and feeling relate to one another as thesis to antithesis. They therefore represent antagonistic but complementary options. Broadly speaking, classicism stands for rational restraint and order, whereas romanticism upholds imaginative and emotional abandon. An individual or society that embraces either alternative at the expense of the other is, by definition, unbalanced. Though this Western cultural dichotomy has profoundly shaped the American experience, as I hope to demonstrate, it is seldom explicitly factored into an understanding of our political history. The fourth and final unifying theme of this book is therefore the presentation of the Gothic imagination as a synthesis of classicism and romanticism. Similar to all such syntheses, it constitutes a transcendent dynamic that supercedes both its thesis (classicism) and its antithesis (romanticism). In short, America's finest, most representative Gothic minds advocate a *synergy,* or dynamic equilibrium, between classical and romantic tendencies in the American experience.

When the Gothic imagination presents itself primarily in terms of metaphysical abstractions and broadly based social theories, it represents the *philosophical Gothic.* When it focuses on theories regarding interior and interpersonal conflicts and contradictions, it exemplifies the *psychological Gothic,* and when it deals with perverse power relationships, dialectical inequalities within our system of constitutional checks and balances, hidden histories, and conspiratorial scenarios, it gives expression to the *political Gothic.* Often these three categories overlap. In the popular *X-Files* television series, for instance, the imaginative romanticism of agent Fox Mulder and the rigid classicism of agent Dana Scully personify these opposing orientations philosophically as well as psychologically. Primarily, however, philosophical Gothic focuses on narrowly defined conceptions of sanity and madness, i.e., consensus standards of thought and behavior deemed normative or aberrant.

The Newtonian paradigm, a scientific-technological-mechanistic model of reality named after the great seventeenth-century English scientist and mathematician, Sir Isaac Newton, tends to discount input from modes of perception that complement or, perhaps, even transcend rationality, such as intuition, imagination, emotion, inspiration, and revelation. Philosophical Gothic narratives, therefore, seek to correct the excesses, reductions, and omissions of science in its radically classical, i.e., Newtonian, aspect (sometimes referred to as scientism). Needless to say, the greatest scientists, including Newton himself as a younger man, achieved a balanced perspective informed by both imagination and reason, romanticism as well as classicism. Indeed, some modern popularizers of quantum physics such as Paul Davies (*The Mind of God*) or Fred Alan Wolf (*Parallel Universes*) speak a language informed by a Gothic synergy of perspective that pre-twentieth-century scientists would not have understood and latter-day exponents of scientism still vehemently reject. While the philosophical Gothic pertains to wide versus narrow conceptions of reason and reality, psychological Gothic as well as political Gothic are concerned with a sadomasochistic impulse focused on dominance, destruction, and vengeance versus a transcendent potential for cooperation, creativity, and compassion. Psychological Gothic deals with interpersonal manifestations of this conflict whereas political Gothic focuses on its broad national and international implications. Both exist in a dialectical relationship to each other.

The function of the political Gothic is to uncover dystopian elements in our national experience, i.e., elements that contradict America's utopian dream of a just, humane, and open society. Those elements can be unleashed by either a deficiency or an excess of idealism. A deficiency in this regard is apt to replace a greater good, such as the fair distribution of wealth, with a lesser one, such as material prosperity. Excessive idealism, meanwhile, is likely to pursue a greater good, such as the triumph of freedom over totalitarianism, with a single-minded obsession that ultimately sacrifices its own principles to some lesser good, such as political victory over an enemy nation. Excessive idealism turned the Salem judiciary into a witch-hunt; it turned the fanatical defense of democracy against Sino-Soviet communism during the Cold

War into a political witch-hunt, and it turned Dr. Jekyll into Mr. Hyde. Typically, the outcome of either imbalance is a reversal into the opposite that Swiss psychologist C. G. Jung termed *enantiodromia*.

Such a reversal derives from a tendency to be consumed by the very evil one most deplores, a tendency that results from a denial of the potential for such evil within ourselves. Jung called this *archetypal* potential for evil the *Shadow*. The concomitant of denial, according to Jung, is *projection,* i.e., the tendency to project one's own undesirable traits, one's shadow side, onto a scapegoat that then becomes the enemy and standard against which one's self, race, or nation is defined. The obvious flaw in this insidious form of self-deception is that the "enemy" is, in reality, an aspect of ourselves. By seeking its annihilation, we unknowingly pursue a course that leads inevitably to our own destruction. From the perspective of the political-Gothic imagination, however, this self-destructive tendency and its creative counterpart, when properly aligned, constitute a *synergistic balance* in the American experience. For a more elaborate explanation of the Jungian terminology italicized above see Edward C. Whitmont, *The Symbolic Quest: Basic Concepts of Analytical Psychology.*

Gothic Perspectives on the American Experience will argue that, at its best, the Gothic imagination is motivated by an uncompromising quest for synergistic balance, a quest that is essential to our sense of individual and collective well-being. Psychologically, the twin poles of this dialectical balance are pessimism and optimism. Politically, they are dystopianism and utopianism. Philosophically, they are romanticism and classicism. Ultimately, the Gothic imagination seeks to reconcile these dialectical extremes, much as differences between agents Mulder and Scully are reconciled in Chris Carter's televised saga of the paranormal. Indeed, dialectical pairings of the sort personified by agents Mulder and Scully are a commonplace of political Gothic storytelling. A mutual desire on the part of these dialectically paired characters to achieve psychosocial synthesis through constructive dialogue is, in part, what defines them as Gothic heroes. Synergy, understood as a dynamic equilibrium in which negative and positive impulses together yield an awareness that neither would be capable of yielding alone, remains the goal, regardless of which category of the Gothic imagination (philosophical, psychological, or political) predominates. Throughout our nation's history the quest to reconcile classicism with romanticism, optimism with pessimism, and utopianism with dystopianism has been thwarted by a conception of the American dream that shuns synthesis in pursuit of quite different philosophical and political objectives. I refer to this alternative version of the American dream as *covert fascism.*

A fifth unifying concept of this book is that our Gothic arts share a common vision, articulated at the nation's founding, of what defines the authentic American dream, an ideal that has been clouded by an unwarranted assumption. According to this assumption, democracy and capitalism are engines of social progress that necessarily run on parallel tracks toward a common destination. The Gothic imagination suggests that, on the contrary, American history is largely a chronicle of the ways in which capitalism, allied with covert fascism, has contradicted and undermined democracy. Indeed, Gothic utopianism invites us to compare democracy as it is with democracy as it should be, whereas Gothic dystopianism alerts us to contradictions of the sort posed by unrestrained capitalism that threatens to transform the authentic American dream into a nightmare of corporate greed, cultural mediocrity, and predatory nationalism.

As regards the use of the adjective *authentic* with reference to Federalist conceptions of America, it is my belief that adjectives such as "dead," white," male," and "European," are not proscriptive. They in no way diminish the political wisdom and visionary genius of the Founding Fathers, or our indebtedness to them. Thomas Jefferson's understanding of an enlightened democracy will therefore be presented as definitive of the authentic American dream. That is not to say his vision of a just, humane, and open society was original, in the sense of being historically unprecedented. Nor was it complete, in the sense of being perfectly realized. Moreover, my respect for Jefferson and the others who assisted at the birthing of our nation is not premised on hero-worship (it should go without saying that the Founding Fathers were clay-footed mortals like the rest of us, not infallible demigods). The authenticity I attribute to their perspective derives from the fundamental nature of the American experiment itself. That experiment is about balancing individual freedoms against civic obligations, majority rule against minority rights, nationalistic claims of tribal identity and custom against universal claims of human brother-and-sisterhood, a self-centered, competitive drive toward economic increase against values that foster a sense of mutual responsibility, and the undoubted advantages of scientific, technological, and administrative efficiency against the equally important benefits of intellectual, ethical, and aesthetic cultivation.

While virtually all the social architects of the American experiment advocated just such a balance, in many ways Jefferson dramatized the difficult quest to attain it with particular vividness. He was a philosopher as well as a farmer, a political theorist as well as an effective administrator, a musician as well as a botanical scientist, an educator as well as a legislator, and a literary stylist as well as a soldier. Within his own multifaceted psyche, Jefferson personified America's dystopian-utopian predilections, and in his complex personal and civic response to this dialectic, he foreshadowed America's Gothic dilemma as well as the potential for transcendence latent within the authentic American dream. In their private and public documents, as in their administrative decisions, Jefferson and other Founding Fathers provided a compelling, if unfinished, picture of what such an experiment in social equilibrium might look like and how it might best be achieved. Today's consensus in favor of unity, tolerance, affluence, diversity, security, and equality is commendable in that, depending on how they are defined and applied, these values are valid components of what is commonly referred to as the American dream. Viewed separately, however, each one of them is contingent, not absolute, in its value. To the extent that they combine to undermine the precarious political and philosophical balances that define an enlightened democracy, such values become, in their misapplication, undemocratic or even antidemocratic.

In searching for an intellectual compass with which to navigate the maze of self-conceptions currently vying for our loyalty, twenty-first-century Americans may well wish to re-examine, from a fresh perspective, i.e., a Gothic perspective, the guidelines set forth in our foundational documents, such as *The Declaration of Independence,* the *Constitution,* and the *Bill of Rights*—guidelines that have to do with equality before the law, the limitations of governmental power, and the responsibilities imposed by individual freedom. Those guidelines are authentic in that they embody one of the earliest, most lucid expositions of America's political and philosophical aspirations. Moreover, they provide a national identity, a theoretical standard against which our nation's Gothic artists have assessed a conception of the American experience that questions the political and philosophical aspirations of the founding. This alternative conception, best understood as a social-democratic variation on a democratic theme, constitutes a discordant element in our national life that has been in competition with the authentic American dream for as long as that dream has been in existence. Arguably, this alternative standard defines the political *status quo* of early twenty-first-century America.

On a global scale, American covert fascism substitutes values endorsed at the founding for a quite different set of its own. For instance, it substitutes paternalism, global economic feudalism, and racism for human equality, economic self-determination, and national sovereignty. Moreover, it promotes an egalitarian cultural mediocrity over an elitism that was intended to insure equality of opportunity as a means of discovering and nurturing individual excellence. A theocratic ideal based on an eccentric and questionable brand of "Christian" morality is substituted for the spirit of tolerance implicit in Jeffersonian formulations concerning church and state. A tribal nationalism replaces universal human rights. Rule by an economic elite that favors indiscriminate consumption, environmental depredation, and ruthless competition (plutocracy) takes precedence over an economic ethic that places the public welfare ahead of private and corporate gain (Martin Luther King's "beloved community"). The means to an end (technology) usurps the end itself (liberty). Finally, this undemocratic standard substitutes covert military and diplomatic action (cryptocracy, i.e., rule by secrecy) for statesmanship supported by informed public debate, an open political process, and uncompromising adherence to the rule of law (constitutional democracy).

In short, Gothic perspectives on the American experience impugn a standard in our national life that is easier to reconcile with the tenets of Hitler and Mussolini than with those of Thomas Jefferson and John Adams. Frankly speaking, this covertly fascist dream of America is not merely at odds with the authentic American dream, i.e., the sort of psychosocial synergy envisioned by the founders, it is discordant with any conception of democracy attuned to what historian Richard Hofstadter refers to as "the Anglo-American ethos of popular political action (Hofstadter 183)." It signals a dangerous Jekyll and Hyde duality in our political psyche, a fissure that widens periodically, threatening to swallow our inalienable human rights, privileges, and freedoms. As we shall see, this "monstrous" duality and the competition it has spawned between irreconcilable conceptions of the American dream is the subject matter of American Gothic arts.

America's political Gothic artists, whether their vision is dystopian or utopian, pessimistic or optimistic, are ultimately informed by the strictures of democratic idealism and Federalist-era republicanism that define the authentic American dream. As stated above, those strictures stand in sharp contrast to a loosely related cluster of social and ethical values, manifested throughout our history, that constitute an ideology akin to twentieth-century fascism. Though associated with German and Italian political movements in the 1930s and 1940s, fascist ideology is a belief system whose historical precedents include Malthusian economics, Manifest Destiny, "the white man's burden," social democracy, philosophical nihilism, and cultural Darwinism. These conceptions were, and are, incompatible with any historically or philosophically justifiable formulation of America's experiment in enlightened participatory government.

Thus, *Gothic Perspectives on the American Experience* presents our nation's history, communicated through its arts, as an unfolding narrative whose dark plot centers on a common motif, that of the *doppelgänger* or split personality. Technically, this creature from German folklore is a spectral replica rather than a distinct alter ego, but in popular usage the term often signifies a sinister dualism rather than an exact mirror image. The dualistic plot of America's Gothic history involves a conflict between antagonistic perceptions of the American experiment. Throughout our history, these incompatible versions of the American dream have co-existed uneasily within our national consciousness, occasionally erupting into open confrontation. One is a vision of limited personal freedom in pursuit of educational and cultural excellence facilitated by governmental activism. The other is a dream of unlimited economic freedom in pursuit of private wealth and corporate power frustrated by governmental interference. In this latter cultural-Darwinist version of the American dream, federal authority is seen as an indispensable, if silent, partner to business interests abroad and as a thoroughly meddlesome impediment to those same interests at home. Accordingly, the entrepreneurial community thinks itself entitled to ask what the federal government can do to protect its corporate investments abroad with legislation and military might, or so it would appear. However, this same community acknowledges no corresponding obligation to uphold democratic standards of social justice in the workplace or civic participation and ethical restraint in the culture at large. Its conception of the American dream is summarized by Calvin Coolidge's well-known dictum "The business of America is business." Its uncivic-minded mantra is concisely expressed by Gordon Gekko, the unscrupulous corporate tycoon in Oliver Stone's cinematic exposé of

Ronald Reagan's America, *Wall Street:* "Greed, for want of a better word, is good." The Jeffersonian alternative to this self-serving distortion of the authentic American dream enjoins us to place the welfare of the community ahead of individual ambition. Its motto is "Ask not what your country can do for you."

One of the supreme ironies of American history is that pro-business propaganda has been successful in convincing many of us for a long period of time that the capitalist dream and the American dream are identical. The cornerstone of the capitalist creed preached and practiced by men like Henry Ford, who was a pronounced anti-Semite and an outspoken proponent of Hitler's Nazi experiment (see Neil Baldwin's *Henry Ford and the Jews: The Mass Production of Hate*), contends that what is good for business is good for America. On the contrary, what is good for the Henry Fords of our culture, according to its utopian visionaries and dystopian artists alike, is often very bad indeed for America and vice versa. One of the much needed benefits to be anticipated from our Pyrrhic victories over the principle twentieth-century totalitarianisms, Nazism and Soviet Communism, may well be a twenty-first century freedom to distinguish American patriotism from tribal loyalty and American democracy from corporate capitalism without fear of being misunderstood. Only when such freedom is accorded will it be possible to assess the extent to which capitalism has conspired against democracy.

Undoubtedly, the most controversial feature of this work is the attention it lavishes on conspiracy theories of one sort or another—a sixth unifying concept—especially those pertaining to the untimely death of President Kennedy. For the most part, the academic community and the mainstream media have shunned unofficial inquiries into the Kennedy killing, most of which pursue a conspiratorial alternative to the lone assassin theory promoted in the Warren Commission's findings. Indeed, conspiracy is arguably one of the few taboos still in force among historians, political scientists, criminologists, and practitioners of journalism. From the perspective of the Gothic imagination, that is precisely why it merits our attention. In this regard, the iconoclasm and subjectivity of the New Left historians and the triumphalism and studied objectivity of old left-wing and right-wing historians of the 1940s and 1950s is a distinction without a difference. Both schools of thought profess an equal disdain for conspiracy theories that see Kennedy's death as a defining moment—a hideous deformity rather than an unfortunate *class paranoia and conspiracy theory* [handwritten annotation]

blemish on the face of American history. To paraphrase Chesterton, however, one suspects that such theories have not been tried and found wanting, but that they have been found ideologically distasteful and left untried. My hunch is that a great many academics and journalists are, at best, superficially acquainted with assassination research literature. The Gothic imagination has always served as a venue for protest against expressions of consensus reality, particularly those that suggest the existence of hidden or alternative histories. Consequently, the red threads of conspiracy and denial have been closely woven into the very fabric of European and American Gothic arts.

In point of fact, the conspiratorial narratives of Charles Brockden Brown, the founding father of American Gothic storytelling, and those of its more recent exponents, such as Chris Carter, Don DeLillo and Oliver Stone, can be said to frame the American experience. Brown's novels expose discrepancies between America's Enlightenment self-conception and its social practice during the Federalist era. In a similar manner, modern literary and cinematic exponents of the Gothic frequently track the ascendancy of cryptocracy over democracy in America to a tragic conflict between the centrist agenda of JFK (a sincere, if deeply flawed, proponent of the authentic American dream) and the covertly fascist agenda of a Cold War establishment that was hostile to his outlook.

According to the Gothic mythology of this alternative to consensus history, the United States intelligence community was initially stitched together from remnants of a Nazi intelligence apparatus, the Gehlen Organization, to address the threat of communism (see chapter 5). Its primary mandate was to engage in covert activities, or "black operations," not simple intelligence gathering, as its adherents claim. The CIA, for example, in addition to its fascist mentors, quickly assimilated new, equally undemocratic elements, e.g., organized crime lords, ultraconservative oil barons, disaffected Cuban counterrevolutionaries, and rabid anti-communists, thereby mutating into an uncontrollable projection of Cold War paranoia. Historically speaking, it thus became "an American Gestapo," to cite President Truman's revealing characterization (*Conspiracies*, A&E Home Video, 1996).

Metaphorically speaking, the anti-communist hysteria of this country's power structures summoned into existence a political Frankenstein, a monster from the id, i.e., the shadow side of America's collective psyche. Indeed, the intelligence community is commonly referred to as a "shadow government." Comparable to the *doppelgängers* of German folklore (the most famous being *Peter Schlemihl,* Chamisso's protagonist who loses his shadow with disastrous consequences), it both mirrors and inverts the values and practices of its other and better self, distorting the ideals of constitutional democracy into a grotesque, covertly fascist parody of the American dream. Since 1947, this protean political entity has metastasized into a wide array of formal and informal power structures and paralegal processes. These structures and processes have arguably come to outweigh democratically sanctioned alternatives, thereby creating a Gothic imbalance within a supposedly open, law-abiding culture that often seems dysfunctional in relation to the authentic American dream, more a commercially driven dystopia than a republican utopia mindful of its own ideals. According to its Gothic detractors, shadow governments throughout the 1950s and 1960s frequently set rather than served the agendas of a comparatively impotent and impoverished federal government, on occasion substituting bullets for ballots, promoting dictatorial regimes favorable to America's corporate elite, and operating beyond the effective control of federal oversight.

As we will see, Oliver Stone's countercultural mythology draws heavily on the conventions of broad Gothic literature. His dark narratives of subversion contend that the de facto fascist implications of America's "shadow government" were recognized and unsuccessfully challenged by Kennedy at the height of the Cold War era, that the ideological shift to the right in America's political center of gravity subsequent to Kennedy's assassination was anticipated by those who engineered this crime, and that the legitimacy of the democratic electoral process was seriously injured, if not mortally wounded, by our failure to discover and punish its perpetrators. Today's guardians of intellectual consensus, those who live in denial of speculation that threatens entrenched attitudes concerning Cold War and post–Cold War America, are not just skeptical but frankly contemptuous of such theories, dismissing them as wild, damaging, or revisionist. A residual distaste for right wing hysteria over unreal Jewish and communist conspiracies propagated in the first half of the twentieth century no doubt enters into their response. During that era, only fascists and anti-communist extremists of the "better-dead-than-red" variety lent credence to such theories. Ironically, this very circumstance may have been instrumental in forming a climate of opinion that not only led to real right-wing conspiracies, but prompted moderates and leftists to filter out perceptions that would tend to substantiate their existence.

Ultimately, however, resistance to conspiratorial interpretations of history is perhaps rooted in deep-seated objections that have more to do with style than substance. From the perspective of those wedded to the Newtonian paradigm, the Gothic imagination is tainted at its source by sensationalism, hyperbole, and emotionalism, attributes that offend rationalist sensibilities. So many of those who belong to professions that shape and/or reflect consensus opinion, e.g., journalists, academics, and lawyers, see themselves as emotionally detached observers, not subjective participants in the events to which they respond. Accordingly, they see history and politics as complex social systems, i.e., Newtonian machines, governed by predictable laws of cause and effect. Such systems, they contend, are immune to the whimsical influences implicit in many, though by no means all, conspiracy scenarios. In effect, their devotion to an epistemological theory transforms the living tissue of history into something as lifeless and impersonal as the archetypal monsters that stalk the pages of Gothic literature.

College professors do not teach politics, they teach political science. Moreover, the "-o-l-o-g-y" Greek suffix that attaches to many people-oriented academic disciplines such as psych*ology* and soci*ology* suggests their allegiance to scientific procedures and models of reality. Although other humanistic disciplines that once ranged freely across the cultural landscape have not, like political studies, been explicitly reduced to the status of adjectives, implicitly many of those who practice them seem to approach their subjects as lab-coated technicians mesmerized by the narrow standards of scientism that define the Newtonian paradigm. However, the vehemence with which social scientists uphold the current consensus (a vehemence bordering on the irrational) suggests an anxious determination on their part. This characterization pertains not only to individuals who support that consensus. It pertains equally to those who do not, but who nevertheless scoff at Gothic mythologies regarding its genesis. Some prominent and otherwise admirable members of the assassination research community itself have scoffed the loudest.

From time to time, one also encounters individuals who remain open to conspiratorial speculations, but who would strip them of their subversive content. From the perspective of the Gothic imagination, the unlitigated murder of an American president is nothing less than a treasonous stab at the very heart of the authentic American dream. However, from the perspective commended by today's pervasive mood of cynicism, it is merely an instance of routine political corruption. The young, in whom the spirit of truth marches on, according to Oliver Stone, often seem as blasé as their elders in this regard. Having been raised in a postmodern culture dismissive of history, acclimated to violence (the cinematic variety, at least), and distrustful of authority, many undergraduates appear to be closet nihilists with regard to the American political process in general and the atrocities of the 1960s in particular. Never having acquired the civic conscience appropriate to citizens, they often seem to exhibit an apathy appropriate to slaves. Sadly, that is perhaps what they are, and what the rest of us have become. The impassioned, time-haunted narratives of our modern Gothic artists pose a challenge to the apparent complacence of "Gen-X." They are no less challenging, however, to the seasoned acceptance of a Cold War generation jaded by the barrage of political trauma that characterized the 1960s. Those narratives remind us that the truth we are most intent on denying is occasionally the truth we are most in need of discovering. In doing so, they necessarily impugn the patriotism and integrity of those who, like King Claudius in *Hamlet,* would have us shed prematurely our stubborn and unprevailing woe.

Some of the films discussed in this book will already be familiar to most readers. Those that are not can be rented or, ideally, added to permanent university library collections. Emmy-award-winning producer Michael Rhodes has produced a series of filmstrips for educational use, *The Spirit of America* series, that raise many of the ethical issues broached in this text (see the combined bibliography/filmography at the back of this volume). Apropos the literature cited, most of the authors and quite a few of the shorter pieces discussed, are anthologized in *American Gothic Tales,* edited and introduced by Joyce Carol Oates. In the following pages, I have cited this anthology whenever possible (see chapter 3). When it has not been possible to do so, I have selected stories that are readily available otherwise. Similarly, the longer works discussed here are easily obtainable. Finally, a word about the selection criteria used for materials covered in this volume: No book of comparable scope can hope to be either thorough or comprehensive, particularly not one that is interdisciplinary in nature. My choice of materials was dictated by two overriding considerations, availability and aptness to the theme on which I determined to focus, i.e., the political Gothic imagination in American culture. On the assumption that authors write best about what they know and love, whenever possible I selected artists and works that have special meaning for me. That other, and perhaps better, choices might have been made is a proposition I am not at all inclined to dispute.

Although this book focuses specifically on political expressions of the Gothic imagination, the omnipresence of the Gothic, in all of its manifestations, is self-evident. Television programs such as *The X-Files* command a large audience. Science fiction, a subset of the Gothic, has its own channel. The supernatural has become an accepted theme on day-time soap operas. Apropos the undead, perhaps the most popular and stylish example of what might be termed adolescent Gothic is Joss Whedon's *Buffy the Vampire Slayer* series. Such obvious examples do not take into account the vast amount of Gothic entertainment premised on crime and disaster, referred to collectively as "reality television."

Instances of Gothic cinema, everything from slasher films and supernatural thrillers to burlesque-Gothic parodies such as Mel Brooks's *Young Frankenstein,* are similarly numerous, as a visit to the nearest Blockbuster video rental or an attentive eye to any local motion picture marquee will attest. Perhaps half the inventory of chain bookstores such as Waldenbooks or B. Dalton is devoted to horror, fantasy, science fiction, and detective fiction, all subcategories of the Gothic. Moreover, these subsets, once again, do not account for secular or religious apocalyptic literature, supernatural romance, kiddy-Gothic such as the sensationally popular *Harry Potter,* works dealing with serial killers, cannibalism, and other manifestations of abnormal psychology, nor do they account for literary classics such as Mary Shelley's *Frankenstein* and Bram Stoker's *Dracula.* Novels such as Charlotte Brontë's *Jane Eyre* or Mark Twain's *Huckleberry Finn* also make ample use of Gothic conventions, though such works may not immediately come to mind as examples of Gothic literature. Finally, one should not underestimate the Gothic content of network television news broadcasts. "Perhaps the most influential apocalyptic-Gothic production in the 1990s American culture," writes Gothic cultural historian Mark Edmundson, "is nothing other than the evening news....TV news gives more than 50 percent of its air-time, on average, to covering crime and disaster" (Edmundson 30).

Despite its unprecedented popularity, the term *Gothic* is problematic in academic circles. As in the case of *romantic,* a genre designation with which it is closely allied, *Gothic* is a label that is protean in its definition and controversial in its historical origin. Indeed, it is defined differently within different disciplines. To art historians, Gothic signifies medieval cathedrals and illuminated manuscripts. To students of literature, it signifies a late eighteenth- and nineteenth-century genre that has to do mostly with "things that go bump in the night." For musicians, the term hardly exists, except in reference to certain items of nineteenth-century program music inspired by motifs borrowed from Gothic literature, such as Saint-Saëns's *Dance Macabre*. Indeed, the very etymology of the term *Gothic* is in dispute. The academically accepted origin of *Gothic* as a genre designation is that the term was originally applied to the ecclesiastical architecture of the Middle Ages by Renaissance art critics who found it as crude and objectionable as the Goths who had destroyed ancient Rome. An alternative, but largely unaccepted, etymology holds that Gothic is a corruption of the Greek *goetik,* meaning something magical. According to this interpretation, the comparatively sudden, unprecedented engineering marvels of great medieval structures such as Chartres were made possible by a secret body of knowledge discovered in the Holy Lands. The Knights Templar, a quasi-military religious order, allegedly uncovered the fabled treasure of King Solomon while serving in the Holy Lands during one of the early Crusades. The esoteric knowledge with which they returned to Europe, and which formed the basis of a magically new and complex style of architecture, was a part of that treasure (Marrs 287).

European Gothic in literature is customarily conceived of as a set of conventional themes, moods, settings, plot types, and characters. The following is a fairly comprehensive catalogue of Gothic elements: darkness, pain, fear, disorientation, death, supernatural ghosts and monsters, primeval forests, German or Italian castles, dungeons, labyrinths, vortices, violence, concealed documents, dreams, omens, portents, torrents and tempests, lunar imagery, fairies and other elemental spirits, alienation, plots that revolve around hidden histories, mistaken or concealed identities or conspiratorial agendas, and stock characters that include a hero-villain and a pristine heroine. Gothic hero-villains are proud, sardonic, world weary, strong but sensitive, alienated, and conversant with alternate realities. Gothic heroines are exceptionally noble, vulnerable, and sexually menaced (often by hero-villains who belong to either an authoritarian Catholic church or a tyrannical aristocracy). All these are recognizable constituents of the Gothic. The question raised by such a diverse list is obvious: What do they have in common, and in what sense are they definitive?

It was Victorian essayist and art critic John Ruskin (1819–1900) who supplied the most famous definition of the Gothic. While Ruskin's subject was medieval Gothic architecture, his definition suggests a conception that could be applied equally to other art mediums. In the central chapter of *Stones of Venice,* entitled *The Nature of the Gothic,* he offers the following short list of Gothic elements: savageness, changefulness, naturalism, grotesqueness, rigidity, and redundancy. Drawing upon a chemical analogy, he compares the constituent parts of a mineral to those of the Gothic imagination:

> It is not one or the other of them that can make up the mineral, says but the union of all....So in the various mental characteristics that make up the soul of the Gothic. It is not one or the other that produces it; but their union in certain measures. Each one of them is found in many other architectures beside the Gothic; but Gothic cannot exist where they are not found, or at least, where their place is not in some way supplied. Only there is this great difference between the composition of the mineral and of the architectural style, that if we withdraw one of the elements from the stone, its form is utterly changed, and its existence is destroyed; but if we withdraw one of the elements from the Gothic style, it is only a little less Gothic than it was before. (Ruskin 79)

According to Ruskin's analogy, the essence of the Gothic is preserved even when the sum of its parts is diminished. In other words, just as a soup will preserve its distinctive flavor even when this or that ingredient is added or subtracted, the Gothic flavor of a building, literary text, musical score, painter's canvas, or film is preserved, even though the number and blend of ingredients that characterize Gothic arts vary from one work to the next. By extending this analogy to mediums other than architecture, the "soul of the Gothic" in literature, music, and film can be synthesized into a comparable list of constituent "mental elements" or artistic conventions.

As literary critic Teresa A. Goddu observes, however, "American Gothic depends less on the particular set of conventions it establishes than on those it disrupts" (Goddu 4). Her point is that American artists, in appropriating the ingredients listed in our original Gothic catalogue, were faced with certain inherent difficulties; e.g., no castles, no state-sponsored Catholic church, no tyrannical aristocracy, no venerable tradition of haunted locales, and so forth. American Gothic writers have, therefore, been required to either shift their settings geographically to a more suitable locale or else find indigenous substitutes for the conventions of European Gothic arts. Moreover, American practitioners of the Gothic were faced with another inherent difficulty, namely, how to distinguish the Gothic from other genres that make use of the same constituent elements...as many do.

A narrative genre comprised of stock characters and situations, i.e., interchangeable components in the manner of a literary erector set, not only lays itself open to parody, but inevitably raises doubts as to its authenticity. That is why, for some, the stylized, highly formulaic aspects of Gothic arts summon the twin specters of lexical imprecision and categorical impurity. How, they ask, is the Gothic to be distinguished from the romantic, and how, from such a diverse list of defining elements, can one ever hope to extrapolate criteria for separating Gothic *kitsch* from genuine Gothic art, the merely fashionable from the artistically meaningful? In short, how is one to create a reliable Gothic canon? The issue is concisely stated by Ms. Goddu: "Whether establishing a distinction between Romantic and Gothic or between the popular Gothic and the more serious works it inspired, the critical aim is a clean canon" (Goddu 6).

To its detractors, the Gothic is most definitely an unclean canon comparable to Victor Frankenstein's infamous monster, a foul thing plundered from the rhetorical conventions of other narrative genres and stitched together into a literary hybrid devoid of aesthetic authenticity or merit. Ironically, what these detractors fail to realize is that the very incongruities and conventionalities with which they fault Gothic arts attest to their extraordinary unity of form and content. The structural anomalies embodied by the monsters of Gothic literature and film and the hybrid character of the genre they inhabit exemplify the incongruities of the rational paradigm that gave them birth. Their very makeup subverts the conventionality of a science that divides reality into discrete categories and clearly defined units of perception for the sake of convenience and then treats such arbitrary divisions as inviolable laws of nature. Gothic narratives, in their eclecticism and resistance to easy classification, as well as in the aberrant characteristics of the mythic archetypes that inhabit them, embody the very precepts that they espouse. Moreover, Gothic arts have been uniquely able to bridge the widening gap between "highbrow" and "lowbrow," pop culture and classical culture. In this regard, they are democratic, as attested by the universality of their appeal and by their ability to attract artists ranging from Walter Gibson (the author of *The Shadow* pulp fiction novels), on the lowbrow end of the spectrum, to Shakespeare, and from Mark Snow (the composer of music for the *X-Files*) to Beethoven. Perhaps the explanation lies in the fact that, as with all genuinely mythic creations, Gothic arts seem to well up from an inexhaustible reservoir of shared human thought and feeling, a circumstance that imbues them with a vitality and interest beyond the reach of purely aesthetic considerations. The great twentieth-century Swiss psychoanalyst Carl Gustav Jung termed this reservoir of common experience the *collective unconscious.*

Writing on the philosophy of horror, Noël Carroll comments on three structural principles according to which Gothic monsters are fashioned: fusion, fission, and magnification. "A fusion figure," writes Carroll, "is a composite that unites attributes held to be categorically distinct." Mummies and vampires, for example, are a composite of the living and the dead, categories that are clearly distinguishable in nature. Conversely, a fission figure is one that is either divided in time or multiplied in space. The protagonist in Robert Louis Stevenson's classic tale, *Dr. Jekyll and Mr. Hyde,* must divide his time between good and evil aspects of himself. Similarly, the werewolf is a fission figure who apportions his time sequentially between his animal and human selves. Spatial fission, as distinct from temporal fission, occurs whenever a single character is multiplied into two or more entities that exist concurrently, such as Dorian and his portrait in Oscar Wilde's Gothic masterpiece, *The Picture of Dorian Gray.* In German Gothic narratives, such manifestations are referred to as *doppelgängers* (Carroll 42–52).

Particularly during the age of above-ground nuclear testing, Hollywood made extensive use of "magnification," Carroll's third principle. Throughout the 1950s, cinema's special effects wizards routinely mutated ants, spiders, and grasshoppers into gigantic versions of themselves. These mutations were invariably attributed to atomic radiation by Hollywood Gothic scriptwriters. The dinosaurs in Crichton/Spielberg's *Jurassic Park* are recent examples of both magnification and fusion in that the terror they invoke is a function of their unnatural synthesis of prehistory with history, as well as their gargantuan size. In all of these space-age parables, the cautionary subtext has to do with the limitations of science and the rational mind, of which the scientific enterprise is one of our culture's most representative expressions. Their Gothic message is that the neat biological, spatial, and temporal categories into which the rational mind divides reality are convenient fictions, nothing more. Reality itself is not so fixed, predictable, or manageable as the hubris of scientism would have us believe. Consequently, scientists are often depicted in Gothic narratives as socially irresponsible zombies, self-absorbed monomaniacs indifferent to the ethical and political implications of their discoveries.

The essential failing of scientism is precisely identified by actor Jeff Goldblum, who portrays a chaos theoretician in the film version of Michael Crichton's sci-fi Gothic tale, *Jurassic Park:* "Your scientists were so preoccupied with whether or not they could, that they didn't stop to think if they should." Although the focus of this volume is American political Gothic, it is important to understand that, in the larger context of Western culture, the Gothic imagination presents a challenge to the rationalist-scientific world view out of which modern democractic theory arose. No one expressed and popularized the confident but reductive mentality of science prior to Einstein more effectively than the great seventeenth-century mathematician, Sir Isaac Newton.

It was Newton's model of reality against which later British and American Gothic artists such as William Blake and Edgar Allan Poe had to contend. The familiar lines of Blake's "The Tyger," present a cosmology that rejects the tidy structural metaphors of the Newtonian paradigm, such as geometric symmetry, linear progression, and unbroken continuity. Newton envisioned a universe that was rationally ordered, geometric in its regularity, machine-like in its design, predictable in its functioning, and positively corpse-like in its stasis. His view of the cosmos led ultimately to the Enlightenment, a cultural phase in European history that gave birth to the political tenets of Anglo-American liberalism upon which our own democratic system was founded. In short, the rationalism of Newton influenced the worlds of art and politics as well as that of science. Jefferson's geometrically designed Palladian home at Monticello, his cadenced Ciceronian prose style, and his revolutionary vision of America as a latter-day blend of Athenian wisdom and Roman civic virtue all owe something to the ordered teleology of Newton's universe. It was, after all, Jefferson's Newtonian confidence in the potency of reason that informed his neoclassical sensibilities and political outlook.

Jefferson's own nature, however, also shared something of the Gothic impulse that motivated William Blake. Blake's pointed rejection of the Newtonian order is well documented. In *William Blake: The Politics of Vision,* for example, Mark Schorer writes:

> Blake needed to construct a picture of the world that was in some sense a counterpart of his experience of life; and the Newtonian order, in its

mathematical denial of that dynamic expansiveness and fluidity which energy connotes, was almost literally "death." (Schorer 35)

If the world was to awaken from what Blake called "Newton's sleep," it would first have to acknowledge what it had become under Newton's influence. As Morris Berman, quoting from Christopher Hill's *The World Turned Upside Down*, points out:

> Blake may have been right to see Locke and Newton as symbols of repression. Sir Isaac's twisted, buttoned-up personality may help us to grasp what was wrong with the society which deified him.... This society, which on the surface, appeared so rational, so relaxed, might perhaps have been healthier if it had not been so tidy, if it had not pushed all its contradictions underground. (Berman 123)

America's Gothic imagination is best understood as an attempt to expose and confront our own repressed contradictions. It is an internalized dialectic between two philosophical impulses: the rational-mechanistic, which seeks to impose order on the unruly forces of nature (including human nature) and the transcendent, which both registers the inherent dangers of the rationalist enterprise and seeks to overcome them. In some measure at least, American history may be read as an externalized projection of our efforts to achieve a synergistic balance of power between these oppositional forces. This achievement is complicated by the dual nature of the Gothic itself, which counsels us to heed both our utopian dreams and our dystopian nightmares. The fact that the Gothic imagination signifies an impulse toward individual or collective (i.e., utopian) transcendence as well as annihilation is too often overlooked. Typically, Gothic pessimism is presented as an alternative, rather than a corollary, to utopian optimism. In the words of Mark Edmundson, "The visionary writers often knew what our culture has forgotten: that the purposes of cultural vitality ask for a conjunction of dark and renovating energies, that the two traditions, now split, might be joined once more" (Edmundson 163). In fact, these traditions, separated in thought, are inseparable in practice. Historically, both have shaped the American experience.

According to the Enlightenment ethos that gave rise to America's optimism, the rational powers of the human mind are more than a match for the irrationalities of nature. Whereas this relationship is inverted in many of his tales, in a comparatively little known science fiction short story entitled "A Descent into the Maelstrom," America's premier proponent of psychological Gothic, Edgar Allan Poe, offers a compelling metaphor of transcendence achieved through an ideal balance between the rational, which he calls "ratiocination," and the chaotic forces of life. At the heart of this short story lies a sublimely terrifying vortex of water, a "terrific funnel...whose interior, as far as the eye could fathom it, was a smooth, shining, and jet-black wall of water...sending forth to the winds an appalling voice, half shriek, half roar, such as not even the mighty cataract of Niagara ever lifts up in its agony to Heaven" (Poe 228). Poe could scarcely have imagined a structural metaphor less evocative of Newton's precisely regulated clockwork universe. Poe's protagonist is a Scandinavian sailor whose skiff is sucked into the maelstrom owing to an inattentive skipper intent on the day's catch. He manages to outlast his ordeal by calmly noting other objects caught in the vortex and observing a pattern favorable to survival. While his unfortunate shipmates succumb to their own mounting sense of terror and are lost accordingly, Poe's Gothic hero uses his frail but effective powers of ratiocination to prevail against the seeming chaos of nature.

The seventeenth-century French philosopher and mathematician Blaise Pascal (1623–1662) characterized humanity as a thinking reed (see Jacques Barzun's *Romanticism and the Modern Ego,* 24–26). John F. Kennedy kept a plaque in the oval office that carried a similar message: "Oh God, Thy Sea Is So Large and My Boat Is So Small." Kennedy's performance during the Cuban missile crisis of October 1962, as faithfully dramatized in Roger Donaldson's cinematic docudrama *Thirteen Days,* represented the triumph of reason and restraint over irrational passions and the momentum of history. While Pascal's words accentuate reason's frail light compared with the vast darkness of incomprehensibility by which it is surrounded, Kennedy's plaque emphasizes the comparable frailty of human aspiration when confronted by overwhelming forces of physical nature and divine providence. Nevertheless, both men were clearly informed by a keen awareness of humanity's risk in the face of life's Gothic mysteries, which is the central theme of Poe's short story as well. Indeed, America's most eloquent artistic and political minds have typically appealed to humanity's surprising potential for transcendence despite, or perhaps owing to, our common mortality. In the words of John F. Kennedy's famous American University speech, in which he summoned his fellow citizens to transcend their xenophobic fear of the Soviet Union: "We all inhabit this same small planet, we all breath the same air, and we are all mortal." In order to assess American culture in light of its idealistic aspirations, it is therefore necessary to sound the depths of its Gothic counterculture. To do so, however, one must first acknowledge the interdisciplinary scope and breadth of outlook encompassed by the Gothic imagination.

Educational theorists Julie Thompson Klein and William H. Newell define an interdisciplinary exploration as "a process of answering a question, solving a problem, or addressing a topic that is too broad or complex to be dealt with adequately by a single discipline or profession" (Newell 21). Clearly, the Gothic imagination is such a topic in that the problems it addresses encompass a great many historical eras, professions, art mediums, and academic disciplines. With that understanding in mind, it is perhaps time to venture a comprehensive statement as to the nature and purpose of a perspective that encompasses a substantial segment of human thought and feeling: *The Gothic imagination gives expression and meaning to life's darkly mysterious, painful, frightening, and seemingly irrational experiences by embracing them as a potential source of insight and transcendence.*

The implication of this statement, as it applies to American political and cultural history, is that our dystopian nightmares and our utopian dreams are inseparably linked. In essence, the search for a correct and thorough understanding of our Gothic predicament, however difficult it is to sustain, and the search for an authentic alternative to that predicament, however difficult it is to envision, are synonymous. They arise from the same impulse and function as complementary aspects of a single dialectic. This dialectic provides an early warning system, alerting us to danger whenever impurities within the body politic reach toxic levels. Similarly to the physical pain we experience when our bodily health is in jeopardy, the collective dis-ease associated with the political Gothic is an index of the extent to which we have endangered our health as a nation. The Gothic imagination therefore offers a potentially renovative, if disturbing, diagnosis of the psychological and political pathologies to which our nation is prone. Accordingly, practitioners of the Gothic imagination, like all shamans, are healers as well as prophets. The remedies they prescribe, however distasteful, tend to a beneficial end, namely the restoration of America to the kind of psychosocial balance envisioned by its founders.

Writing of the late-nineteenth, early-twentieth-century Gothic artist Ambrose Bierce, literary critic Clifton Fadiman observes that "the dominating tendency of American literature and social thought, from

Benjamin Franklin to Sinclair Lewis, has been optimistic....This has been the stronger current. But along with it there has coursed a narrow current, the shadowed stream of pessimism" (as quoted in Bierce vii–viii). The somewhat unorthodox thesis of this work is that the great divide in American thought and cultural expression is not between dystopian pessimism and utopian optimism, but between a dystopian-utopian dialectic and an alternative orientation in American thought and social practice with which that dialectic is in conflict.

American optimism offers rational, sometimes naively rational, solutions to social problems that prove resistant to its idealistic panaceas. Premised on an inadequate reckoning of the complexities and irrationalities arrayed against them, these rationalist panaceas, in turn, give rise to a pessimistic response. Nevertheless, many of America's celebrated thinkers, its pessimistic dystopians as well as its idealistic utopians, share the same underlying commitment to a just, humane, and open society. However, there is another, covertly fascist thought-stream in our cultural history that does not share that commitment. Indeed, it runs retrograde to the ideological course set for America by its founders. As one might expect, the political priorities churned up by this retrograde stream are antithetical to the dystopian-utopian synergy, represented by both America's Gothic artists and its Founding Fathers. This alternative to the authentic American dream is a thought-stream that flows between the banks of predatory capitalism, on the one side, and tribalistic chauvinism, on the other. Arguably, its waters have defiled the current of American idealism set in motion at the founding. The essential purity of that current, however murky its origins, is one that our most representative political leaders have sought to protect. Political Gothic artists in this country have therefore directed their heaviest assault against America's own fascism, and the denials on which it thrives.

Discussion Topics and Questions

1. In what sense can the democratic idealism of the Founding Fathers be regarded as definitive of the American dream?
2. What evidence is there of the prevalence of the Gothic in contemporary American culture?
3. Discuss the "somewhat unorthodox" division in American social and political thought that forms the premise of this book.
4. Identify the three structural principles behind the classic monsters of film, as well as the cautionary subtext that Hollywood monsters serve.
5. Discuss the Newtonian paradigm in relation to the Gothic imagination.

2 Narratives of Subversion and Conspiracy

In a chapter entitled "Conspiracy, Subversion, Supernaturalism," literary critic E. J. Clery quotes a passage from the Marquis de Sade's essay "Reflections on the Novel," in which he links the rise of Gothic literature to the political turmoil of late eighteenth-century Europe. Because the principal expressions of that turmoil were the French and American revolutions, his comments apply equally to the advent of American Gothic literature. The body of work he has in mind consists primarily of novels by Horace Walpole, Mrs. Radcliff, and Mathew "Monk" Lewis. "This genre," writes de Sade "was the inevitable product of the revolutionary shocks with which the whole of Europe resounded." Commenting on the sensationalism of the Gothic novel and the emotional and psychological needs it addressed, de Sade goes on to observe that "there was nobody left who had not experienced more misfortunes in four or five years than could be depicted in a century by literature's most famous novelists; it was [therefore] necessary to call upon hell for aid in order to arouse interest" (Clery 156). In the same chapter in which he cites de Sade's observations, Clery discusses various conspiratorial speculations that were rife during the Enlightenment era, and the Gothic narratives they inspired. These involved quasi-secret societies such as Freemasons, Jacobins, deists, and Bavarian Illuminati that were widely suspected of having manipulated political events on both sides of the Atlantic (Clery 156–71).

Other authors and works besides those of English Gothic artists gave rise to closely related literary movements. These included the German *Sturm und Drang* ("Storm and Stress") movement epitomized by Schiller. Goethe was also involved with *Sturm und Drang* and Gothic romanticism in works such as *The Sorrows of Young Werther* and *Faust*. Other literary achievements that reinforced the ethos of the Gothic included the sentimental novels of Richardson and Sterne in England, the writings of Rousseau in France, and the novels of Jean Paul Richter in Germany. Finally, this same period encompassed the nascent romanticism of the Jena group in Germany and the Lake Poets of England, as well as the romantic generation of Byron, Keats, and Shelley. James MacPherson's pseudo-Celtic literary forgery, i.e., a work penned by MacPherson himself but presented as an authentic example of primitive epic poetry, *Ossian,* and the ghostly tales of Sir Walter Scott, represent Scotland's most importable and enduring expressions of the fledgling Gothic genre. *Ossian,* incidentally, figures in both Goethe's *Werther* and in Mary Shelley's *Frankenstein.* What all these interrelated movements have in common is an implicit or explicit rejection of Enlightenment rationality and restraint in favor of a newly emergent cult of sensibility and sensationalism.

Moreover, as the term itself implies, the neo-Gothic impulse of the eighteenth century was but a renewal of interest in the heroic, the marvelous, and the impassioned. Earlier authors such as Homer, Virgil, the Greek tragedians (Aeschylus, Sophocles, Euripides), Dante, Shakespeare, and Milton and earlier genres such as Judeo-Christian religious lore and Romance literature of the Medieval era (Arthurian legends and Grail lore), all made significant contributions to the broad Gothic imagination. Taken together, this body of literature provided both a tradition upon which American Gothic intellectuals could draw and a standard against which they could rebel. Whereas the violence and upheaval of revolution may have been the principle catalyst for a Gothic revival on both sides of the Atlantic, the appearance of a characteristically American version of the Gothic was prompted by other factors as well. One of these was the competing political ideologies of republicanism and economic liberalism that vied for preeminence in the decades immediately following the War of Independence. To explain the genesis of a uniquely American Gothic imagination, it is necessary to understand both the democratic idealism of the American founding and the economic liberalism that quickly replaced it. Please note that here, as elsewhere throughout this book, republican with a lower case "r" refers to the philosophical and political tenets adopted by the Founding Fathers, whereas *Republican* refers to one of the two political parties that have been dominant in American politics since the Civil War era.

Revisionist Versions of America's Founding

According to the political Gothic imagination, nations as well as individuals are susceptible to internal contradictions and patterns of denial that, if left unacknowledged or unresolved, will provoke an identity crisis. A correct understanding of America's current malaise hinges on the unacknowledged but long-standing conflict between democratic idealism and Anglo-American libertarianism, which embraces the spirit of the marketplace and opposes all form of governmental activism. This is particularly true in light of the fact that the republican agenda of the Founding Fathers, which is presented here as definitive of the authentic American dream, has its current detractors on both ends of the political spectrum. For left-wing critics of the founding, the issue is not how to restore the authentic American dream, but how to expose its pretensions and hypocrisies. "It isn't simply a question of whether democracy can survive," says one cultural historian, "But the deeper question, of course, is whether democracy deserves to survive" (Lasch 86). For these detractors, the hidden history that haunts the American psyche is not about the lost republican ideal of Thomas Jefferson and those who shared his vision, it is about the suppressed realization that the "idealism" of the founding was itself a cynical cover for a Machiavellian *coup d'etat*. According to this view, an agrarian society of affluent, all-white-male colonialists hypocritically pursued its own political and economic self-interest in the name of liberty and "brotherhood"—an exclusionary and sexist term, say their critics. Meanwhile, right-wing defenders of the founding seek to promote an equally slanted view of America's original intentions. By their account, a capitalistic, libertarian, and xenophobic version of democracy, sometimes referred to as "fortress America," is what Jefferson and the others had in mind all along. This book contends that neither view will withstand careful scrutiny.

Modern liberal revisionists of the American Revolution argue that the founding was elitist and sexist, as well as racist. The rhetorical question posed by historian Howard Zinn and those who share his perspective is this: "Were the Founding Fathers wise and just men trying to achieve a good balance? In fact, they did not want a balance, except one that kept things as they were, a balance among the dominant forces at the time. They certainly did not want a balance between slaves and masters, propertyless and property holders, Indians and whites [or women]" (Zinn, A *People's History of the United States*, 101). Zinn, who helped bring about a national consensus in favor of ending the Vietnam War with his *Vietnam: The Logic of Withdrawal,* and whose cynicism about the founding is perhaps traceable to his resentment over that cruel and unnecessary conflict, is partially correct. However, what his criticism amounts to, in essence, is that the Founding Fathers failed to bring about at once what their thoughts and deeds have made possible, and will hopefully continue to make possible, in the fullness of time. Without their contribution to American political theory, the social reforms they set in motion, and continued to inspire, might never have occurred.

Could the founders have acted with greater dispatch? That question is undoubtedly an entertaining and valid source of speculation. However, the conclusions so confidently inferred from such a scenario by those who would not hesitate to answer in the affirmative are unwarranted. Admittedly, among Jefferson's contemporaries there were some who advocated policies that seem preferable to his in retrospect—the immediate abolition of slavery for example. While their fervor was sincere and their intentions admirable, such individuals exercised no real power and therefore incurred no real risk, either to themselves or to their fledgling country. Jefferson, who did exercise real power, chose a different course: "I am sensible how far I fall short of effecting all the reformation which reason would suggest, and experience approve, were I free to do whatever I thought best; but when we reflect how difficult it is to move or inflect the great machine of society, how impossible to advance the notions of a whole people suddenly to ideal right, we see the wisdom of Solon's remark, that no more good must be attempted than the nation can bear" (as quoted in Padover 35). A patriot who had waged everything to achieve independence from Great Britain—reputation, fortune, and life itself—could ill afford the luxury of indulging his private conscience at the expense of national survival. To accuse such a man of being overly cautious is one thing. To accuse him of cynical manipulation and moral cowardice is another. The former charge, though not compelling in my view, is at least plausible. The latter seems to me ungenerous to the point of being unjust.

Admittedly, the men who began the American Revolution did not finish it, and undeniably they *were* men. "The generation that commences a revolution," says Jefferson, "rarely completes it" (as quoted in Padover 21). In contrast to present-day radicals who denigrate their achievement, however, the Founding Fathers did unquestionably begin a revolution, not a culture war. Furthermore, that beginning was elitist in its conception and execution because it was engineered and implemented by an extraordinary convergence of America's best educated, most accomplished citizens. Arguably, it succeeded, to the extent that it did, for that very reason. Men like Jefferson believed unabashedly in intellectual distinction. They were exponents of republican democracy, not social democracy. They advocated equality, not egalitarianism. The elitism of the founders sought to raise the intellectual, moral, and cultural tone of American civilization to the level of the highest, not the lowest, common denominator of private and civic virtue. Their devotion to cultural excellence was implicit in their commitment to their vision of America as the shining city on the hill—a latter-day Athens. Undoubtedly, their mind-set had more in common with the elitism of Plato's philosopher kings than with that of today's corporate boardrooms, partisan think tanks, and political bureaucracies. Nevertheless, what distinguished Jefferson's ideal republic from the *The Republic* of Plato is that the former envisioned a society open to the possibility that a philosopher king might arise from any class, race, economic strata, or ethnic background, given sufficient ability, educational opportunity, and social incentive.

Paradoxically, to the extent that it is legitimate, our modern distrust of *elitism* stems from a subconscious respect for Jefferson's elitist ideals. Perhaps more than any of the other founders, he and Franklin implanted an archetypal image in American political consciousness of the model citizen as rustic philosopher, a sturdy, morally upright yeoman—an image that is strikingly at odds now with the partisan lobbyists, and indistinguishable party hacks who overpopulate America's corporate and political corridors of power. Unlike Jefferson, a republican elitist who desired the services of America's best and brightest to formulate a national policy grounded in the consent of the governed, today's elitists comprise a culture of philistines who desire the services of those as one-dimensional as themselves to circumvent the will of the governed whenever it is found expedient to do so. Manifestly devoid of philosophical, historical, or aesthetic cultivation, its representatives pay lip service to the importance of education while fostering a political and economic climate that affords little incentive to those who would seek a civic outlet for intellectual or artistic distinction. From the perspective of the political Gothic imagination, these bureaucratic spawns of Victor Frankenstein's mad-science seek to create and control a Brave New World of economic globalization, nuclear and biochemical terrorism, information technology, and media-imposed conformity of thought. Moreover, they hope to accomplish their objectives with minimal participation or consent from the rest of us. Arguably, the principal role assigned to the populace at large by today's power elite is to fund their activities while continuing to shore up the façade of participatory democracy. This is a role that we the people routinely fulfill by voting for the candidate of somebody else's choice—an increasingly empty ritual in which citizens are called upon to select from a carefully screened slate of party regulars representing a range of political options so narrow as to be virtually meaningless (see Lasch 161–75).

The power elite envisioned by Jefferson was, paradoxically, popular in that it comprised a disparate collection of the most refined, expansive, and liberal minds gleaned from the general populace. At Jefferson's Banquet of Democracy, there was to be no reserved seating. Ideally, those who occupied the head of the table did so in recognition of special gifts and extraordinary accomplishments. Ultimately, they were selected by virtue of the trust they inspired in those who elevated them to public office. Moreover, all were encouraged to strive for a place of distinction. While modern elitism is exclusionary and conspiratorial in spirit, the republican elitism of the Founding Fathers was conceived in the spirit of an open invitation. Our defining documents suggest that all who are willing to accept the responsibilities of citizenship are not only welcome at the community table but eligible to vie for a position at its head. I would encourage those for whom this as yet inadequately realized democratic ideal seems hypocritical to compare it with the ideal vision that has informed other political systems. They might search in vain, for example, to discover a comparable mandate under which their Jewish or African American brothers and sisters could have gained a seat at the table of German National Socialism—much less a place of honor. Regrettably, African Americans, Native Americans, women, and the "propertyless" were excluded from the first course at Democracy's Banquet. However, provided we shun the councils of covert fascism by adhering to the authentic American dream, they will not be excluded from the last. Their eventual appearance on the guest list is made mandatory by the very terms of the invitation itself.

As a well-educated man of the Enlightenment, Jefferson realized that intellectual distinction and aesthetic discrimination, which is the by-product of intellectual distinction, are as difficult to achieve as they are to preserve. He believed that these fragile flowers of democracy should therefore be cultivated and nurtured in the public interest and at the public's expense. With this end in view, he advocated the establishment of institutions of higher learning that were to be liberal arts centers of philosophical, historical, and aesthetic inquiry, not vocational training. These, in turn, were intended to serve as a feeder system for public service. Jefferson understood that a discerning, involved, and well-informed electorate was, in the final analysis, democracy's best safeguard against tyranny, as well as its only true source of legitimacy.

In today's pop culture world, that which is refined, intellectual, or sophisticated is widely viewed as inherently elitist and undemocratic. Whereas the founders sought to liberate the uncommon individual whose exceptional gifts were often trapped behind social and political barriers to public service, the ideal citizen of modern America seems to be the boorish, often unlettered, individual content with personal and cultural mediocrity and unambitious as regards civic service. Arguably, it is the champions of Ebonics, foul speech masking itself as free speech, and other pseudo-proletarian movements that are insincere in their devotion to the democratic ideal. The tendency of their demagoguery is to undermine the verbal clarity, precision, and eloquence practiced by our most notable statesmen from Jefferson and Lincoln to John F. Kennedy. In reality, our pop culture fear of elitism and highbrow culture contains a veiled insult to the much-heralded Common Man. It arrogantly assumes that he (or she) is attracted only by that which is inferior.

One manifestation of today's postmodern obscurantism is that our media celebrities, i.e., athletes, movie stars, and pop musicians, are licensed to speak the rude argot, not of the street, but of the sewer. All too often well-educated adults, seeking to establish their own egalitarian credentials, curry favor with the young by following suit. "Profanity, who really cares," challenged Bob Dylan in the early 1960s. At that particular moment in time, when the experiential obscenities of warfare and political assassination were cloaked by those careful to avoid unsavory language (in public, at least), there was poetic point and justice in Dylan's nonconformist message. However, forty years of linguistic thought pollution later, there is a clear answer to Dylan's rhetorical question: Anyone cares about the pervasive and mindless use of profanity who still values precision of thought and expression or the appropriate use of the English language as a tool of insight and communication. In my view, the strongest argument to be made against today's casual use of profanity is political rather than moral or aesthetic. In the words of George Orwell, "the decline of a language must ultimately have political and economic causes.... It becomes ugly and inaccurate because our thoughts are foolish, but the slovenliness of our language makes it easier for us to have foolish thoughts ... to think clearly is a necessary first step towards political regeneration: so that the fight against bad English is not frivolous and is not the exclusive concern of professional writers" (Orwell 163).

Though held to a marginally higher standard than our media celebrities, political leaders are routinely excused from any expectation of carefully nuanced thought or stylish expression. These same inarticulate politicians—many of whom are, themselves, semi-literate at best—point an accusing finger at underpaid educators and overburdened school systems for the breakdown of literacy in America. They are justified only to the extent that teacher training programs place far too much emphasis on *how* to teach at the expense of *what* to teach—a problem that gratuitous testing, higher standards of accountability, and merit-based pay incentives will not address. One can only hope that the general public who fund our school programs will heed the appeal from professional educators for greater student and parent accountability rather than the expedient, but far less pertinent, hue and cry of politicians for increased teacher accountability. The intellectual clarity and transparency of self-evident truth is a foundation of republican democracy. If an intellectually stunted culture addicted to four-letter words, televised sound bites, and four-word sentences is incapable of differentiating legitimate thought from bumper sticker slogans or of discriminating between authentic eloquence and recycled campaign rhetoric, democracy cannot prosper. English author C. S. Lewis writes:

> The demand for equality has two sources. One of them is among the noblest, the other is the basest of human emotions. The noble source is the desire for fair play. But the other source is hatred of superiority. Equality (outside mathematics) is a purely social conception. It applies to man as a political and economic animal. It has no place in the world of the mind. Beauty is not democratic; she reveals herself more to the few than to the many....Virtue is not democratic; she is achieved by those who pursue her more hotly than most men. Truth is not democratic; she demands special talents and special industry in those to whom she gives her favors. Political democracy is doomed if it tries to extend its demand for equality into these higher spheres. (C. S. Lewis 54)

The remaining two "liberal" charges against the republican ideal, sexism and racism, though equally plausible at first blush, are equally hollow upon closer consideration. The feminist critique of the founding is that women were denied the vote by white male supremacists who believed them to be inherently irrational. This misrepresentation is supported by historians such as Marc Kruman who is quoted by Thomas G. West to the effect that, "Women were excluded because of a presumed incapacity for sound reasoning" (West 85). The second charge is that of racism. The founders refrained from abolishing slavery; therefore they did not truly believe in human equality or the brotherhood of man. "Blacks," writes Kruman, "were seen as incapable of civic virtue, white men as naturally virtuous" (West 27). Such views, though fashionable and superficially plausible, prove to be examples of what Civil War historian James M. McPherson terms "presentism," which he defines as "a tendency to read history backwards, measuring change over time from the point of arrival rather than the point of departure" (McPherson 16). Though slavery was not abolished and women were not enfranchised at the founding, the principles it established paved the way for these later developments. Moreover, an unbiased appraisal of the scruples that informed the founders suggests that they were motivated by prudence rather than cynicism, racism, or sexism.

Left-wing revisionists such as Howard Zinn have provoked a spirited defense of the founding from right-wing intellectuals. That defense, however, is itself revisionist in its contention that the founders shared the enthusiasm of late twentieth-century conservatives for the precepts of *laissez-faire* economics. Jefferson is sometimes quoted in support of this claim. For example, conservative historian Thomas G. West supports his own devotion to the ethos of capitalism with a quotation from Jefferson's First Inaugural Address of 1801: "A wise and frugal government ... shall leave them [the people] otherwise free to regulate their own pursuits of industry and improvement, and shall not take from the mouth of labor the bread it has earned" (West 39). This argument sounds convincing until one considers that in modeling the *Declaration of Independence* after John Locke's famous *Second Treatise on Government*, Jefferson intentionally substituted the phrase "life, liberty, and the pursuit of *happiness*" for Locke's "life, liberty, and *property*" [italics mine]. To a neoclassicist such as Jefferson, happiness could only have meant "the exercise of vital powers along lines of excellence in a life affording them scope" (Hamilton 35). This ancient Greek definition of happiness—one that John F. Kennedy would later be fond of quoting—sets an intellectual limit on the sanctity of private property, a limit that doctrinaire conservatives seem unwilling to set.

West then goes on to dispel what he regards as the *myth* of the late-nineteenth-century robber barons by claiming that, "The worst abuses of the period were committed not by businesses like Standard Oil operating in the free market, but by businessmen granted special privileges or

monopolies by government, such as some of the railroad companies"
(West 41). He is, of course, correct in his larger argument that the now
pervasive alliance between corporate capitalism and government was and
is contrary to the republican ideal. In the words of Kalle Lasn, "The
United States of America was born of a revolt not just against British
monarchs and the British parliament, but against British corporations.
We tend to think of corporations as ... the legacy of the Rockefellers and
the Carnegies. In fact, the corporate presence in pre-Revolutionary
America was almost as conspicuous as it is today ... the colonies
resisted" (Lasn 52). What West's free-market conservatism fails to
acknowledge, however, is that it was businessmen who sought an
alliance with government in the first place, and that throughout our
history men like them have been more than willing to exploit their
advantage, usually at the expense of participatory democracy. In the
words of Noam Chomsky, one of corporate capitalism's most trenchant
critics, "Roughly speaking, a society is democratic to the extent that
people in it have meaningful opportunities to take part in the formation
of public policy.... Fascism is a term from the political domain, so it
doesn't apply strictly to corporations.... But corporations are more
totalitarian [in their lack of participatory democracy] than most
institutions we call totalitarian in the political arena" (Chomsky 9).

The willingness of corporate capitalism to use legislative and
judiciary branches of government to subvert democracy arises directly
from an ethos of ruthless competition and unrestrained greed. Ultimately,
that ethos refutes the civic virtue and self-restraint promoted by both
republicanism and classical liberalism. Such conservative propaganda as
the views of West cited above would have us believe that the American
citizen and the American consumer are synonymous terms. The Gothic
imaginations of Charles Brockden Brown, Charles Dickens (an English
master of the political Gothic imagination who wrote extensively about
America), Nathaniel Hawthorne, and, closer to our times, filmmakers
Orson Welles and Oliver Stone have been expended on demonstrating
that they are not. With few exceptions, American Gothic arts have sought
to preserve the republican ideals of the founders against both its overt
enemies and a politico-economic status quo that, to some extent, had
already formed by the time Andrew Jackson became president in 1828.
Based on an alliance between governmental and business interests, the
status quo to which I refer is one that America's Gothic counterculture
deems inimical to the authentic American dream.

The Shadow Side of Thomas Jefferson

Perhaps no one is better qualified to speak for the republican ideal on what constitutes the authentic American dream than Thomas Jefferson. In the words of one literary critic, "Jeffersonian thought, though stemming from the European Enlightenment, represents an Americanization of the Enlightenment.... Jefferson, political engineer as well as thinker, embodied certain peculiar American contradictions latent in Enlightenment thought.... embodied a national temperament, reflected cultural assumptions, and personified an outlook so representative that his name became the stamp of an era" (Christophersen 116). At an official reception for winners of the Pulitzer Prize, John F. Kennedy quipped that he was addressing the largest single gathering of native talent ever assembled at the White House, with the possible exception of when Jefferson dined there alone. It was by virtue of Jefferson's emotional and intellectual diversity, humorously invoked by Kennedy, that he was uniquely qualified to articulate the authentic American dream. However, these same qualities are what enabled Jefferson to empathize with the novelistic subversion of that dream penned by the founding father of American Gothic literature, Charles Brockden Brown. Understandably, the Gothic nuances and romantic ambiguities that marked Jefferson's domestic life are recorded in his personal correspondence and private notebooks rather than his public writings. In many ways, these intimate sources provide a fascinating counterpoint to his classically inspired political rhetoric and Palladian public persona.

Jefferson's utopianism envisioned a modern republic that was to be a synthesis of the philosophical and aesthetic traditions of ancient Athens with the administrative and civic virtues of republican Rome. Being himself part warrior, farmer, orator, administrator, politician, classical violinist, naturalist, educational philosopher, avid reader, and student of history, he envisioned the kind of nation (and world) congenial to his own level of cultivation. He professed a belief in equality of justice and educational opportunity for all, regardless of race, religious preference, or economic class. He also believed that individuals would appropriate that opportunity differently according to their innate gifts. Ultimately, he sought to create a society that would extend educational and cultural advantages previously reserved for members of the feudal aristocracy to every qualified citizen.

In Jefferson's thought world the individual human will is entrusted with absolute autonomy and guided by the innate moral compass of reason. He therefore believed that the state is obligated to seek out and nurture its most gifted citizens, i.e., those who by virtue of superior intellectual and artistic gifts belong to what he termed an "aristocracy of nature." According to Jefferson, that government governs best that furnishes conditions under which individual talent, tempered by patriotic ambition, can best flourish. He clearly advocated more than an American revolution on behalf of political rights and freedoms. Such rights and freedoms were understood to be the precondition for a quality of civilization that was, ultimately, beyond the reach of politics. Indeed, he advocated an American renaissance of mind and spirit. At times, Jefferson, along with his sometime political opponent John Adams, seems to consider "an aesthetic education as the ultimate benefit to be derived from the social reforms set in motion by the American Revolution, not material gains, or even political rights" (Pepetone 10).

The ultimate objective, as far as these founders were concerned, was to create a paternalistic society governed by its democratically selected philosopher kings, a humanist haven peopled with happy and enlightened horticulturalists who would till the earth by day and read classical literature and history by night. This may sound more like a caricature than a valid characterization, but in point of fact, one of Jefferson's proudest boasts to foreigners was that, "America was the only country in which you could find farmers who read Homer" (Lehman 38). From our vantage point in time, Jefferson's idyllic conception seems akin to the escapist fantasies of flower power in the 1960s and the back-to- nature movement it spawned.

That Jefferson himself was anything but a spinner of impractical daydreams, however, is evidenced by his impressive list of public and private accomplishments. What distinguishes Jefferson's American utopianism from later varieties is that it was grounded in a real understanding of husbandry and practical affairs as well as a keen susceptibility of heart and mind. Nevertheless, the practical, rationalistic Jefferson was clearly offset and balanced by another, more Gothic Jefferson. This other Jefferson was deeply affected by the rhapsodic emotionalism of *Ossian,* prone to passionately romantic involvement with married as well as unmarried women, inspired by the great classical music of the eighteenth century, and genuinely approving of novels by America's first important exponent of the Gothic imagination—Charles

Brockden Brown—even though his own neoclassical agenda was called into question by them.

At one point in his life, Jefferson devoted no fewer than five hours daily to mastering his musical instrument of choice, rumored to have been an Amati, a handcrafted Baroque violin of enormous quality. In the days when musical manuscripts were comparatively rare, his extensive music library featured works by Purcell, Handel, Corelli, Vivaldi, Boccherini, and Haydn. In 1785, as quoted in Padover, he wrote from Paris to a friend:

> Were I to proceed to tell you how much I enjoy their architecture, sculpture, painting, and music, I should want words. It is in their arts that they shine, The last of them particularly [music] is an enjoyment, the deprivation of which with us, cannot be calculated. (Padover 139)

Ironically, this ecstatic approval comes from the same isolationist statesman who repeatedly warns against the depravities of European culture and the dangers of foreign entanglements. Writing of Jefferson's almost obsessive attachment to *Ossian,* biographer Andrew Burstein states:

> The images of Ossian never entirely receded from his imagination. The lengths to which he would go to explore Ossian's world, the fact that this self-demanding student who had undertaken to read Homer in the original now desired to learn Gaelic for this one purpose, indicates the depth of his interest. The dark and mysterious heroic tale stayed with him from colonial times through old age. (Burstein 31)

Perhaps Jefferson's most fervent and revealing personal document is a twelve page love letter to Maria Cosway, "a dialogue between the Head and the Heart." It runs to more than four thousand words and he labored over it "with the same intensity he brought to the Declaration of Independence" (Ellis 112). This Jekyll and Hyde epistle refutes the stern man of reason image that attaches to Jefferson's public persona. The confident, self-satisfied face that Jefferson wore in public is consistent with the tidy rationalisms of the Newtonian paradigm. The Jefferson it portrays, i.e., the republican Jefferson, is the one that many of us learned about in school. The other face, evident in his love letter to Maria Cosway, reveals the hidden facets of Jefferson's Gothic psyche. It presents the lineaments of a man at odds with himself and with a seemingly smug Enlightenment ethos of poise, serenity, and rational self-sufficiency. It suggests that, in reality, the neoclassical thought world that sustained the neurotic personalities of Locke and Newton was little more than a fragile, if ingenious, façade. Many of that era's most representative figures, such as Samuel Johnson and Wolfgang Amadeus Mozart, privately harbored the same psychological complexities and contradictions that characterized the private Thomas Jefferson. Indeed, it would not be unfair to conclude that the Age of Reason to which Jefferson belonged was, in certain respects, manifestly irrational. This is significant because Jefferson's conflicted alter ego, i.e., his shadow side, embodies the contradictions of a fledgling American nation that was, to an extent, a projection of his own divided psyche. The conflicts latent in that psyche were to open a rich vein of unacknowledged thought and feeling that would later be mined by literary, musical, and cinematic artists. Indeed, Charles Brockden Brown (1771–1810), America's first professional writer in the Gothic vein, initiated that process during Jefferson's lifetime.

Brown's Gothic Subversion of Jefferson's Utopian Dream

In 1798, Jefferson received an unusual gift from an unlikely source. The gift was a complimentary copy of a newly published American novel entitled *Wieland, or the Transformation,* and it prompted an uncharacteristic response. The source was its unknown twenty-seven-year-old author, Charles Brockden Brown. Jefferson's generous response reveals a hidden facet of his intellect. In that response he confesses to taking pleasure in novels and expounds on the freedom to embellish the facts that imaginative fiction enjoys over history. He goes on to say that the chief advantage of the former is that fiction is free to paint virtue and vice in their most extreme forms (Christophersen 115). What renders this observation surprising is the approving tone it adopts toward a literary genre that was regarded by the intelligentsia of his time in much the same way as comic strips, Hollywood films, and popular music were, until recently, regarded by most modern intellectuals. Indeed, the novel, and in particular the Gothic novel, is an early manifestation of what today would be called popular culture. Moreover, *Wieland,* which deals with madness, incestuous murder, conspiracy, and religious fanaticism, portrays an America that is essentially the antithesis of Jefferson's republican City on the Hill.

The questions raised by this episode are many: Why would Brown, an untried author, have sought Jefferson's approval, or if that was not his motive, why would he intentionally seek to provoke his disapproval? Similarly to other intellectuals of his generation, Brown began as an enthusiastic radical who supported Jefferson's utopian aims, but ended as a conservative critic of both Jefferson and his republican agenda. Such ideological shifts would recur at later crisis points in American history. For instance, many apostate radicals of the 1930s and early 1940s who initially sympathized with the Soviet experiment became ardent anti-communists during the Cold War era, just as certain anti-Establishment radicals of the 1960s turned into Reaganite conservatives during the 1970s and 1980s. Quite possibly, the answer to the riddle of Brown's gift and Jefferson's acceptance of it lies in the latent romanticism of the age of reason and classical restraint to which they both belonged. The early years of the new republic were fraught with tensions between republicanism and federalism, populism and elitism, slavery and freedom, humanism and Calvinism, civic virtue and emergent capitalism, hawks and doves. As Brown scholar Bill Christophersen observes, the nation was experiencing shocking and revolutionary changes that influenced all facets of life—economic, political, and cultural. These traumatic events produced new anxieties, among which were anxieties occasioned by the fear of political and religious conspiracies. He describes the spirit of the times as "a heady, rationalistic optimism tempered by, then traumatized by a succession of political shocks" (Chistophersen 7). This description of the Spirit of 1776 once again evokes the spirit of our own times in the wake of the thwarted radicalism and violence of the 1960s. Anxieties relating to suspicions of conspiracy and fear of military invasion in the early days of the Republic exerted a considerable influence on America's political and social agendas.

In response to war and rumors of war, the wolf man syndrome latent in the American psyche (i.e., our Jeffersonian psychic split between head and heart, rational restraint and violence) was soon unleashed. It was summoned this time by our fear of the British lion, which by 1812 was on the prowl once again. However, before a succession of post-revolutionary conflicts with the parent country, there came another, more urgent, trauma over events transpiring across the ocean, events that were, to an extent, legitimized by our example. The French Revolution of 1789 and the Reign of Terror to which it gave rise sent tremors throughout the western world. "The chief index to the national temperament in the

1790s—and, arguably, to the American psyche in general—was the French Revolution. That American-inspired revolution, whose amalgam of ideals and atrocities put political choices, for better or worse, at the head of society's agenda, was a glass in which America read her own distorted likeness" (Christophersen 12).

For many people, including notable poets and writers such as William Wordsworth in England and Washington Irving in America, the French Terror was both a retribution and a cautionary fable against the political *hubris* of an age that sought to create a new political entity (as Mary Shelley's Dr. Frankenstein would later seek to create a new human entity) by the light of its own, unregenerate reason. To find in subsequent European history a psychic eruption of comparable magnitude, one would have to reference the impact of the twentieth century's two world wars. In American history, comparable traumas are associated with the Civil War, the political and economic insecurities of the 1930s, and those of the period between the assassination of President Kennedy and the end of the Vietnam War. Each of these societal traumas was preceded by a resurgence of idealism—a romantic confidence in humanity's capacity to shape its own destiny—and each gave rise to a reactionary backlash. The basis of Charles Brockden Brown's rejection of Jefferson's republicanism was ultimately rooted in his reaction to war-related fears and traumas of the late eighteenth century.

In addition to these fears and traumas, however, postrevolutionary America also underwent a socioeconomic transformation with implications that would subsequently define America's Gothic dilemma. Brown's biographer Steven Watts writes, "The decades between independence from Great Britain and the Panic of 1819 framed the consolidation of a market economy and market society in the United States. The ascendancy of 'liberal capitalism,' as the process has been defined, entangled growing numbers of citizens in complex webs of commodification and profit seeking that enshrined the competing individual [i.e., Economic Man rather than Republican Man] as a social ideal" (Watts 2). In light of this shift from republican idealism to liberal capitalism, Brown's subtitle for his first Gothic novel, *Wieland, or The Transformation,* is suggestive. Just as the rationalizing hero in another of Brown's Gothic novels, *Arthur Meryn,* concedes certain principles to the demands of private necessity, Jefferson as president made certain concessions to federalism in order to preserve a union threatened by internal dissention and foreign aggression. He thereby sacrificed his democratic ideals to political necessity, or so his critics, including Brockden Brown, believed. (Christophersen 123). It was a time when everything seemed to be at stake and the country was divided between proponents of individual liberty and federal authority. Both sides predicted dire consequences, either tyranny or anarchy, if their opponents prevailed (Burstein 204).

Some, including Charles Brockden Brown, saw the Louisiana Purchase, the strengthening of a National Bank, war with Britain on commercial grounds, and the suppression of indigenous uprisings by a federal militia, as unprincipled acts of political expediency. An alternative interpretation suggests that they were assertions of the principle of "positive liberty," the so-called "guarantee clause" of the Constitution, Article IV, Section 4 that reads, "the United States shall guarantee to every state in the Union a Republican Form of Government." Ironically, this principle, enshrined in the Constitution and in six of the first seven post–Civil War amendments to the Constitution, originated as a corollary to the negative conception of liberty in eleven of the first twelve amendments and in the doctrine of "states rights" (McPherson 140). Nevertheless, it has been invoked in justification of federal initiative on behalf of democratic idealism at every major crisis point in American history, i.e., the first revolution against Britain, the second revolution or Civil War against southern secession, the New Deal realignment of political and economic power, and the New Frontier's aborted third revolution against the Cold War establishment. Each of these crises, in turn, has given rise to a significant Gothic response.

Parallels between the Republicanism of Jefferson and Kennedy

In retrospect, it is not difficult to explain John F. Kennedy's sympathy and admiration for his illustrious predecessor, Thomas Jefferson. Both men served during a period in which the very survival of America and democracy seemed to be at stake. In a manner reminiscent of Jefferson, Kennedy sought to achieve a dynamic equilibrium between oppositional forces both without and within the American government over which he presided. In Kennedy's case, tensions were caused by his resistance to external pressures for war from the Soviets as well as internal pressures from Pentagon officials and hard-line cold warriors within his own administration. In Jefferson's case, a comparable tension resulted from his well-known republicanism in the face of pressures posed by the danger of foreign aggression from Great Britain and Federalist opposition at home. Both men were viewed as weaklings by their friends and traitors by their enemies, including those who saw the world in conspiratorial terms.

In Kennedy's case, the paranoia of those who misinterpreted his motives may well have prompted them to adopt extreme measures. Both men served at a time when reasonable and enlightened people believed in the existence of powerful conspiracies, a belief that so-called reasonable and enlightened historians of our own era find it convenient to dismiss (Burstein 204). After all, the rumor of conspiracy, like the rumor of war, can be as provocative as conspiracy itself. The political consequences of such theories are nullified, in the eyes of skeptical historians, simply by demonstrating to their satisfaction that the original rumor is baseless. These biased exponents of the Newtonian paradigm would do well to heed Brown's suggestion that human perception is limited by human prejudice and that, as Brown suggests, people often see what they are predisposed to see rather than what is actually present (Christophersen 121).

Just as there were those in the wake of the French Terror who believed that Jefferson and his republican proponents were the dupes of the radicals, there were those in the wake of the Stalinist terror who believed that Kennedy was a dupe of Soviet Communism. His cautious response to anti-Soviet paranoia within his own ranks therefore presented a clear and present danger, from the perspective of those who shared that paranoia. A truly committed cold warrior, given the opportunity, might not have scrupled to remove that danger by whatever means necessary. Just as Jefferson's eastern establishment version of the American dream was replaced by Andrew Jackson's frontier conception of democracy in the nineteenth century, Kennedy's neo-Jeffersonian outlook was supplanted by the Wild-West mentality of Lyndon Johnson's frontier constituency in the twentieth century (see Carl Oglesby's *The Yankee and Cowboy War*). Given these circumstances, it is not difficult to understand why the conspiratorial narratives of Charles Brockden Brown and Oliver Stone historically bracket American expressions of the political Gothic imagination.

Ironically, it was Brown, not Jefferson, who would finally spurn the republican vision. Later in life, he renounced his youthful radicalism, at the same time abandoning a literary agenda that had originated in his desire to understand and transcend what he saw as America's utopian-dream-turned-dystopian-nightmare. He tried his hand at writing sentimental novels and then took up journalism. However, the nature of the nightmare he had chronicled, and by implication the nature of the utopian dream of which it was a distortion, is clearly delineated in two of his earlier productions, *Wieland, or the Transformation* and *Edgar Huntly, or the Sleepwalker*. Just as the subtitle of the former carries wider implications though it primarily concerns the fate that overtakes its principle character, the subtitle of the latter carries a connotative as well as a denotative meaning. At the denotative level, it refers to a pathological condition with which two of its principal characters are afflicted. At the connotative level it expresses its author's profound skepticism concerning the future of a society premised on humanity's capacity for rational self-government.

Wieland's Gothic Transformation and Huntly's Sleep of Reason

Theodore Wieland, the protagonist of Brown's first Gothic novel, begins as an exemplar of Jefferson's virtuous republican. His education "had been modeled on no religious standard" (*Wieland* 30), i.e., like Jefferson he was a humanist by educational training whose Enlightened religion was free of guilty superstition. Wieland's profession was to be agriculture, Jefferson's democratic vocation par excellence, and his rationalistic optimism was such that "Time was supposed to have only new delights in store" (*Wieland* 29). His home is reminiscent of Jefferson's rural retreat, in that it is described in terms reminiscent of the Palladian style favored by Enlightenment architectural taste. Situated on a hilltop, like Monticello, it features a neoclassical temple to humane learning. The entrance to this temple is adorned with a bust of Cicero, one of Jefferson's intellectual heroes (see Burstein 117). Opposite to this bust is a harpsichord, similar to the one that graced the music room in Jefferson's home.

Wieland's eighteen-year-old sister serves as the narrator of Brown's novel. The glimpse she provides of their lifestyle before her brother's sinister transformation, and her own, is likewise reminiscent of Jefferson's documented activities at Monticello:

> This was the place of resort in the evenings of summer. Here we sung, and talked, and read, and occasionally banqueted.... Here the performances of our musical and poetic ancestors were rehearsed [Ossian perhaps?] ... here a thousand conversations pregnant with delight and improvement took place ...

My brother was an indefatigable student. The authors he read were numerous,
but the chief object of his veneration was Cicero. (Brown, *Wieland* 32)

In view of these parallels, it is possible that Jefferson served as a model
for Wieland and his utopian rationality. Both *Wieland* and *Edgar Huntly*
are initiation stories, "the account of a young man who begins by looking
for guilt in others and ends finding it in himself; who starts out in search
of answers but is finally satisfied with having defined a deeper riddle
than those he attempted to solve" (Fiedler 157).

In Wieland's case, the guilt he looks for in others concerns the
unsolved mystery of his father's death from unknown causes that
curiously resemble instances of so-called spontaneous combustion.
Eventually the rationalistic Wieland comes to attribute this tragedy to a
supernatural agency. In a scenario that is uncomfortably suggestive of
the Charles Manson murders in 1969, Wieland's transformation from
Jeffersonian rationalist to religious fanatic climaxes with his successful
attempt to murder nearly every member of his immediate family,
supposedly at the prompting of a supernatural voice. Incidentally, the
chilling murder in chapter 19 surely owes something of its maniacal
intensity to the famous bedroom scene in that earlier masterpiece of the
broad Gothic imagination, Shakespeare's *Othello*. We learn subsequently
that the "voice of God" heard by Wieland belongs to an evil ventriloquist
named Carwin, a European schemer intent on seducing Wieland's sister.

To be more precise, while the reader is encouraged to accept this
naturalistic explanation, Brown utilizes a supernaturalistic loophole
whereby the issue of who was speaking to Wieland, in every instance, is
left unresolved. Such unresolved ambiguities are a commonplace of
Gothic narrative. The *X-Files* episode entitled "Grotesque," for example,
similarly explores the issue of madness versus possession. In this
intriguing episode, first aired in 1996, Agent Mulder is stalked by a serial
killer. In the end, the killer turns out to be Mulder's former mentor, FBI
Agent Patterson. Though a brilliant criminologist, Patterson is also a
dogmatically rational man of science. Consequently, in attempting to
find the killer by entering imaginatively into his grotesque thought
world, he ends up losing himself. His rationalistic sensibilities, unable to
cope with the dark allure and ambiguity of the Gothic, render him
susceptible to either madness or demonic possession—perhaps by his
discarded other self, i.e., a bestial and irrational *doppelgänger* that
manifests as a medieval gargoyle. The principle suspect, a sculptor
named Mostow, is obsessed with creating images of gargoyles, some of

which prove to be dismembered victims covered in clay. Agent Mulder, who has successfully aligned the classical and romantic components of his well-balanced psyche, employs Patterson's intuitive methods to expose his mentor's guilt. Ironically, as the tragic plot unfolds we learn that Patterson, in a moment of intuitive transcendence, covertly requested that Mulder, whom he secretly admires, be assigned to the case. Clearly, his subconscious motive in doing so was to bring his own homicidal rampage to an end. Ultimately, Agent Patterson is captured and imprisoned—behind walls of rational denial as well as those made of brick and mortar. In a chilling epilogue, the final scene offers a close-up of the once confident man of science—a man who was rudely disdainful of his former student's openness to the paranormal—rattling the bars of his prison cage and raving incoherently of his innocence. The moral painted by this haunting image is clear: A closed mind offers the worst possible defense against life's Gothic mysteries, either supernatural or political. By implication, the cause of Patterson's insanity, if indeed he is mad, is the very rationality that prevents him from recognizing his own schizophrenic condition.

Significantly, the sinister "biloquist," i.e., ventriloquist, in Charles Brockden Brown's narrative turns out to be a political subversive, as well as a would-be seducer. He is exposed as a member of the notorious Bavarian Illuminati, an enigmatic secret society suspected, in some quarters, of having instigated the American and French Revolutions of the eighteenth century (see Marrs's *Rule by Secrecy*). Wieland, whose earlier commitment to Enlightenment tenets of rationality has left him vulnerable to the same kind of psychic dissociation experienced by Agent Patterson, is similarly unable to acknowledge his guilt. At the very conclusion of the novel, however, Carwin, exhorts his victim in the following terms: "Man of errors! cease to cherish thy delusion; not heaven or hell, but thy senses have misled thee to commit these acts" (*Wieland* 259). Rendered suddenly aware of his own insupportable guilt, Wieland, "transformed at once into the man of sorrows," takes his own life. However, Wieland's subconscious burden of guilt is evident long before Carwin triggers this belated acknowledgment.

Though he blames himself, Wieland is not actually responsible for his father's unexplained demise, which occurs anterior to the events of the novel. Figuratively, however, in having abandoned the Calvinistic faith of his forefathers in preference for the new republican faith in human reason, he stands convicted in his own tortured mind of an apostasy deserving of divine retribution. "The temple was no longer assigned to its ancient use," laments Wieland's sister Clara in reference to the Monticello-like structure that adjoins her brother's home. Historically a place of religious worship, the neoclassical temple was converted during the Enlightenment into an architectural symbol of secular humanism. Wieland's "neglect" of the temple signals his denial of an ancient religious heritage, and by extension symbolizes an act of philosophical and political patricide. Under the influence of his own guilty conscience and the machinations of the evil conspirator Carwin, Wieland himself is ultimately transformed from a model of Enlightenment rationality into a homicidal lunatic.

Edgar Huntly, the hero of Charles Brockden Brown's second Gothic novel, also undertakes an ambiguous journey of Enlightenment that leads to a similar outcome. His home stands on the border between civilized Federalist America and frontier America, which, symbolically and psychologically, is equivalent to the border between Jeffersonian rationality and transparency, at one extreme, and the Gothic wilderness of untamed passion and savagery, at the other. "The Gothic," writes literary critic Teresa A. Goddu, "challenges the critical narratives of American literary history and.... unsettles the nation's cultural identity" (Guddu 10). Early Gothic writings did so, in part, by challenging the regional stereotypes with which Federalist Americans sought to distance themselves and their form of government from Gothic contamination.

James, the epistolary hero of John de Crèvecoeur's *Letters from an American Farmer* (1782), for example, is a prototypical republican agriculturalist suggestive of Jefferson's rustic ideal. In one of his neoclassically phrased letters, he reports on the condition of frontier America. In a passage dealing with Crèvecoeur, Goddu writes, "Turning from the industrious Americans who live near the sea and in the middle colonies, James discovers in the frontiersmen of the west 'the most hideous' part of American society: they are 'a mongrel breed, half civilized, half savage,' and live a lawless, 'licentious idle life'...they are not the 'true' representatives of American society" (Goddu 17). Perhaps not, but they would nevertheless soon replace Jefferson's industrious, though literate, rustic as a type of genuine Americana. In 1828, that transition was ratified with the election of Andrew Jackson to the presidency. Speaking of the Jacksonian constituency, historian Henry Steele Commager writes, "They did not believe for a minute that the great prizes of public life were reserved for the rich, the well born, and the educated. The coon hunter has as good a right to them as the Harvard graduate" (Nevins and Commager 166).

Jacksonian democracy, in its egalitarian insistence on unconditional, i.e., unmerited, equality of opportunity, bore a superficial resemblance to Jeffersonian democracy, just as Lyndon Johnson's "Great Society" bore a superficial resemblance to John Kennedy's "New Frontier." Jackson's brutal pogroms against Native Americans, however, suggest that he was a very different stamp than Jefferson or Kennedy, men whose use of power was tempered by a tolerance and restraint born of historical perspective and personal cultivation. In effect, the election of President Jackson signaled the demise of Jefferson's aristocracy of nature as an ideal on which to model democratic governance. Needless to say, Jefferson's ideal, restated a half century later by Ralph Waldo Emerson, does not, as some would maintain, call for government by college professors. Such a conclusion is mere caricature. What it does call for is a government by "Man Thinking," i.e., the well-rounded humanist suited to many callings by a deep and genuine commitment to the world of ideas as well as to the world of practical actions and outcomes (see Emerson's essay, "The American Scholar"). Although this humanist ideal would resurface periodically—most recently during the administration of President Kennedy—with the election of Andrew Jackson, the faltering torch of Jefferson's populist elitism had indeed been passed to a new and very different generation of Americans.

Similarly to Wieland and Agent Patterson, Edgar Huntly sets out to solve a crime only to discover, in the end, that *he* is the perpetrator. More precisely, he discovers that he is capable of the same insensate violence as those who were responsible for committing the crime. In this instance, the actual deed is perpetrated by a band of renegade Native Americans frustrated by the encroachment of white settlers. In the process of confronting these renegade "savages," Huntly must confront a savage penchant for violence within himself, as Wieland did. In the Gothic tradition of Universal's horror film classic *The Wolf Man*, Huntly, anticipating film actor Lon Chaney Jr. by almost two centuries, is portrayed as a prototype of the pathetic hero-villain, a Gothic everyman at the mercy of an irrational propensity to sleepwalk and an even more disturbing tendency to transform into a mindless primitive when confronted with life-threatening situations. As one Brown scholar points out, Edgar is stoical, alienated, and deadly, a type that later writers, such as D. H. Lawrence, would depict as the quintessential American

(Christophersen 127). An ingenuous subplot, by the way, centers on the essentially innocent character of Clithero, a name suggestively similar to Cicero, who like Huntly nearly succeeds in destroying those he most loves. Tragically, Clithero is manipulated into taking his own life rather than face existence as the inmate of a lunatic asylum. Was this episode an attempt on the part of the author to suggest that Jefferson's commitment to classical order, reason, and republicanism, as symbolized by his devotion to Cicero, was tainted at the source, or that, similarly to both Wieland and Clithero, he was being manipulated by sinister forces?

Brown's tangled plots, though tragic in nature, are as difficult to unravel as a Shakespearean comedy, and often for the same reason. Both authors rely heavily on disguised, fragmented, or mistaken identities. Wieland, for example, is shadowed by his intensely rational alter ego, a character named Henry Pleyel. Comparing the two men, Clara notes, "Their creeds were in many respects opposite" (33). She goes on to explain: "Where one discovered only confirmations of his faith, the other could find nothing but reasons for doubt. Moral necessity and Calvinistic inspiration were the props on which my brother thought proper to repose. Pleyel was the champion of intellectual liberty" (33, 34). Edgar Huntly and Clithero are *doppelgangers,* or mirror images, of one another. Appropriately, they share a similar fate. Characters appear and reappear, both in and out of disguise. In the process, unsuspected and often perverse power relationships are revealed and concealed crimes, i.e., hidden histories, are exposed.

American Gothic themes and settings abound in *Edgar Huntly* as well: Brown's use of "the abyss" as a broad Gothic symbol of sublime nature, for instance, suggests Poe's later use of the vortex in *The Descent into the Maelstrom.* Coincidences multiply, and unexpected twists and turns of plot hinge on concealed or ambiguous documents. The literary outcome is a kaleidoscope of constantly shifting situations and personalities in which a stockpiling of sensational incidents, often violent in nature, imparts an almost hallucinatory energy and vividness. Significantly, Clara Wieland, and other characters from American Gothic fiction such as Hester Prynn from Hawthorne's *The Scarlet Letter,* ultimately take up residence in Europe, thereby reversing the archetypal journey to the New World. Clearly there is more going on here than an author's innocent desire to provide his readers with a beguiling pastime. This something more gives rise to certain questions: What is the motivating force behind Charles Brockden Brown's dark parables of the

American experience at the founding, and what self-congratulatory version of early American history do his stories subvert?

To answer these questions, we must think back for a moment to the almost painfully obvious parallels between Wieland's temple of reason and Jefferson's Monticello. Think back also to the guilty self-awareness shared by Brown's Gothic hero-villains. The American Revolution, and to an even greater extent, the French Revolution were acts of political patricide. Even though the famous tumbrels did not roll on this side of the Atlantic, nor did the heads of those favored by Madame Guillotine (as the cruel machinery of the French Terror was sardonically called), all Americans who sided with the revolutionists were nevertheless implicated in an Oedipal crime against their parent country. The tragedy of Oedipus, as related by Sophocles, is another political murder mystery in which the hero is also the criminal, though he does not realize his own guilt until the catastrophe has overtaken him. All three Gothic heroes, Oedipus, Wieland, and Huntly, are ultimately responsible for the death of their friends and family. Both *Oedipus Rex* and Brown's third Gothic novel, *Arthur Mervyn*, open with terrible plagues that have inexplicably gripped the land. These plagues symbolize unresolved Gothic dilemmas, i.e., hidden histories, that must be openly acknowledged if the well-being of society is to be restored. In effect, they are the festering outcome of chronic denial.

Even after the blind oracle Teiresias has accused him, however, Oedipus continues to deny the terrible truths of his own past. Just as Wieland at his trial for murder enters a plea of "not guilty" and stubbornly persists in maintaining his innocence, Oedipus remains adamant long after his subjects have come to accept his guilt as factual. Moreover, he attempts to shift the blame onto another by accusing his brother-in-law Creon of engaging in a political conspiracy against the throne. Creon's outraged counteraccusation is that his brother-in-law is dreaming. In his Gothic novels of subversion, Brown implies that Jefferson's dream of democracy, i.e., the authentic American dream, is similarly delusional. Moreover, he implies that unless Jefferson, and the republic over which he presides, can be persuaded to balance their utopian impulses against a more realistic appraisal of the limitations imposed by human nature and America's buried but still potent past, their Enlightenment delusions may well involve their fellow citizens in a fate similar to that experienced by Oedipus and the citizens of Thebes. He warns that just as the murder of a parent or a wife will bring with it a well-merited downfall, whether the perpetrator is cognizant of his crimes or not, America's symbolic murder of its Puritan heritage and its paternalistic British rule is destined to bring about a comparable downfall.

According to one commentator, sleepwalking is an obvious metaphor of our human tendency to hide from unflattering truth by rationalizing our motives (Christophersen 138). For instance, we may deceive ourselves into believing that our theocratic past is behind us. However, the separation trauma that inevitably attends so radical a change as a political revolution continues to haunt us. No matter how deeply we attempt to bury our inherited sense of guilt beneath layers of Enlightenment rationalization, suggests Brown, the specter of our unacknowledged past will continue to stalk America, even as the specter of Hamlet's father continued to stalk the ramparts at Elsinore. For Charles Brockden Brown, it was plausibly the guilt occasioned by the excesses of the Reign of Terror, as well as the war insecurities and philosophical conflicts of the early republic, that unexpectedly exhumed traumas associated with America's recently discarded past. However, in all likelihood there was another subterranean chamber in our national psyche reserved for an even more profound level of guilt. Commenting on this uniquely American predicament, Leslie A. Fiedler, America's foremost literary critic of the Gothic, writes:

> In the United States, certain special guilts awaited projection in the Gothic form. A dream of innocence had sent Europeans across the ocean to build a new society immune to the compound evil of the past from which no one in Europe could ever feel free. But the slaughter of the Indians, who would not yield their lands to the carriers of utopia, and the abominations of the slave trade, in which the black man, rum, and money were inextricably entwined in a knot of guilt, provided new evidence that evil did not remain with the world that had been left behind.... How could one tell where the American dream ended and the Faustian nightmare began. (Fiedler 143)

America began not as a secular nation-state devoted to rational self-government, but as a collection of theocratic city-states consecrated to the God of Abraham and burdened by a strong Calvinistic sense of sin and predestination. In denying that heritage, Brown implies, the new republic reenacted the Oedipal crime on a political plane. In effect, our revolution symbolically killed not only the king of Britain, but also the King of Kings. It signified not just the murder of our geopolitical parent across the Atlantic ocean but, by extension, the murder of "our Father who art in heaven." Small wonder that Wieland, the apostate rationalist, should be haunted and possessed by a demonic manifestation of this discarded deity, a deity who is, in reality, a projection of his Gothic alter ego. One of the essential insights of American political Gothic is that in our headlong pursuit of progress—or conversely our desperate flight from history—the unassimilated self we choose to deny will inevitably return in a distorted form, often one that is destructive. C. G. Jung's term for this tragic reversal into the opposite is *enantiodromia*.

Apropos our theocratic origin and the separation trauma associated with it, the alleged connection between Protestant religion and capitalism, well established in certain academic circles, requires some qualification. This is particularly true in light of my thesis that democracy and capitalism represent belief systems that are difficult to reconcile in the American experience. In reference to this alleged connection, cultural historian Michael A. Ledeen writes:

> Nearly a century after Tocqueville, the great sociologist Max Weber reached the same conclusion: "The spirit of capitalism.... was present before the capitalistic order." ... In Weber's famous theory, our relentless drive to create wealth came from the terrible inner tensions created by the Calvinist doctrine of predestination: not knowing whether we are saved or damned, we desperately seek some sign that we are among the chosen, and material success is taken to be such a sign. (Ledeen 80)

Even if Tocqueville and Weber are correct and this brand of "Christian triumphalism" does figure importantly in American thought and social practice, its theological pedigree is extremely questionable. The cry for social justice from abusive economic and political power is a leitmotif of the Old Testament prophets from Isaiah to Micah: "Learn to do good, search for justice, help the oppressed, be just to the orphan, plead for the widow" (*Isaiah* I: 17). Amos warns that those who have built them will not live to inhabit their luxurious homes "since you have trampled on the poor man" (*Amos* 5:11); and in a passage that would later be cited by Martin Luther King, he expresses his prophetic yearning in the following terms, "Let justice flow like water and integrity like an unfailing stream" (*Amos* 5:24). For a time at least, Job is by no means spared the pains of poverty despite his righteousness; and, in a passage that is often cited as a summary statement of Old Testament theology, the prophet Micah asks, "What does the Lord require of you but to do justice, and love kindness, and to walk humbly with your God" (*Micah*

6:1–8), not a formula for success likely to be echoed in America's corporate boardrooms and corridors of political power.

The New Testament, meanwhile, is no less stinting of passages that place greed, callousness, and competitiveness at variance with Christian morality. The early Christian community shared its property equally and made no allowance for the individual initiative deemed essential to social progress by modern champions of commercial culture (*Acts* 2:14, 36–47). One of the few occasions on which Jesus is provoked to anger in the Gospel accounts of his life concerns the blasphemy of the money changers, and in the Lukan version of the *Beatitudes,* he says "Blessed are the poor," thereby standing Christian triumphalism on its head. Such passages, which could be multiplied many times over, all tend to the same conclusion: The Pilgrim fathers were theologically mistaken in their belief that material prosperity is a special mark of divine favor. On the contrary, the Bible teaches that it is a special temptation to unwarranted power against which an enlightened Christianity might well seek to guard itself. From the perspective of the authentic American dream, it is a temptation against which an enlightened American patriotism might also seek protection.

Jefferson, who no doubt saw America's natural abundance as a blessing and property as a natural right, nevertheless made material prosperity secondary to the requirements of civic culture. In essence, he saw individual rights, including property rights, as subordinate to a more fundamental consideration, i.e., the self-evident right of individuals to live in a just society. "A right to property," says Jefferson, "is founded in our natural wants, in the means with which we are endowed to satisfy these wants, and the right to what we acquire by those means without violating the similar rights of other sensible beings.... Justice is the fundamental law of society" (as quoted in Padover 18). In other words, Jefferson's authentic American dream comprises a system of ethical checks and balances between cooperation and competition, individualism and civic conscience. The spirit of capitalism, which acknowledges no such ethical limit on either ambition or acquisitiveness, may well have been present in America before the capitalist order was established, but it was never entirely in accord with the spirit of democratic idealism, a fact that our Gothic storytellers, beginning with Charles Brockden Brown, were prompt to seize upon.

The early American theocracies, so vividly portrayed in the Gothic novels and short stories of Nathaniel Hawthorne, were conformist and austere in comparison with the later colonial structures that replaced them. The transplanted Whig aristocracy of the British colonial era, though oppressively paternalistic, was confident in its power, relaxed in its mores, and worldly in its avoidance of mystery. In short, it was an elegantly secular world better suited to the materialistic philosophy of Horatio than to the Gothic mysticism of Hamlet. The Federalist era that replaced it was even more so. Jefferson's generation was skeptical of ghosts and shadows. It was a generation committed to neoclassical standards of order and rationality that excluded the insights of the Gothic imagination. As Fiedler suggests, it is small wonder the American pioneer in Gothic fiction, Charles Brockden Brown, was driven to renounce the Gothic and ultimately to abandon novel writing altogether. (Fiedler 144). Before doing so, however, he produced a series of American prototypes that would instruct and pave the way for the later American dispensers of both Gothic and utopian literature such as Washington Irving, Nathaniel Hawthorne, Herman Melville, Edgar Allan Poe, Charlotte Perkins Gilman, Ambrose Bierce, Stephen Crane, Ignatius Donelley, Ralph Waldo Emerson, Henry David Thoreau, and Edward Bellamy.

Discussion Topics and Questions

1. Explain the close connection between Anglo-European Gothic arts and politics.
2. Summarize the revisionist interpretations of the Founding Fathers at both ends of the ideological spectrum (right-wing/left-wing) and discuss their respective strengths and weaknesses in relation to the "authentic American dream."
3. What are the internal contradictions within our national self-image that have given rise to a Gothic perspective on the American experience?
4. Discuss the American frontier as a symbol of the Gothic and explain how the political ethos of the American wilderness, personified by Andrew Jackson in the nineteenth century and Lyndon Baines Johnson in the twentieth century, is antagonistic to the republican ethos of Thomas Jefferson and John Kennedy.
5. Compare prominent themes in both *Wieland* and *Edgar Huntly* with those encountered in two dramatic masterpieces of the broad Gothic imagination, *Oedipus Rex* and *Hamlet*.

3 Nineteenth-Century Political Gothic

While Charles Brockden Brown was the founding father of American Gothic literature, Washington Irving (1783–1859) was its first transcontinental celebrity. His solution to the problems posed by a callow republic that could neither sustain the conventions of European Gothic nor confront its own internal contradictions, was to create an original subcategory of the Gothic, hereafter referred to as *burlesque Gothic*. His most familiar examples, *The Legend of Sleepy Hollow* and *Rip Van Winkle*, are tales of haunting and possession suited to a bustling, pragmatic society that does not truly believe in either ghosts or demons, least of all those from its own political and religious past. Irving's two celebrated folktales are narrated with tongue-firmly-in-cheek, though a thread of serious commentary runs through both—their common theme being the psychic displacement produced by rapid social change and mobility. "There is no encouragement for ghosts in most of our villages," observes Irving's narrator wryly "for they have scarcely had time to finish their nap, and turn themselves in their graves, before their surviving friends have traveled away from the neighborhood ... this is perhaps the reason why we so seldom hear of ghosts" (Irving/Joyce Carol Oates 37). Rip Van Winkle, meanwhile, awakens, not from death but from a preternaturally prolonged nap, to find himself a veritable ghost haunting an alien social and political landscape. From his perspective, that landscape has changed overnight. As one commentator observes, the protagonists of Washington Irving's *Rip Van Winkle* and Brown's *Wieland* are both caught in the throes of a social and political transition, a transition that calls their identities into question and challenges their capacity to understand and adapt (Christophersen 172).

When Irving wishes to create a more conventional Gothic narrative, as he does in *The Adventure of the German Student*, the setting shifts from upstate New York to England, France, and Spain, locales in which he spent much of his adult life. This particular tale is set in revolutionary Paris at the time of the French Terror. It tells of a serious young man, somewhat incongruously drawn to both the visionary doctrines of Swedenborg and the liberated views of the *philosophes*. He encounters a beautiful but distraught young woman late one night at "the Place de

Gréve, the square where public executions are performed." In defiance of traditional mores, he takes her back to his apartment. "It was a time for wild theories and wild actions," writes Irving. "Old prejudices and superstitions were done away; everything was under the sway of the 'Goddess of Reason.'" The following day he awakens next to her decapitated corpse. Realizing that he was seduced by a cadaver, he shrieks, "I am lost forever!" His belief in the rational certainties of the Enlightenment shattered, he lapses into madness and dies, like Wieland and Clithero in Brown's earlier novels (Irving 223–27). This melodramatic parable of republican hubris and damnation once again underscores the political origins of the Gothic imagination as well as the extent to which the specter of the French Revolution haunted a youthful republic. Of course, the most vivid specimen of Gothic literature inspired by the French Revolution, *A Tale of Two Cities,* was penned not by an American or even a Frenchman, but by the celebrated Victorian author Charles Dickens (1812–1870).

Dickensian America: "Not the Republic of My Imagination"

Dickens was responsible for two books that pointedly addressed America's schizophrenic adherence to republican and capitalist ideologies. He traveled to America in 1842 in order to present a series of public readings of his own works, fraternize with illustrious colleagues such as Irving, Emerson, and Poe, and gather raw data for a contemplated travelogue that he would eventually entitle *Notes on America.* His observations on the American experiment were also chronicled in *Martin Chuzzlewit,* the last full-length novel of his early period. Dickens came to this country confident of finding his democratic dreams realized. He brought impeccable credentials as a crusader against British abuses of the common welfare committed in the name of *laissez–faire* economics. Those libertarians who wish to disprove that America's economic difficulties stem from governmental interference would be well advised to review the history of the early industrial revolution in England. An unbiased survey of that era will quickly demonstrate that governmental deregulation does not foster an ethos of compassionate conservatism. On the contrary, in the best historical test case available, the social consequences of freeing the business community to follow its own devises reveals a record of Regency/Victorian England's inhumanity to man that rivals the atrocities of Nazi Germany. That record took the form of punitive "poor laws," exploitive labor practices, cruelty to children, and the creation of a permanent economic underclass forced to endure life in squalid urban ghettos rife with crime, disease, and poverty. In works such as *A Christmas Carol*, which owes much to the burlesque Gothic vein opened by Irving, Dickens attacked these British abuses of wealth and privilege with an eloquence on behalf of democratic idealism that is unsurpassed in the annals of political Gothic literature.

He was no more sparing of America's inhumanity to man. His principle target was slavery, an institution the English abolished in 1833, but one that was condoned by many Americans in the name of economic self-interest. Dickens intuited that the institution of slavery was linked to an ethos of selfishness and commercial dealing that was fundamentally incompatible with the republican aspirations of the founding. The boastful jingoism he frequently encountered in the New World conveniently ignored elements of our national life that negated democratic principles. He was therefore dismissive of such braggadocio and contemptuous of its unwarranted pretensions to democratic idealism, though he did form many warm personal attachments and found much to admire in the confidant vitality of the comparatively youthful republic. Moreover, his estimate of Americans in the aggregate was guardedly hopeful. In *Martin Chuzzlewit*, for example, the protagonist and his manservant, Mark Tapley, after visiting America for several harrowing months, engage in the following pertinent exchange on the eve of their return to England:

> "Why, Cook! what are you thinking of so steadily?" said Martin. "Why, I was thinking, sir," returned Mark, "that if I was a painter and was called upon to paint the American Eagle, how should I do it?" "Paint is as like an eagle as you could, I suppose." "No," said Mark. "That wouldn't do for me, sir. I should want to draw it like a Bat, for its short-sightedness; like a Bantam, for its bragging; like a Magpie, for its honesty; like a Peacock, for its vanity; like an Ostrich, for its putting its head in the mud, and thinking nobody sees it." "And like a Phoenix, for its power of springing from the ashes of its faults and vices, and soaring up anew into the sky! Well, Mark. Let us hope so." (547)

Nevertheless, Dickens returned to England in June of 1842 with a strong impression that America was not the republic of his imagination and that, by the failure of its example, it would one day deal a fatal blow to democracy. In addition to slavery and obsessive commercialism, Dickens also targeted the philistinism of American culture, i.e., its neglect of art and intellect. He found evidence for this in low standards of American journalism, in public indifference to the establishment of a just copyright law, and in the general lack of mental cultivation and introspection that marked the speech and demeanor of the average citizen. Both of his American-inspired books created a public outcry on this side of the Atlantic that only served to document their accuracy. In the words of one biographer, "Most of what Dickens said about America ... was true in essence. That was why it hurt" (Johnson 445).

    Even Dickens, however, despite his abhorrence of slavery, could not see past the conflict between competing forms of capitalism, i.e., "Yankee capitalist bourgeoisie" versus "southern planter aristocracy" (McPherson 8) to the deeper issues at stake in America's Civil War. He regarded the cause of abolition as a mere rationalization. "Any reasonable creature may know, if willing," wrote Dickens to William de Cerjat, "that the North hates the Negro, and that until it was convenient to make a pretense that sympathy with him was the cause of the war, it hated the abolitionists and derided them up hill and down dale" (Johnson 1002). For Dickens, the Northern cause was synonymous with the cynical ambition of Economic Man and the Scrooge-like spirit of expediency and soulless commercialism that motivated him. To an extent, of course, he was justified in this opinion. As noted Civil War historian James McPherson points out, the war between the states was, in part, an economic revolution on behalf of Northern entrepreneurial capitalism. In contrast to Lincoln, however, who saw very clearly that the South was fighting for the right to reject "the universal liberty of mankind" and that its invocation of the Spirit of 1776 was therefore bogus, Dickens viewed the North's objection to Southern secession as a hypocritical rejection of a precedent established by the War of Independence, as did Hawthorne. What both men failed to realize was that the South was inverting the republican argument on behalf of "natural human rights" and that "Secession was not just a revolution, but an unjust counterrevolution" (McPherson 28). The issue, as Lincoln expressed it succinctly in the Gettysburg Address, was whether a divided nation dedicated to the proposition that all men are created equal could endure. In retrospect, Lincoln's concern is clearly justified. Few modern historians believe that had the Union rather than slavery been abolished, the American experiment would have survived. Ironically, the deadly blow to democracy that Dickens feared America would one day deliver might well have been dealt with his tacit approval.

This section on mid-century Gothic writers begins with Dickens, rather than Hawthorne or Poe, because the America he visited twice was essentially the utopian-dream-turned-Gothic-nightmare that Brockden Brown surveyed in the Federalist era and that Dickens's literary cousins in the New World would attempt to map with considerably less impact on the international reading public. Dickens, the preeminent Gothic novelist of the Victorian era, commanded a much larger audience than his American contemporaries and predecessors. However, the roots of America's democratic dilemma eluded not only England's most astute and ardent democrat, but its own most gifted writers as well, with the possible exceptions of Emerson, Thoreau, and Twain. Only one of our great literary stylists, who happens to have been also one of our most revered presidents, was fully able to grasp and master the issues at stake. Abraham Lincoln, whose thought and character stamped the Civil War era much as Jefferson's thought and character stamped the Federalist era, defended the authentic American dream against conservative proponents of states' rights and human slavery. Just as Jefferson before him, and Woodrow Wilson, Franklin D. Roosevelt, and John F. Kennedy after him, were able to transcend conservative traditions of their culture in order to defend that dream, Lincoln transcended not only the conventional wisdom of his times but his own personal reservations and previously held convictions to actuate a moral imperative. It is important to realize that the protest lodged by the geniuses of American Gothic is primarily moral in nature. Commenting on Dickens, George Orwell, author of *1984*, one of the twentieth century's most widely read dystopian novels, notes that "Dickens's attitude is at bottom not even destructive.... It would be difficult to point anywhere in his books to a passage suggesting that the economic system is wrong *as a system*" (Orwell 58). America's Gothic artists and political figures have likewise advocated not revolution, but a synergistic balance between the claims of democratic idealism and capitalism, civic conscience and individualism.

Transcendentalists and the Coming Political Crisis

Of the generation of utopian writers who either straddled the Civil War era or came of age artistically in the decades immediately preceding it, Ralph Waldo Emerson (1803–1882) and his disciple Henry David Thoreau (1817–1862) made the greatest contribution to America's dystopian/utopian dialectic. No two writers commented more incisively on the social and political issues that emerged from an America drifting inevitably toward civil war, or better illustrated the ways in which those divisive issues were internalized. Both seemed to echo the buoyant optimism of Jefferson's public persona, and yet both cultivated a dark shadow side to their rationalist outlook that not only deepened their message but challenged the political and economic status quo of mid-century America.

In "The American Scholar," a commencement address delivered at Harvard in 1837, Emerson charted a progressive course for his country's intellectual life. Sometimes referred to as America's "intellectual Declaration of Independence," this summons to educational reform proclaims that "The eyes of man are set in his forehead not in his hindhead" (Emerson 47). Emerson's insistence that there is no inviolable canon of great literature and that the achievements of the past are of value only to the extent that they inspire innovative thinking in the present strikes a Jeffersonian note of iconoclasm that is still contemporary. He asserts that the function of scholarship is "to guide men by showing them facts amidst appearances," and goes on to issue a Gothic warning that the true history of any period is hidden or buried under layers of conventional wisdom and self-delusion:

> The world of any moment is the merest appearance. Some great decorum, some fetish of a government, some ephemeral trade, or war, or man, is cried up by half mankind and cried down by the other half, as if all depended on this particular up or down. The odds are that the whole question is not worth the poorest thought which the scholar has lost in listening to the controversy. Let him not quit his belief that a popgun is a popgun, though the ancient and honorable of the earth affirm it to be the crack of doom. (53)

He follows this ringing endorsement for independent thought with a confident assertion that "In self-trust all the virtues are comprehended.... In yourself slumbers the whole of Reason" (59). He insists that the great enemy of truth and freedom is fear: "Fear always springs from ignorance. It is a shame to him ... if he seek a temporary peace by the diversion of his thoughts from politics or vexed questions, hiding his head like an ostrich ... to keep his courage up. So is the danger a danger still; so is the fear worse" (54). Discounting Franklin Delano Roosevelt's famous dictum, "The only thing we have to fear is fear itself," it would be difficult to find anywhere in American social thought a more vigorous or insightful denunciation of our human tendency to engage in denial, i.e., to escape from a painful truth by accepting a less painful lie or half-truth.

At several points in his earlier essays, Emerson applied his own insight to the dangers of an economic spirit that was threatening to swamp the spirit of democracy. In the early essay cited above, he had already come to lament the influence of the commercial spirit on American scholarship: "Public and private avarice (sic) make the air we breathe thick and fat," complains Emerson. "The scholar is decent, indolent, complaisant. See already the tragic consequence. The mind of this country, taught to aim at low objects, eats upon itself" (59). As with many of the Gothic images imbedded in Emerson's utopian thought, the self-cannibalism of that last image is easily missed. In *Politics,* published in 1844, he argues that "persons and property" are "the two objects for which government exists," but that the seemingly self-evident principle that proprietors should be granted "more elective franchise than non-proprietors ... no longer looks so self-evident." He goes on to point out that "doubts have arisen whether too much weight had not been allowed in the laws of property" and that "the whole constitution of property on its present tenures, is injurious, and its influence on persons deteriorating and degrading" (380).

Emerson, however, encourages no political remedy for "public and private avarice." In keeping with the essentially conservative tradition of American political philosophy up to the period of Reconstruction, Emerson, like Jefferson before him, is distrustful of government. "The less government we have the better—the fewer laws, and the less confided power." His antidote to the "abuse of formal government" is "the influence of private character" (386). In order to transcend America's Gothic dilemmas, however, America's greatest political leaders, e.g., Jefferson, Lincoln, Wilson, Franklin Roosevelt, and Kennedy, were able to surmount their reservations with regard to the use of governmental power. At the major crisis points in American history, they set aside their devotion to the principle of "negative liberty" in favor of the doctrine of "positive liberty" (see chapter 2, 43). Ultimately, America's premier transcendentalists did likewise.

In Emerson's case, the impetus to transcend his innate conservatism was provided by the Civil War and his own abolitionist sympathies. In his 1862 essay entitled *The Emancipation Proclamation,* Emerson endorses Lincoln's application of the principle of positive liberty to the issue of slavery: "Liberty is a slow fruit. It comes, like religion, for short periods, and in rare conditions, as if awaiting a culture of the race which shall make it organic and permanent. Such moments of expansion in modern history were ... the Declaration of Independence ... and now, eminently, President Lincoln's Proclamation" (801). At this moment of political crisis, he accepted the proposition that strong governmental action, not the "influence of private character" was an appropriate remedy for the evils of slavery.

In doing so, Emerson was making his own transcendent leap of faith on behalf of a principle that was "over and above" the principle of "negative liberty." The democratic principal in question was the utopian "instinct of man to rise, and the instinct to love and help his brother" (786). Lincoln used the full power of his office to preserve the ideals of democracy, much as Jefferson had done earlier. You will recall that it was Jefferson's federalism that prompted Charles Brockden Brown's ultimate repudiation of republicanism. What Emerson was able to see as moments of transcendence in American history, men such as Charles Brockden Brown and John Wilkes Booth saw only as moments of betrayal. The bold initiatives of Roosevelt's "New Deal" and Kennedy's "New Frontier" were similarly interpreted by many contemporaries as reckless extensions of executive and legislative power rather than transcendent acts of leadership. Contrary to what today's conservatism would have us believe, however, the issue is not between big versus small government or an imperial versus a subservient presidency, but between the use of governmental authority to either promote or thwart the authentic American dream. Sadly, Lincoln and Kennedy paid with their lives for a willingness to place considerations of democratic idealism ahead of those dictated by political expediency, covertly fascist racial theories, and conservative fear of government.

Emerson, who knew Lincoln personally, was stricken by the news of his untimely death. Even had this personal bond not existed, the murder of a president, like that of a king, invokes the sin of Oedipus. Our presidents are frequently father (or grandfather) figures. "What haunts the psyche?" asks cultural historian Mark Edmundson rhetorically. His answer: "Its traumatic past, and particularly the past relations with parents" (Edmundson 32). In cadenced Gothic prose worthy of comparison with the elegiac poetry of Whitman's *When lilacs last in dooryard bloomed*, Emerson expressed his grief and sense of personal loss at a memorial service held shortly after the assassination: "We meet under the gloom of a calamity which darkens down over the minds of good men in all civil society, as the fearful tidings travel over sea, over land, from country to country, like the shadow of an uncalculated eclipse over the planet.... In this country, on Saturday, every one was struck dumb, and saw only deep below deep, as he meditated on the ghastly blow." At this point, Emerson's eulogy undergoes a jarringly abrupt transition from a minor to a major tonality. Just two sentences later he writes, "Yes, but that first despair was brief: the man was not so to be mourned. He was the most active and hopeful of men; and his work had not perished: but acclamations of praise for the task he had accomplished burst out into a song of triumph, which even tears for his death cannot keep down" (Emerson, *Abraham Lincoln* 829). The strained nature of Emerson's sudden shift from genuine despair to a forced and artificial triumph is obvious. Its implications will be considered below.

Curiously, Lincoln's violent death, like that of Kennedy a century later, inspired few such distinguished examples of Gothic literature and political Gothic commentary. It did, however, give rise to doubts and speculations of a conspiratorial nature. As pointed out earlier, conspiracy theories have occupied the Gothic imagination throughout its history, and are inseparable from the neo-Gothic revival in European literature that was initiated by Horace Walpole in 1764. Indeed, the Gothic perspective is fundamentally conspiratorial in its assumption that human history is inexplicable as a closed system subject to predictable laws and patterns. Our cultural beliefs, i.e., the intellectual status quo with regard to the way in which we conceptualize forces that define our place in the universe is a social construct determined, in part, by cultural and personal expediency. The more elaborate the construct, the more likely it is to collide with the very realities it was designed to cloak. The Gothic imagination therefore appeals to that part of our awareness that anticipates such collisions and attempts to interpret them.

America's social construct—its perception of its place in the political universe—is that of a nation premised on the rule of law, due process, and the orderly transition of power. Beneath the surface of that utopian self-conception, however, there lurks a submerged dystopian counter culture of political paranoia. That paranoia tends to surface in the aftermath of national traumas such as revolution, war (foreign or civil), and political assassination. The question naturally arises: to what extent is this paranoia justified? In one sense, of course, this question is irrelevant. The sociological and aesthetic impact of conspiratorial anxieties are unaffected by the issue of whether or not they are factually warranted. Like *Ossian*, the fraudulent Celtic epic that appealed so strongly to the suppressed romanticism of Jefferson's generation, conspiracy theories surrounding the Lincoln and Kennedy assassinations have dipped into a witches' cauldron of fear, suspicion, and emotional need that clearly requires an outlet. This cauldron is periodically replenished and brought to a boil by historical forces that we can neither control nor comprehend. Alternatively, the very existence of such a cauldron bears witness to our collective yearning for the kind of closure that only factual knowledge can provide. If our fears have stampeded us into settling for "a temporary peace" purchased at the price of denial, as Emerson's response suggests that he was stampeded into denial by Lincoln's death, we have indeed traded our republican birthright for a mess of pottage, i.e., our idealistic commitment to truth and justice for a false and unsustainable sense of well-being. As Emerson, who was unable to benefit from his own earlier insight, warned: "So is the danger a danger still."

Conspiracy Buffs and Scholarly Bluffs

Conspiracy theories, like prescription medicines, come in many sizes and shapes, some more palatable than others. To those who suffer from a low tolerance for Gothic ambiguity or who are immune to temporary suspensions of disbelief, there is simply no such thing as a palatable conspiracy theory. However, as historian Richard Hofstadter notes, there is a great difference between recognizing that conspiracies do sometimes occur in history and perceiving history itself as a tissue of conspiracies, evil plots, and official deceptions (Hofstadter 71). Some people take such medication as needed, but only in small doses and to evaluate its efficacy on a case-by-case basis. However, they may have the greatest difficulty swallowing larger pills. Scenarios that claim history is controlled by super-secret societies endowed with unlimited resources stretch credibility to the breaking point... or beyond. Consequently, when Jim Marrs, a dispenser of very large pills indeed, hints darkly that John Wilkes Booth was connected to the Knights of the Golden Circle, Bavarian Illuminati, and the Italian *Carbonari*, one is easily persuaded to decline his prescriptions (Marrs 212).

The theories presented in *The Lincoln Conspiracy* by David Balsinger and Charles E. Sellier Jr., on the other hand, seemingly merit closer consideration. Though less grandiose, they are ostensibly more plausible. Essentially, they posit a sequence of overlapping plots sponsored by Maryland planters, Northern capitalists, Confederate officials, and Radical Republicans in Washington led by Lincoln's own war secretary, Edwin M. Stanton. Admittedly, this scenario is presented as pop-culture docudrama rather than scholarly history. Admittedly also, it was written at a time when the soil had been sown for just such a fresh crop of conspiratorial speculation by public pressure for an official reinvestigation into the murders of JFK and MLK (not to mention public skepticism in the wake of Watergate). This linkage is explicitly acknowledged by the authors who maintain that, "In writing this book, the premise taken is that 1865 official statements might not be true, in light of what is now known about the Warren Commission investigation of the Kennedy assassination and the Watergate cover-up" (9).

Though intriguing, a verdict of insufficient evidence seems warranted with regard to this theory as well, were it not for the curious rush to judgment with which eminent historians have dismissed it. A short book review of *The Lincoln Conspiracy* by Lincoln biographer Stephen B. Oates will serve as an example. If the theories put forward by Balsinger and Sellier are so ill founded as this noted Civil War historian suggests, why could so eminent an authority not have provided a reasoned rebuttal rather than an inaccurate *ad hominem* attack? For instance, Oates contends that the allegedly incriminating missing pages from Booth's diary, supposedly discovered by one Joseph Lynch, do not exist ("The 'missing' diary pages were never released and doubtless do not exist"). He declines to say on what basis he makes this claim (Stephen Oates, *Abraham Lincoln: The Man Behind the Myths* 171). Why would a distinguished Civil War historian investigating so potentially significant a discovery demand certain verification that these documents are spurious? The number of missing pages is also in dispute. Oates insists there are thirty-seven; Balsinger and Selliers mention eighteen. Admittedly, the latter figure raises certain and obvious suspicion in light of the crucial eighteen minute lacuna that had recently been discovered in one of Richard Nixon's incriminating Watergate tapes. Oates also insists that hard evidence for the Lincoln conspiracy scenario is based exclusively on these missing pages. Balsinger and Sellier, on the other hand, cite several other documents and scientific tests as the basis for their conclusions. If Oates is correct, it should have been easy for him to have authoritatively discredited these other sources. Why didn't he?

Oates also misrepresents the plot, or plots, as outlined in the book. Balsinger and Sellier do not accuse Stanton of being the mastermind behind the assassination, as Oates maintains. Stanton is accused of being implicated in an abduction plot that was hijacked by the fanatical and murderous Booth, a plot that went bad and had then to be covered up. According to this scenario, Radical Republicans, fearful that Lincoln would lose his reelection bid to the Democrats, thereby turning Reconstruction over to their political enemies, arranged for a coup. Here is how the plot is described: "Members of Lincoln's own party are going to have him kidnapped and kept out of sight [not assassinated] until fake charges are arranged to impeach him. Meanwhile the Radicals will set up a system to run the executive branch" (Balsinger and Sellier 48).

Commenting on this plot, Balsinger and Sellier write, "No legal precedent existed for the action planned. The Constitution contained no provision for a committee to run the country, to appoint an interim president, or to declare that a legally elected president could not be inaugurated. The whole American system of government was to be disrupted in a game of politics without equal in history. Kidnapping, *possible* murder [italics mine], and the circumvention of the people's will were all in the plan" (51). If this was the plot in which Stanton was involved, its motivation need not have hinged, as Oates contends, on disagreements over Reconstruction policy within the Republican party, nor does such a plan preclude the possibility that Stanton was personally devoted to Lincoln and genuinely fearful for his life. Robert Kennedy was genuinely devoted to his brother but may well have played an inadvertent role in his assassination by encouraging CIA plots against Castro. If so, his grief was no doubt as genuine as his sense of guilt was warranted.

Moreover, Stanton is not accused of arranging for the missing guard Parker to leave his post. According to Balsinger and Sellier, Parker left to watch the play. Nor did Joseph Lynch discover the disputed missing pages in 1977, as Oates inaccurately states (according to the book, it was in 1974). Apart from his *ad hominem* attacks on CBS, Jack Anderson, Balsinger, Sellier, and, by extension, anyone who would dare to entertain the Stanton thesis, Oates's argument boils down to the fact that Stanton was a good man, an able war secretary, and an undoubted friend to Lincoln. Perhaps he was all of these and more, but I seem to recall that Caesar's assassins were also honorable men who, though they may have smiled upon their leader in public, are justifiably condemned by history as "damned villains." Furthermore, if Oates and those who share his disdain for Lincoln "conspiracy buffs" are truly interested in defending

Stanton against a charge they deem slanderous, their best recourse is surely to offer a meticulous, point-by-point refutation rather than a slashing counter-slander. The hysterical tone often adopted by defenders of consensus history against conspiriologists tends to confirm rather than dispel one's suspicions. If Stanton was such a good friend, solicitous of Lincoln's safety, why did he discourage the burly Major Eckert from protecting Lincoln the night of the assassination without making an alternative arrangement?

One also wonders if Lincoln and the Radicals led by Stanton were truly in agreement as to the best method of implementing a firm but conciliatory policy of reconstruction, as Oates suggests. Perhaps Johnson respected his predecessor's intentions far better than Stanton. One suspects that, with regard to this particular issue, Lincoln and Johnson were ethically at odds with their own party, much as John and Robert Kennedy were fundamentally at odds with many of their fellow democrats vis-à-vis issues pertaining to civil rights and the Cold War. Was the Washington telegraph service truly inoperative in the crucial hours following the assassination? Did the War Office truly block off all viable escape routes from Washington except those most likely to be used by Booth and his cohorts? Did Booth shave his mustache, as one of the accused conspirators (Dr. Mudd) claimed, and was the corpse officially identified as Booth possessed of a mustache? Were Booth's fellow conspirators isolated and mistreated in accordance with Stanton's express orders? Was Stanton unduly anxious to secure a military rather than a civilian trial for the conspirators? Is the apparent confession of conspiracy penned in doggerel by Col. Lafayette Baker, head of the NDP, America's Secret Service during this period, historically authentic?

These are not "cheap rhetorical questions," and perhaps Dr. Oates can supply unequivocal answers to all of them. If so, one final question remains: Why didn't he? Just as the public has an obligation to shun historical sensationalism, the scholar, whose task it is "to guide men by showing them facts amidst appearances," has an obligation to use his public forum to instruct rather than ridicule. Is the alleged continuity between Lincoln's and Stanton's views on reconstruction more appearance than fact? If it is, just how paranoid should we be with regard to the history of these events? Professional guidance in this matter would be appreciated. Unfortunately, many professional historians seem content to either dismiss such questions with little more than a sneer or ignore them entirely. Consequently, concerned citizens have no responsible option but to accept, provisionally at least, the cautionary aphorism in "Unusual Suspects," a conspiracy episode from Chris Carter's *X-Files* series: "No matter how paranoid you are, you're not paranoid enough."

Though modern Civil War historians seem content to endorse the orthodox version of Lincoln's assassination, dogmatically for the most part, William Hanchett, the Gerald Posner of the Lincoln conspiracy controversy, is an exception. His interpretation of Lincoln's murder does furnish a point-by-point refutation of at least some issues raised by earlier exponents of the Stanton conspiracy thesis, such as Otto Eisenschiml, author of *Why Was Lincoln Murdered,* on which Balsinger and Sellier based their work. Hanchett also offers a credible repudiation of the "new" documentation cited in *The Lincoln Conspiracy.* Some of his answers to the questions raised above are compelling. Others are disingenuous. For instance, he contends that Stanton refused to honor Lincoln's request that the burly Major Eckert accompany him to the Ford Theater out of a desire to discourage Lincoln from attending. Perhaps he did, but surely the issue is not why Stanton balked at Lincoln's request but why, once he realized that Lincoln was determined to attend, he failed to provide ample protection. Hanchett's willingness to depart from the historical record when it suits his purpose, a charge he and other historians frequently level against conspiracy buffs, is also noteworthy. For example, he chooses to refute Eisenschiml's contention that one of Stanton's agents was ordered to silence Booth, speculating that someone else might have fired the fatal shot. The historical record, however, indicates that the other soldiers were ordered to position themselves thirty yards from the burning barn in which Booth was stationed, well out of gunshot range. "It is true," argues Hanchett, "that Corbett and the other soldiers had been originally ordered to assume positions that far away, but it is easy to imagine that as the drama neared its fiery climax the temptation to move in for a close look would have been overpowering" (Hanchett 177–78). The relevant point here is not that defenders of consensus history should be censured for engaging in unconfirmed speculation, but that the same latitude should be accorded to conspiriologists. Moreover, Hanchett's premature assertion that in discrediting the documentation used by Balsinger and Sellier, exponents of consensus history have conclusively disposed of the Stanton thesis suggests a rush to judgment that belies his professed dedication to strict standards of historical objectivity.

Before leaving this controversial subject, there is one additional Gothic element to Lincoln's final days that is uncontested. Just days prior to the assassination, he experienced what appears to have been a premonitory dream. In this dream he wandered from room to room late at night without seeing anyone until finally he came to the East Room where his own body was lying in state. A guard standing watch informed him that the president had been assassinated. Precognition was not Lincoln's only brush with the paranormal. Earlier in life, in 1862 following the death of his son Willie, he dabbled in spiritualism, though his involvement seems to have been largely prompted by his distraught wife. Commenting on this episode, Oates maintains, in his classic biography (*With Malice Towards None*), "Ultimately it was Lincoln's own fatalism that eased his sorrow and helped him to cope with his dreams and memories.... 'I have all my life been a fatalist,' he told a congressman one day, and said he agreed with Hamlet that 'there is a divinity that shapes our ends'" (Stephen Oates, *Malice* 317). The importance of Shakespeare, *Hamlet* in particular, to the political Gothic imagination will become apparent as America's political-Gothic history unfolds. In his verbal portrait of Lincoln (*Lincoln the Literary Artist*), cultural historian Jacques Barzun depicts a young man suggestive of Shakespeare's immortal Dane: "His strangely detached attitude towards himself, his premonitions and depressions, his morbid regard for truth and abnormal suppression of aggressive impulses, suggest that he hugged a secret wound which ultimately made out of an apparently common man the unique figure of an artist-saint" (Barzun, *The Barzun Reader* 297).

Lincoln's Hamlet-like fatalism is well attested by his attitude toward his own possible assassination, as reported by Stephen B. Oates: "Lincoln agreed with Seward. 'Assassination,' Seward declared, 'is not an American practice or habit, and one so vicious and desperate cannot be engrafted into our political system'" (*Malice* 452). Despite mounting evidence to the contrary, this same argument still represents the consensus wisdom among professional historians and journalists. Apropos Lincoln's uncanny dream, the twentieth-century British author J. B. Priestley, who rejected the conclusions of the Warren Commission and devoted much of his life to exploring time anomalies, has this to say: "I for one can no longer accept it as a precognitive dream, as I understand precognitive dreams. No actual scene in the near future is being described.... During the last phase of the Civil War, Lincoln, hated in the South and disliked by various factions in the North, was constantly

receiving letters that were insanely abusive and threatening. He may
have shrugged them away but that does not mean they would have no
effect on his unconscious, which finally created for him the dream he
described" (Priestley 83). Though persuasive up to a point, this
explanation ignores the possibility that Lincoln's dream was an
expression of a more than private anxiety. It was perhaps also a
subconscious attempt to transcend his fearful and fatalistic denial that a
"vicious and desperate" habit was about to be engrafted unto the
American political system.

Emerson's Reversal into the Opposite

Returning to a consideration of Emerson's memorial address on
Lincoln, Mark Edmundson writes, "To be sure, Emerson is a philosopher
of novelty, of the American capacity to begin anew; but the cost for such
innovation, he continually informs us, can be appalling, and it is a cost
that each must bear himself." He goes on to say that "Emerson, in short,
refuses mourning, or strains to make short work of it.... To Emerson 'the
only sin is limitation'—the only sin is Gothic bondage to the past (160–
61). Emerson's almost brutal refusal of mourning is very clear in the
passage, cited above, in which he transitions so abruptly from grief to
triumph. Even so, is such a forced and unnatural suppression of grief
indicative of authentic transcendence or does it suggest Gothic denial?
    In Emerson's later essays, one detects a marked change of attitude.
The challenge to democratic idealism posed by an ethos of prosperity
and those who value property rights above human rights is no longer
disparaged. From denouncing the "deteriorating and degrading" effects
of wealth and property, as he did in 1844, Emerson goes on by 1860 to
become a mouthpiece for the commercial spirit he had earlier deplored.
In *Conduct of Life* he writes admiringly of Dickens's Economic Man:
"Commerce is a game of skill, which every man cannot play, which few
men can play well.... Wealth brings with it its own checks and balances.
The basis of political economy is non-interference. The only safe rule
found is the self-adjusting meter of supply and demand" (637). Notice
the Newtonian, mechanistic metaphor of the "self-regulating meter." The
ethos out of which Emerson is speaking here is one that would have been
applauded by the diabolical mill-owner Bach from Melville's *The
Tartarus of Maids,* a work that will be discussed below. It would not
have been applauded by Emerson's disciple Thoreau or by Emerson's

own younger, more idealistic self. So what had happened to dampen Emerson's youthful ardor for economic justice and democracy? What had become of the man who once wrote: "Let men cultivate the moral affections, lead manly independent lives; let them make riches the means and not the end of existence, and we shall hear no more of the commercial spirit" or "The power of love, as the basis of a State, has never been tried" (Emerson, *Politics* 388)? One possible answer is encompassed in the Gothic realities of war and death. Those realities would run through Emerson's portion of American history like a surging torrent, gaining momentum with the passage of time. The mounting casualties of The Mexican War and the Civil War, the death of a beloved child, the assassination of a beloved president, the execution of Emerson's abolitionist friend, John Brown—an extensive catalogue of strife and conflict to which the name of one more casualty must be added—that of Emerson himself. In the end, he had endured a flood tide of national and personal trauma. What remained when the waters receded was an enormous burden of undischarged pain and grief. How long and often can any individual, even one as fundamentally hopeful and optimistic as Emerson, stare into the face of the Gorgon without turning to stone? My point is not that Emerson became a man of Gothic sensibilities, but that in attempting to repress such sensibilities he became an object lesson in the psychological dangers of denial.

As Edmundson points out, Emerson's way of dealing with grief was to suppress his sense of loss, to heroically deny its dark trinity of pain, memory, and longing and the redemption it affords. As Emerson's younger self realized, however, the psychic dangers posed by such a strategy are undiminished by our denial of them. Indeed, they are magnified by it. One of the most persistent insights of the Gothic imagination suggests that only by acknowledging one's Gothic dilemma and examining it thoroughly is authentic transcendence possible. As psychologists such as Freud and Jung have repeatedly warned, the discarded self invariably returns, usually in the archetypal guise of a devouring monster. It feeds off our denial, gaining strength in direct proportion to the strength we exert in the acting to suppress it. Once again, the Gothic price tag on Emerson's brand of pseudo transcendence is *enantiodromia,* Jung's reversal into the opposite. In 1846, Thoreau went to jail as a conscientious objector to America's unjust war with Mexico. Having paid Thoreau's bail against his wishes, Emerson visited his former student at the jailhouse: "Henry, what are you doing in jail?"

Thoreau replied, "Waldo, what are you doing out of jail?" History leaves little room for doubt as to which man was truly imprisoned.

Thoreau's Gothic Transcendentalism

When Thoreau came out of jail, he was a changed man—changed in his attitude toward his friend Emerson, his government, and his neighbors. Though traditionally associated with the utopian optimism of the transcendentalist movement, he obviously underwent a psychological conversion not unlike that experienced by the somber protagonist of Hawthorne's Gothic tale *Young Goodman Brown,* in which he dreams of seeing his fellow citizens, including those on whose virtue he had implicitly relied, assembled in a forest to attend a witches' Sabbath. Commenting on the internal revolution this visionary experience produces, Hawthorne writes, "A stern, a sad, a darkly meditative, a distrustful, if not a desperate man did he become from the night of that fearful dream" (Hawthorne/Joyce Carol Oates 63). Compare this with the following quotation from Thoreau's essay on *Civil Disobedience:* "Action from principle, the perception and the performance of right, changes things and relations; it is essentially revolutionary, and does not consist wholly with anything which was. It not only divides states and churches, it divides families; ay, it divides the individual, separating the diabolical in him from the divine" (Thoreau 91). Thoreau elaborates in the same essay: "I saw yet more distinctly the State in which they lived. I saw to what extent the people among whom I lived could be trusted as good neighbors and friends; that their friendship was for summer weather only; that they did not greatly propose to do right" (Thoreau 99).

Clearly, Hawthorne's central message, as stated by the devil himself, is the more fatalistic of the two. "Evil, says Satan, "is the nature of mankind." Thoreau affirms his transcendentalist belief in the sanctity of individual human conscience and in the power that comes of bearing witness to the truth. "Any man more right than his neighbors," asserts Thoreau, "constitutes a majority of one already." However, what both writers have in common is a Gothic perception of one's neighbor as a divided being potentially capable of being overshadowed by an evil self, as Dr. Jekyll is by Mr. Hyde in Stevenson's fable and as the enlightened spirit of JFK is overshadowed by its dark alter ego, Richard Nixon in Oliver Stone's cinematic cycle of conspiracy films.

Transcendentalism and the American Founding

[handwritten annotation in right margin]

If America's dystopian/utopian impulses are complementary rather than antagonistic, as this book contends, it is appropriate to ask in what way and to what extent did Thoreau's utopianism ratify or subvert Jefferson's republican agenda? At a glance, Thoreau's call to passive resistance and Jefferson's call to public service seem antithetical; but are they? Thoreau derived his political philosophy from his mentor Emerson who writes, "The less government we have the better." In a famous defense of radical conservatism, the student surpasses the master: "That government is best that governs not at all" (Thoreau 85). The mentor affirms, "with the appearance of the wise man the State expires. The appearance of character makes the State unnecessary" (Emerson 386). The student rejoins, "There will never be a really free and enlightened State until the State comes to recognize the individual as a higher and independent power, from which all its own power and authority are derived" (Thoreau 104).

Both men are clearly distrustful of institutional power, but then so was Jefferson who writes, "Our General Governments may be reduced to a very simple organization and a very unexpensive (sic) one" (as quoted in Padover 30). All three men, in theory, supported the principle of negative liberty; and yet, at critical junctures in their lives, all three embraced its opposite. Jefferson, as indicated earlier, adopted an expansive, pro-active approach to governance while he occupied the White House. Emerson backed Lincoln's stand against secession, slavery, and states' rights. The pacifist Thoreau, in his outrage at the return of a slave to his master in 1854, was stung into the following admission that were the state to become the champion rather than the opponent of human rights, he would take up arms in its defense: "Show me a free state and a court truly of justice, and I will fight for them, if need be" (Thoreau 15). The explanation for this apparent inconsistency is that all three of these idealists were convinced that government could not create freedom, only the conditions under which freedom may be expected to flourish. In other words, they acknowledged a higher good, i.e., an impulse toward cooperation, creativity, and compassion, that is superior to the claims of the state. Jefferson identified this impulse with reason, Emerson and Thoreau identified it with conscience, but they were referring to the same transcendent reality. Ultimately, all three men envisioned the possibility of a political entity founded on moral virtue rather than force.

It was their flexible, imaginative alter egos, i.e., their Gothic imaginations, that permitted them to exorcise their own rationalist hobgoblins of inconsistency in order to affirm a deeper commitment to political and economic human rights. That is why the unconditional devotion to small government and *laissez-faire* economics that defines modern conservatism is historically and theoretically bogus. It seems to track back to these patron saints of the American heritage but, on closer inspection, proves to be a misguided expression of the same Gothic fear and skepticism that all three men, at critical junctures, were able to overcome. In addition to a common capacity for transcendence, Jefferson, Emerson, and Thoreau shared other characteristics as well. All three exhibited a romantic reverence for nature, i.e., the organic as opposed to the mechanistic, all three recognized the dangers to progress posed by an overly cultivated sense of tradition, all three endorsed a view that the ultimate benefits of the American experiment had to do with personal cultivation rather than political empowerment, and all three equated education with the moral, philosophical, and aesthetic enlightenment of the whole person, not the acquisition of a specialized body of technical skills and practical knowledge.

Clearly, Thoreau recognized the dangers of economic slavery posed by a commercial spirit that reduced the whole person to the one-dimensional status of "consumer." Jefferson, who seems never to have anticipated this development, writes, "The merchants will manage the better, the more they are left free to manage for themselves" (as quoted in Padover 30). Emerson, as we have seen, sounded the alarm in his younger days, but devolved into a propagandist for the same utilitarian spirit that Charles Dickens devoted his literary career to opposing. Thoreau, however, was as much a conscientious objector to the economic war against the human spirit being waged by unrestrained capitalism as he was to America's war of national aggression against Mexico. Both abuses of power were motivated ultimately by considerations of financial gain. "Cold and hunger," writes Thoreau in "Life Without Principle," "seem more friendly to my nature than those methods which men have adopted and advise to ward them off" (360). While applauding the spirit in which these words are offered, one inevitably wonders if Thoreau had ever truly experienced cold and hunger as those who belong to our modern empire of the homeless surely have.

Somewhat later in this same essay he explains, "America is said to be the arena on which the battle of freedom is to be fought; but surely it cannot be freedom in merely a political sense that is meant. Even if we grant that the American has freed himself from a political tyrant, he is still the slave of an economical and moral tyrant" (369). Thoreau identifies the superficiality and provincialism of American culture as the foremost symptom of this economic tyranny: "Just so hollow and ineffectual, for the most part, is our ordinary conversation. Surface meets surface" (366). Under such a system, complains Thoreau, journalism, the exalted Fourth Estate charged with guarding our democratic freedoms, is a mere dispenser of trivial gossip. The danger of attending closely to our "news from nowhere" is stated in the following passage: "Only the character of the hearer determines to which it shall be open, and to which closed. I believe that *the mind can be permanently profaned* by the habit of attending to trivial things, so that all our thoughts shall be tinged with triviality" (368, italics mine). So that there can be no mistake as to the source of our social affliction, he underscores his point by drawing attention to the fact that "We are provincial ... because we are warped and narrowed by an exclusive devotion to trade and commerce and manufactures and agriculture and the like, which are but means, and not the end" (370).

The dystopian implications of Thoreau's insights were fully realized only in the second half of the twentieth century. The shallowness and triviality of which Thoreau complained is now magnified many times over by a pervasive culture of mass consumption. In the words of media critic Neil Postman, "the Founding Fathers did not foresee that tyranny by government might be superseded by another sort of problem altogether, namely, the corporate state, which through television now controls the flow of public discourse in America" (Postman 139). Postman goes on to observe that our Ministry of Culture is Huxleyan, not Orwellian: "It does everything possible to encourage us to watch continuously. But what we watch is a medium which presents information in a form that renders it simplistic, non-substantive, non-historical and non-contextual; that is to say, information packaged as entertainment" (141). In truth, of course, it is both Orwellian in its tendency to rewrite history and Huxleyan in its reliance on hedonism. Postman's book was published before the information "revolution" introduced us to the packaged entertainment of "Quake!" It is somehow difficult to believe that Bill Gates's innovative game technology is contributing to the kind of revolution supported by Jefferson, Emerson, and Thoreau. By the same token, it is difficult to see what the robotic army of acolytes one encounters during a weekend stroll through one of America's many glass-domed cathedrals of commerce has to do with the realization of Jefferson's republican dream.

Hawthorne, Melville, and the Ghost of America's Theocratic Past

Nathaniel Hawthorne (1804–1864) died before the war between the states ended, and Edgar Allan Poe (1809–1849) did not live to see its commencement. In 1862, before Lincoln's *Emancipation Proclamation*, Hawthorne did, however, encounter the president at a public function in Washington, an encounter that he memorialized in the following vivid, though jarringly condescending portrait: "The whole physiognomy is as coarse a one as you would want to meet anywhere in the length and breadth of the States.... A great deal of native sense; no bookish cultivation, no refinement; honest at heart, and thoroughly so, and yet, in some sort, sly.... On the whole, I ... would as lief have Uncle Abe for a ruler as any man whom it would have been practicable to put in his place" (Miller 474). Though one hopes that his professed regard is genuine, Hawthorne's patronizing sense of intellectual superiority toward "Uncle Abe" is evident. Plainly, Hawthorne's regional bias prevented him from seeing past Lincoln's rough frontier façade. Nevertheless, it was Lincoln, not Hawthorne who grasped the republican stakes involved in the South's bid for secession. As one of Hawthorne's recent biographers observes, "At the beginning of the war in April 1861 Hawthorne rejoiced, or so he said, that 'the Union is smashed. We never were one people, and never really had a country since the Constitution was formed.'" He remained convinced that "'amputation' was the better plan and that 'all we ought to fight for is, the liberty of selecting the point where our diseased members should be lopped off'" (Miller 470).

Lacking the political Gothic instincts of Charles Brockden Brown, Hawthorne was ill-equipped to serve as Lincoln's Gothic alter ego as Brown had served Jefferson in that capacity. However, he did, in a sense, pick up the argument where Brown left off in *Wieland*. Brown's dystopian vision of republicanism undone by religious fanaticism and the cash nexus is frequently related to an event in our early history known as the Great Revival, or Second Great Awakening (1797–1800). "Anxiety over the future," says one historian of this social phenomenon, "lay at the heart of the Second Great Awakening" (Christophersen 39). During periods in which levels of democratic participation are low and/or levels of social unrest are high, people look to religion for meaning and consolation. From the extent to which America's writers such as Poe and Hawthorne turned away from the public arena at or near the mid-point of the nineteenth century, focusing on the psychological and the metaphysical rather than contentious social issues, one can infer that American society was ill at ease with its political prospects. Because politics permeates culture, however, no artistic statement is without political implications. The stories and novels of Hawthorne are a prime example.

In "A Man of Adamant," for instance, Hawthorne sounds a recurrent theme, namely the dangers of spiritual or scientific perfectionism. In countless stories such as *Rapaccini's Daughter, Ethan Brand,* and *The Artist of the Beautiful,* the Gothic hero-villain is guilty of intellectual pride. Like Faust or Frankenstein, Hawthorne's protagonists frequently enter into a devil's bargain by adopting inhumane means to achieve ostensibly idealistic ends. In the process, they separate themselves from the redemptive grace of human sympathy and community. Hawthorne's preoccupation with this theme can be read as an autobiographical exploration of the alienated status of the artist in society as well as a commentary on the biblical concept of original sin. However, it can also be interpreted as a theme well suited to a nation premised on the utopian quest for political perfection. Hawthorne warns that the price we pay, as a nation, for a tendency to lapse into a self-congratulatory stance of moral superiority and denial threatens to transform Jefferson's ideal citizen into a man of "adamant."

Denial is, indeed, one of the central themes in Hawthorne's greatest novel, *The Scarlet Letter.* The question it poses is one that perennially haunts the American psyche: What becomes of an individual or a society that attempts to conceal its guilty past, as the Reverend Dimmesdale attempts to conceal his adultery? Is it possible to transcend one's history without openly and publicly acknowledging one's guilt, as Hester Prynne is compelled to do and as Dimmesdale undertakes to do voluntarily? Gothic heroes and villains are typically time-haunted individuals for whom painful memory, i.e., an awareness of past wrongs and evil deeds, becomes an agency of redemption. That is why, in Gothic narratives, memory is not so much a stenographic record as it is a creative faculty whereby human experience is continually deciphered, refigured, and recontextualized in order to sound its deeper meanings. Memory, in short, serves as a catalyst for transcendence.

American culture is sometimes accused of being deficient in its sense of history. According to the Gothic imagination, a culture that suffers from such a deficiency is fated to endlessly recycle its Gothic dilemmas, to experience what Mark Edmundson, in his excellent short survey of American culture, *Nightmare on Main Street,* refers to as "dead-end Gothic." Fate and history are synonymous, warns Edmundson. An insufficient sense of either becomes the mechanism whereby an individual or society is locked into a hopeless cycle of denial, projection, and vengeance. Such a cycle, claims Edmundson, precludes the very possibility of transcendence (Edmundson 72). Commenting on what he terms Hawthorne's "tragic humanism," Leslie Fiedler maintains that Hawthorne seeks to invoke "the blackness of life most men try deliberately to ignore" (Fiedler 432–35).

In Hawthorne's near masterpiece, *The Blithedale Romance,* he seems to adopt a more overtly political subject, a utopian experiment in communal living based on the socialist theories of Charles Fourier. For a short time, Hawthorne took up residence with the lotus-eaters of the Brook Farm experiment a few miles outside of Boston. In his 1852 preface, however, he claims that his "whole treatment of the affair is altogether incidental to the main purpose of the Romance; nor does it put forward the slightest pretensions to illustrate a theory, or elicit a conclusion, favorable or otherwise, in respect to Socialism" (Hawthorne, *Blithedale* 1). Although this is more than a little disingenuous, as many of Hawthorne's critics and biographers have observed, it is nevertheless consistent with the reluctance, noted earlier, of the Gothic imagination to entertain theories of systemic change.

The experiment is clearly depicted as a failure, and the very notion that it could have been anything else was plainly alien to Hawthorne's Calvinistic outlook: In another work, his biographical *Life of Pierce,* as cited in a critical essay by Roy M. Male, Hawthorne writes, "There is no instance in all history of the human will and intellect having perfected any great moral reform by methods which it adapted to that end" (Hawthorne, *Blithedale* 297). In the second paragraph of the opening chapter of *The Scarlet Letter* ("The Prison Door"), Hawthorne makes another public confession of his doubts concerning rationalist schemes for social reform: "The founders of a new colony, whatever Utopia of human virtue and happiness they might originally project, have invariably recognized it among their earliest practical necessities to allot a portion of the virgin soil as a cemetery, and another portion as the site of a prison" (Hawthorne, *Scarlet Letter* 2). As suggested above, this great Gothic novel is haunted by a sense of humanity's inescapable thralldom to the past.

The most overtly Gothic feature of *The Blithedale Romance*, first published in 1852, is its preoccupation with mediumship and mesmerism, subjects that had commanded national attention just a few years earlier. In 1848, the Fox sisters of Hydesville, New York, created a sensation that swelled into an international controversy when they introduced to the world the mysterious pleasures of table-rapping and other psychic manifestations associated with spiritualism (Wilson, *Afterlife* 86). Some critics, such as Irving Howe, dismiss this aspect of Hawthorne's novel as "Gothic flim-flam" (Howe 296). Others, such as Teresa Goddu, see in it a veiled commentary on the tyranny of the marketplace and the culturally ambiguous role assigned to women within a market economy (see Goddu 94–116).

By a strange twist in logic, Goddu concludes that Hawthorne's "pretense" of having escaped the trammels of commodification through his art is ethically inferior to Louisa May Alcott's frank surrender to marketplace values. According to this curious argument, Hawthorne's sincere, if futile, desire to distance himself from Economic Man signals his masculine weakness, whereas Alcott's willingness to produce literary potboilers for the marketplace she despises is a sign of feminine power. According to such feminist reasoning, what is good for the artistic goose, under capitalism, is apparently bad for the artistic gander. However, the mere fact that dozens of communities like Brook Farm sprang up in the pre–Civil War era suggests that while, in one sense, radical republicanism was alive and well, in another, there was a perceived need to seek an alternative to the lifestyle afforded by mainstream American culture. This circumstance, I suspect, prompted Hawthorne's interest and accounts for our own continued involvement with *The Blithedale Romance* as well.

Herman Melville (1819–1891), like Hawthorne, is preoccupied with metaphysics rather than politics in American culture. His basic theme, the inexplicable human propensity for both good and evil, is one that Hawthorne tends to situate in America's theocratic past. Commenting on the role that America's colonial theocracies played in shaping nineteenth-century literary sensibilities, Leslie Fiedler points to three primary lines of development: an "hysterical evangelicalism" that was dismissive of art and intellect, a "Middlebrow Puritanism" that championed the sanctity of the individual human conscience, and a "tragic humanism" that embraced the evangelical doctrine of humanity's innate moral depravity while rejecting its Philistine dismissal of intellectual and aesthetic culture. He concludes that the aesthetic impact of extreme evangelicalism was transitory, though if he had lived to witness the resurgence of fundamentalist Evangelicalism embraced by the conservative constituency of Newt Gingrich and Jerry Falwell, he might have thought differently. Middlebrow Puritanism, claims Fiedler, led to the optimistic utopianism of transcendentalist thinkers such as Emerson and Thoreau. He regards Hawthorne and Melville as the chief representatives of the third line of development, tragic humanism (Fiedler 430–32).

While it is undoubtedly correct to view Melville's classic novels, *Moby Dick* and *Billy Budd,* as Gothic explorations of metaphysical evil (e.g., the Satanic pride epitomized by Captain Ahab, and the motiveless malice epitomized by Claggart) both works are commentaries on social and political evils as well. *Moby-Dick,* for example, which has been humorously characterized as a thousand pages of metaphysics and whale blubber, explores the brutality and monomania with which nineteenth-century capitalists pursued the profits of whaling, one of that era's most lucrative industries. Similarly, the naval vessel that provides the setting for *Billy Budd,* which inevitably suggests the metaphorical "ship of state," chronicles a blatant miscarriage of justice. Melville's tale of official corruption on the high seas is thereby intended as an allegory on the judicial impotence of the state when attempting to protect its citizens against human depravity. To realize the contemporary relevance of Melville's message, one has only to think of the failures of our own judicial system to thoroughly vet the evidence with regard to accused assassins Lee Harvey Oswald, Sirhan Sirhan, and James Earl Ray, the inconclusiveness of the O. J. Simpson trial, the judicially determined outcome of the Bush/Gore presidential race, and the policy of frontier justice that President George W. Bush evidently prefers to that prescribed by international law with regard to Muslim terrorist Osama bin Laden—a distinction that is admittedly academic so long as bin Laden remains at large.

That Melville was sensitive to the economic as well as the metaphysical dimensions of human evil is well attested by his short story, *The Tartarus of Maids*. This mythopoeic tale is offers a prophetic indictment of early American industrialism, though it is equally an indictment against the sexual politics of a culture in which feminine virtues are routinely subjugated to the exigencies of a male-dominated marketplace. At a literal plane, Melville recounts a mundane business transaction between a seed-salesman in need of replenishing his depleted store of envelopes and a paper manufacturer named Bach. Melville's story begins with an intentional invocation of Dante's *Divine Comedy,* a literary landmark of the Gothic imagination in which the protagonist is conducted on a guided tour through hell, purgatory, and paradise. As you may recall, at the core of Dante's underworld lies the frozen lake of Cocytus, a potent symbol for a realm devoid of either human warmth or divine grace.

On a mythic plane, Melville's mountainous New England setting is transformed into a Dantean Inferno of freezing wind, snow, and ice. The protagonist makes his way to the papermill via a road that stands "within a Dantean gateway." He proceeds among "many Plutonian, shaggy-wooded mountains" to a hollow called "the Devil's Dungeon," where he encounters a "strange-colored torrent" known as "Blood River." Finally, he arrives, with frostbitten cheeks, at the isolated papermill itself. The locale through which he passes is compared to both the German Rhineland and the region near the Temple Church, London known as the "Paradise of Bachelors." The "dark-complexioned" mill owner, "Old Bach," bears a German name that translates into English as Brook, a name suggestive of the blood-red torrent mentioned earlier. That circumstance, together with his dark complexion and the designation of the hollow in which the mill is situated (the "Devil's Dungeon") strongly implies the mill-owner's diabolical identity.

This satanic mill, with a single exception, employs only women. Described as "passive-looking" or "sad-looking," these females are forced to serve the factory machines. Melville writes, "Machinery—that vaunted slave of humanity—here stood menially served by human beings, who served mutely and cringingly as the slave serves the Sultan" (Melville/J. C. Oates 70). A young male employee named Cupid, leads the frozen protagonist on a guided tour of Bach's industrial gulag. Of this enigmatic guide, Melville writes, "More tragical and more inscrutably mysterious than any mystic site, human or machine, throughout the factory, was the strange innocence of cruel-heartedness in this usage-hardened boy" (Melville/J. C. Oates 72). The dominant image in

Melville's story, however, is the unfeeling machinery itself, which serves as a metaphor of an unfeeling economic order, "the essence of which is unvarying punctuality and precision." The organizing principle of Bach's operation, implies Melville, is utterly Newtonian—a coldly rational order that maims and dismembers the human spirit as Bach's machines threaten to maim and dismember the human bodies of its female servants. He describes this sinister setting as follows:

> Something of awe stole over me as I gazed upon this inflexible iron animal. Always, more or less, machinery of this ponderous, elaborate sort strikes, in some moods, strange dread into the human heart, as some living, panting Behemoth might. But what made the thing I saw so specially terrible to me was the metallic necessity, the unbudging fatality which governed it. (Melville/J. C. Oates 75)

Like Poe's terrifying maelstrom and Gilman's yellow wallpaper, Melville's "iron animal" symbolizes the values associated with a particular paradigm, or model, of reality. Its Gothic menace is neither supernatural nor altogether natural, just as the unconventional hero-villain of Melville's mechanized inferno is neither a lusting monk nor a power-crazed aristocrat. The true Gothic villain of the *Tartarus of Maids* is a patriarchal and dehumanizing industrial system, personified by the mysterious Mr. Bach. The danger it represents arises from its politically sanctioned disregard for the emotional needs of its employees, male as well as female—though this essentially male-oriented approach to human productivity and social organization is particularly oppressive to females.

Melville's parallel between the Woedolor Mountains of New England and the "Paradise of Bachelors" calls attention to a quarter of London, the Temple, that is closely identified with the legal profession. This symbol, in turn, serves as a convenient shorthand for British justice and officialdom in general. By means of this succinct process of association, Melville conjures an England that is not only the birthplace of the Industrial Revolution, but home to a political establishment as indifferent to the plight of its laboring "hands" as the cruel-hearted Mr. Bach is to the plight of his female employees. In essence, Melville is suggesting that America's increasingly one-sided culture is replicating the institutionally sanctioned sins of Europe against the spirit of liberal democracy.

In the dystopian world of Melville's satanic paper mill, not only women but African Americans, Native Americans, immigrants, and other marginalized groups are further than ever from claiming a seat at democracy's table. Meanwhile, original participants who are unable or unwilling to serve the new arrangement, such as farmers, artists, and intellectuals, find that they are no longer welcome. Indeed, Melville's story foreshadows a world in which Jefferson's refined Banquet of Democracy is replaced by a primitive feeding frenzy unfit for men and women of refinement and goodwill. According to Melville, the barren lifestyle mandated by America's burgeoning capitalism is an emotionally chilling Tartarus, an underworld of the spirit. Such an environment makes little provision for a fully realized life in which the liberty to pursue public service and individual cultivation, i.e., Jefferson's conception of happiness, is recognized as an inalienable human right. Earlier, I suggested that Jefferson seemed unaware of the impending industrial holocaust. In retrospect, however, his untenable determination to preserve America's Arcadian lifestyle was conceivably prompted by a Gothic foreboding. By the end of the nineteenth century, the predatory eagle, symbolizing a new political paradigm based on the alliance of big business with big government, was in full flight. As America's Gothic ravens such as Charles Brockden Brown, Dickens, and Thoreau foresaw, the enlightened and humane spirit of republicanism that Jefferson personified would ultimately be replaced by a spirit analogous to twentieth-century European fascism. Within a century or less, big business would become more menacing to the cause of liberty than big government.

Quoth the Raven

No survey of prominent nineteenth-century Gothic voices would be complete without reference to Edgar Allan Poe and Charlotte Perkins Gilman. The focus of their work is psychological, but similarly to Hawthorne, their narratives often carry political implications. This is demonstrated by two parallel short stories, Poe's *The Black Cat* and Gilman's *The Yellow Wallpaper*. Both are feminist tracts, both are ostensibly unrelated to politics, and yet both offer important insights into the kind of perverse power relationships that exist within a culture characterized by a ruthlessly competitive, male-dominated ethos. Just as Wieland vehemently defends his sanity in Charles Brocken Brown's novel, the nameless protagonist of Poe's "The Black Cat" begins his first-person narrative by emphatically stressing his mental competence:

"For the most wild, yet most homely narrative which I am about to pen, I neither expect nor solicit belief. Mad indeed would I be to expect it....Yet mad am I not" (Poe/ J. C. Oates 78). He goes on to relate how, despite the "docility and humanity" and his special fondness for animals, he eventually tortures and hangs his household cat Pluto "because I felt it had given me no reason for offense" and then goes on to murder his wife with an axe. "Mad I am not?" Clearly, denial is as prominent a theme in Poe as it is in Hawthorne.

Poe's narrator is "of two minds," but where exactly lies the fault line along which this schism appears? The name, as well as the nature of his household pet, suggest a possible answer. Pluto, lord of the underworld in Roman mythology, points the reader to the subterranean realm of the subconscious mind. Moreover, cats are a gendered symbol closely identified with female sexuality and the feminine principle. Traditionally, felines are the familiars of witches. In Poe's day, of course, any explicit reference to sex was prohibited in polite literature. This makes it all the more unlikely that his use of erotically charged symbolism is accidental. For instance, take the fire that consumes his Gothic hero-villain's bed following his drunken assault on the unoffending Pluto: "The curtains of my bed were in flames," writes Poe. "It was with great difficulty that my wife, a servant, and myself, made our escape from the conflagration" (Poe/J. C. Oates 81). The use of fire as a symbolic substitute for sexual passion is a well established convention in nineteenth-century literature. In Dickens's *The Old Curiosity Shop,* for instance, the libidinous Quilp figures as a sexually charismatic dwarf who displays his lust for Little Nell by lolling on her bed while puffing away furiously at his cigar. The character of Bertha Mason in Charlotte Brontë's *Jane Eyre* furnishes another example. Not only is her insanity directly attributed to sexual promiscuity, but she is also a compulsive pyromaniac who, more than once, nearly succeeds at engulfing her husband's bed in flames.

To resume our exploration of Poe's short story, a second cat is introduced into the narrative with similarly unfortunate results. This animal, like its predecessor, is missing an eye—Poe's favorite symbol of consciousness, divine or mortal. It takes an immediate liking to its master. In a passage vividly suggestive of the narrator's mounting sexual hysteria, Poe describes this animal's behavior as follows: "Whenever I sat, it would crouch beneath my chair, or spring upon my knees, covering me with its loathsome caresses.... Although I longed to destroy it with a blow, I was yet withheld from doing so ... by absolute *dread* of the beast"

(Poe/J. C. Oates 83). During a visit to the cellar (a common symbol of the psychic netherworld), the destructive blow finally falls. The axe misses its target, however, burying itself instead in his wife's skull! So implausible a sequence of events invites a flexible approach to interpretation. As usual where Poe is concerned, an event that makes little sense on the literal plane is logical when interpreted symbolically: Cat equals sex, sex equals wife, ergo wife equals cat....a classic Aristotelian syllogism. On an even deeper symbolic plane, moreover, cat and wife together equal self, and murder equals the destruction of the feminine, nurturing, and instinctual aspects of the husband's inordinately masculine psyche.

Speaking of Poe's hero-villain in *The Black Cat* and another male character from a closely parallel short story, Tony Magistrale and Sidney Poger have this to say about the symbolic identities in *The Black Cat:* "Both men seek to destroy that which they cannot control—specifically, the feminine principle. Their respective wives represent those characteristics in themselves that each husband has systematically repressed: sensitivity, a concern and respect for others, artistic expression, an appreciation of the beautiful, the need for social connections" (Magistrale and Poger 74). The Swiss psychologist C. G. Jung labels this feminine principle within the male psyche the *anima*. He posits a psychoanalytic definition of sanity as a balance of oppositional forces within the individual between a male and female component. In *The Black Cat,* Poe anticipates Jungian psychology by half a century (see Edward C. Whitmont's The *Symbolic Quest: Basic Concepts of Analytical Psychology,* chapters 12 and 13). The psycho-political insight towards which he seems to be groping is that in a society of males who abuse their gentler, more nurturing selves—or a society of females dominated by their male animus—one can expect periodic outbreaks of unprovoked hostility and other manifestations of unbalanced behavior.

In her Gothic short story *The Yellow Wallpaper,* Charlotte Perkins Gilman (1860–1935) offers a tale that is reminiscent of Poe in its message as well as in its use of imagery, symbolism, and first-person narrative. Told from the vantage point of an unnamed convalescent woman recovering from childbirth, it traces the narrator's terrifying descent into a maelstrom of insanity. At the same time, however, it treats insanity ambiguously, as an expression of the seeming irrationality that defines the Gothic imagination. The opening of the story establishes the narrator's personality and the Gothic dilemma in which she finds herself.

It also outlines the personality of the two individuals who are chiefly responsible for that dilemma, her husband John and her brother, who is also unidentified by name. The first thing we learn about both men is that they are physicians, i.e., scientists, who attribute her sickness to psychosomatic causes. The narrator, however, offers an alternative diagnosis: "John laughs at me, of course, but one expects that in a man. John is practical in the extreme. He has no patience with faith, an intense horror of superstition, and he scoffs openly at any talk of things not to be felt and seen and put down in figures. John is a physician and *perhaps* ... that is one reason I do not get well faster" (Gilman/J. C. Oates 87). Indeed, the utilitarian, rationalist predisposition of the men by which she is beset throughout the story suggests that her deteriorating physical and psychological condition is a direct outcome of the confinement, humiliation, and emotional starvation imposed by her self-styled male benefactors. She is shut up in a room fitted with bars on the windows, a bed that is attached by screws to the floor, and decorated, of course, with yellow wallpaper.

There is a suggestion that this sterile chamber, which combines the features of a prison and a mental asylum, was previously used as a nursery. Significantly, her husband, who ignores her insights into her own condition and enforces a regime of total inactivity, addresses her in terms of endearment usually reserved for a child, e.g., "little girl," and "Bless her little heart," (Gilman/J. C. Oates 95). She is not allowed to cuddle her own infant, and the ever-solicitous John prohibits even a modest daily session at her writing desk, where her intellect and imagination, if not her physical self, might hope to find some release. "Personally," muses the prisoner, "I believe that congenial work, with excitement and change, would do me good. But what is one to do? I did write for a while in spite of them; but it does exhaust me a good deal— having to be sly about it, or else meet with heavy opposition" (Gilman/J. C. Oates 88). That women are not innately immune to the "practical," i.e., unimaginative and oppressively rationalistic, mind-set, is attested by John's sister Mary, who enforces her brother's policies without question. Similarly to the vortex in Poe's tale, the wallpaper in Gilman's narrative is an analogue to the Gothic paradigm itself—much as the satanic mill in Melville's short story is an analogue to the Newtonian paradigm. In other words, the wallpaper provides a visual representation of the elements that constitute the Gothic imagination. She describes it as follows: "It is dull enough to confuse the eye in following, pronounced enough constantly to irritate and provoke study, and when you follow the lame uncertain curves for a little distance they suddenly commit suicide—plunge off at outrageous angles, destroy themselves in unheard of contradictions" (Gilman/J. C. Oates 89).

Eventually this apparent formlessness resolves itself into a "strange, provoking, formless sort of figure" with two bulbous eyes that stare at her upside-down. In time, this figure transforms again into a "creeping woman" who shakes the wall from behind and escapes on all fours into the moonlit night. "Sometimes," reports the narrator, "I think there are a great many women behind and sometimes only one, and she crawls around fast, and her crawling shakes it all over" (Gilman/J. C. Oates 98). The upshot of all this is that when the narrator's process of mental and emotional dissociation is complete, the reader learns that she and the creeping woman are one and the same person. Trapped inside her husband's severely circumscribed world, her only escape is through the portal of madness. Paradoxically, it is at the height of her insanity that she most clearly recognizes the psychological double-bind into which she has been placed by those who profess to love her: "John knows I don't sleep very well at night, for all I'm so quiet! He asked me all sorts of questions, too, and pretended to be very loving and kind. As if I couldn't see through him" (Gilman/J. C. Oates 100). From his own perspective, of course, her husband's motives are quite possibly pure. One of the unresolved Gothic ambiguities of this story is whether or not his wife's growing paranoia is symptomatic of her condition.

Nevertheless, the reader is finally left with the impression of a woman victimized by a patriarchal culture that denies her most basic needs in the name of chivalry and reason. As indicated by Poe's companion piece, however, this sexually lopsided "rationality" is blind to one half of human wisdom, i.e., the transrational half, sometimes referred to as "lunar knowledge," that is intuitive, mystical, and emotional. The question posed by Gilman's devastating exploration of Gothic madness is this: How reasonable and well balanced can such "rationality" be, in the final analysis, and what does it say about a political culture committed to human equality and justice? Clearly, equality of the sexes in an America that relegates women to the status of passive victims and dependent children is, once again, a Gothic dystopia, a world that reproduces and even celebrates the "unheard of contradictions" symbolized by the yellow wallpaper itself. Moreover, a society in which men as well as women are compelled to either surrender to the masculine principle or become its pawn is, in the final analysis, a psychosexual dystopia that mocks the republican ideal of human equality and synergistic balance within and between individuals. Sexism in American society, understood as male domination in the psychic as well as the professional and political spheres, remains an unresolved problem, along with racism, philistinism, a culture of official secrecy, corporate totalitarianism, and bureaucratic elitism. However, the majority of these unresolved problems only emerge as full-blown Gothic dilemmas in the period from 1850 to 1950.

Clemens, Crane, and the Second American Revolution

George Orwell, the British author of *1984,* one of the political Gothic imagination's most compelling expressions of Cold War paranoia, entertained a low opinion of Samuel Clemens (1834–1910). Orwell maintained that Clemens, better known as Mark Twain, settled for the role of buffoon when, like Dickens, he might have claimed the mantle of Gothic prophet. According to Orwell's indictment, Twain, one of the most lucid minds of his era, lacked the earnestness and moral courage to effectively challenge either the racism of the pre–Civil War South, in which he was born, or the post–Civil War jingoism and economic ruthlessness he lived to witness. Though incisive, Orwell's censure is overly harsh. Twain did in fact speak with a prophetic voice on the issue of race relations in *Huckleberry Finn* and *Pudd'nhead Wilson* (a variation on the *Prince and the Pauper* theme in which a black and white baby are switched at birth and nurtured in accordance with conventional prejudices and expectations). More so than any of his contemporaries, he understood the complex cultural forces that shaped America during a half century of industrialization, territorial expansion, and massive immigration. American historian James M. McPherson notes that the impact of the Civil War, a conflict that toppled centuries-old institutions and otherwise transformed America's political and cultural landscape, "cannot be measured short of two or three generations" (McPherson 24). Twain would have concurred. The trauma of those changes left him saddled with a nostalgic ache for a lost time and place to which, because it had never actually existed, he could never truly return.

For Twain, the childhood and early adulthood of his pre–Civil War youth was magically enshrined in the archetypal image of the journey downriver. The wide waters of the Mississippi evoked, for him, an idyllic freedom from the financially imposed need to address his public in the guise of a rustic clown, i.e., to hide behind a comedic mask fashioned in response to a despairing realization that his genteel bourgeoisie audience would never tolerate a candid revelation of the deep resentments he harbored toward America's betrayal of its idealistic founding. Indeed, one of the most frustrating measures of that betrayal is the extent to which an intellectual such as Twain, who exemplified Jefferson's rustic philosopher and Emerson's Man Thinking, was compelled to hide the idealistic side of his nature behind a façade of sardonic humor. No intellectual of his era better grasped the conformity, chauvinism, greed, and shallow religiosity of the dominant American temper between the Civil War and the Great War (1914–1918). As the spirit of aggressive materialism—embodied economically in the doctrine of laissez-faire, politically in the doctrine of Manifest Destiny, and philosophically in the doctrine of social Darwinism—was successfully promoted by America's robber barons, Twain gave Gothic utterance to his anguish in a short piece entitled *The War Prayer*.

It tells of a church service held on the eve of an unspecified political conflict. The service is interrupted by a divine messenger sent to warn the minister and his congregation that the petition for victory that they were about to offer carries implications of which they are unaware. That congregation includes many young men, confident of success and exhilarated at the prospect of exhibiting their manhood on the battlefield. This messenger's transcendent mission is to articulate the price, in human misery, that will be exacted if their prayer is granted and to afford an opportunity of rescinding it. After listening to his litany of pain, privation, and despair, the stranger is dismissed as a lunatic. Shortly after *The War Prayer* was written, a friend asked Twain if he intended to have it published. He replied, "I have told the whole truth in that, and only dead men can tell the truth in this world" (Twain, *War Prayer* 1). Accordingly, at Twain's request, this anti-war parable was withheld until 1923. By that time, of course, WWI was history and "the American century" it inaugurated was under way. According to academic orthodoxy, the cardinal achievement of that century was the defeat of totalitarianism and the triumph of democracy. The counter-cultural mythologies of the Gothic imagination, however, suggest otherwise. Whichever vision proves to be correct, there is no disputing the fact that the American century, thanks in part to so-called advances in weaponry, was a century of warfare, economic exploitation, and political terrorism on a scale that is without historical precedent.

Toward the end of his life, as his *War Prayer, Letters from the Earth,* and *The Mysterious Stranger* attest, Twain was left feeling emotionally stranded. His condition invites comparison with one of the bemused characters from the pages of Washington Irving or the disoriented protagonist in "A Resumed Identity," a Gothic vignette by one of Twain's contemporary fantasists, Ambrose Bierce, set during the Civil War. An impressionistic blending of the psychological and the political Gothic, it tells of a distraught Union soldier, age twenty-three years, who witnesses a soundless army pass close by on a dusty country road, stops a physician on horseback to ask directions (only to be humored), and finally, upon catching his reflection in a pool of water, realizes that he has been inexplicably transformed into an old man and yields up "the life that had spanned another life" (Bierce 474). This brief Civil War sketch, like Irving's burlesque Gothic folktale *Rip Van Winkle* and Twain's *War Prayer,* deals with the shattering sense of temporal and psychic dislocation imposed by the traumas of war and the accelerated pace of social change by which war is often accompanied. Few American artists have registered that trauma more truly than Samuel Clemens, and even fewer have so thoroughly sounded the depths of self-loathing occasioned by a lifelong habit of denying what they truly felt.

America's preeminent Civil War novel is by an author who adopted a literary credo that precluded Twain's dilemma. Stephen Crane (1871–1900), who was just twenty-four years of age when *The Red Badge of Courage* was published in 1895, subscribed to a modernist belief that "Sentiment is the devil," according to an introduction to that novel by Civil War historian Shelby Foote (Crane xiv). Ironically, he set out thirty years after the thunderclouds of Civil War had dispersed to produce the first modern American novel that looked unblinkingly at the chaos and futility of armed conflict. In a very real sense, as Foote maintains, Crane's subtitle, *An Episode of the American Civil War,* might be changed to read simply *An Episode of War,* without any essential loss of artistic intent. Neither Lincoln, Jefferson Davis, nor any of the other personalities who figured prominently in America's Second Revolution appear in this novel, even peripherally, nor are the political and social issues that made that conflict revolutionary in any way addressed. Indeed, such issues are by implication secondary, if not irrelevant, to Crane's central concern, which is the existential horror of war. Much as utopian socialism is not the essential subject matter of Hawthorne's *Blithedale Romance,* Southern slavery and secession are not the subject of Crane's novel.

Foote characterizes *The Red Badge of Courage* as "Crane's ahistorical historical novel." In his introduction, which is understandably brief, he points out that "Any true work having to do with war is bound by definition to turn out antiwar in its effect, and so of course does this one" (Crane xi). Generally speaking, stories that focus on war, rather than the causes and effects of war, are comparable to stories about sex rather than love relationships. Predictably, they are lacking in drama because they are essentially all the same story. Moreover, it has frequently been suggested that violence of any kind, warfare included, is closely linked to a failure of the imagination and is therefore inherently banal. In effect, the violence of war begins where thinking, statecraft, and political problem solving ends. The American Civil War, for example, began where a fifty-year cycle of utopian social and political fermentation ended. It was at precisely that moment in time, when fear and frustration overtook hope and idealism, that the armed conflict erupted. The possibility of political transcendence hinges on a precarious balance of forces within individuals and societies. Sometimes, as with Lincoln and Kennedy, when that balance is lost to a society as a whole, it is nevertheless preserved by its leaders—unless, of course, they too are lost. From 1861 to 1865, America was deprived of both its social equilibrium and a president in whom that dystopian/utopian balance of oppositional forces was finely balanced. Prospects for a peaceful transformation of relations between races along the lines envisioned, though not acted upon, by its Founding Fathers were consequently suspended until a resurgence of idealism in the 1960s opened another window of opportunity. Crane's views with regard to how and why individuals react under the stress of war's insanity are succinctly stated in a short sequel to his Civil War novel entitled *The Veteran.*

In this sequel, Henry Fleming, the young protagonist of *The Red Badge of Courage,* is now a grandfather. The story opens at the village grocer's where he is being questioned about his Civil War exploits. "Mr. Fleming, you never was frightened much in them battles, was you," asks one of his inquisitors deferentially. When Fleming admits that he was, his young grandson, who is eavesdropping nearby, is troubled. Shortly thereafter the scene shifts to the site of a barn on the Fleming homestead that has caught fire. Time and again, the distraught grandfather rushes into the inferno to save his animals, though his hair is singed and his skin blistered in the process. Finally, the roof of the structure collapses and he is consumed by the flames. The last sentence reads, "The smoke was tinted rose-hue from the flames, and perhaps the unutterable midnights of the universe will have no power to daunt the color of this soul" (Crane 258). Near the conclusion of The *Red Badge of Courage,* the narrator says of the young Henry Fleming, "He had been an animal blistered and sweating in the heat and pain of war" (Crane 246). The connection is obvious, as is Crane's message that the so-called valor of war is apt to be a spontaneous response to a chaotic situation in which human beings are reduced to the condition of terrified animals.

In a sense, the dystopian/utopian terrain first mapped by Jefferson and Charles Brockden Brown, and explored by Twain, Hawthorne, and others was an interior projection of the turmoil and longing that would erupt externally into a second Revolutionary War, i.e., the Civil War, and beyond that to a third American Revolution of sorts during the 1960s. America of the 1850s and 1860s was similar in many ways to the America of the 1790s. The economy was unstable in both eras, there were widespread regional differences and hostilities, slavery remained an unresolved and contentious issue, and doubts as to the validity and durability of the American experiment were rampant (Christophersen 174) In the throes of that turmoil and longing, a national identity was provisionally forged. The dissonance of slavery, though not that of racial prejudice, was resolved by the Civil War, while other discordant elements were not. For the most part, those unresolved discords prompted by territorial expansion and emergent industrialization comprised a standing Gothic agenda. Commenting on that agenda, historians Allan Nevins and Henry Steele Commager point out that America in the second half of the nineteenth century experienced a period of unprecedented change from an agrarian nation to an industrial nation. This change, in turn, created a new and largely unprecedented set of social problems having to do with the distribution of wealth, corporate control of capital, and the preservation of democracy under the stress of an increasingly powerful economic system that was undemocratic in both its aims and methods (Nevins and Commager 137–38).

Until the Civil War, Jefferson's hopes that America would evade the politico-economic pitfalls of industrialized Europe were, for the most part, realized. "A century after the Sage of Monticello went to his well-earned rest, however, the value of manufactured products was five times that of farm products; financial titans and industrial barons dictated policies in Washington, and the farmer seemed in danger of becoming a peasant" (Nevins and Commager 256). A covertly fascist adherence to the ethics of social Darwinism created an economic climate of radical individualism and cut-throat competition that was contrary to the authentic American dream. Drawing upon a familiar Gothic trope, the former governor of New York, Mario Cuomo, identified that post–Civil War ethos as follows: "Especially after the Civil War, what we now call social Darwinism reigned as the dominant social philosophy, squaring solidly with the business interests of the day. But then the abuses began to surface—the ruthless predatory Mr. Hyde heart inside the magnanimous, moralizing Dr. Jekyll that was the Industrial Revolution" (Cuomo 76).

Though the psychic wound opened by this political Gothic split festered until well into the new century, the problems it created took on a new sense of urgency as a tidal wave of European immigration in the late nineteenth and early twentieth centuries came to diversify, complicate, and ultimately enrich our cultural identity. Domestically and internationally, the growing division between rich and poor and the stranglehold of the ethos that supports it noticeably deepened over the next half century. Invoking Dickens's famous novel of the French Revolution, Cuomo, in a plea for compassion based on civic values, aptly characterized that division as *A Tale of Two Cities* (Cuomo, 1984 Keynote Address, Democratic National Convention).

Eventually, the Great Wars of the twentieth century pushed an insular, parochial, and, in some respects, an unprepared America onto the center stage of international affairs. This, more than any other single factor would redefine the dystopian/utopian dialectic that has played so crucial a role in shaping and reflecting our nation's self-image. At the same time, however, it would add new and disturbing elements to our Gothic dilemma. The traditional role of America's countercultural Gothic narratives has been to prick our civic conscience into undertaking a process of self-examination, to provide a critical perspective from which to assess our changing perceptions of the American dream, and to subvert the celebratory narratives of the American experience promoted by a self-serving status quo. As we shall see, the twentieth century provided Gothic artists with abundant raw material for such narratives.

Discussion Topics and Questions

1. Please explain the following statement and justify your explanation with examples cited in this chapter: The political Gothic imagination is essentially moralistic rather than revolutionary.

2. Gothic heroes are often described as "time-haunted." Explain the importance that Gothic artists attach to memory in relation to the theme of Gothic denial.

3. Discuss Melville's *The Maids of Tartarus,* Poe's *The Black Cat,* and Charlotte Gilman Perkin's *The Yellow Wallpaper* as protests against the Newtonian paradigm (i.e., as expressions of philosophical Gothic).

4. In what sense did Lincoln's application of the principle of "positive freedom" with regard to the issue of slavery demonstrate his capacity to transcend America's Gothic dilemma by endorsing America's moral commitment to human equality over considerations of economic or political expediency?

5. Define and discuss the traditional role of American Gothic arts.

4 Pulp Culture and American Politics

Describing the changes that overtook America subsequent to the Civil War, historian Richard Hofstadter chronicles the mutation of capitalism from a partner in the American experiment into something like an adversary: "The rapid development of the big cities, the building of the great industrial plant, the construction of the railroads, the emergence of the corporation as a dominant form of enterprise, transformed the old society and revolutionized the distribution of wealth. During the 1840s there were not twenty millionaires in the entire country; by 1910 there were probably more than twenty millionaires sitting in the United States Senate" (Hofstadter 136). This *Wieland*-like transformation of America from an approximation of Jefferson's agrarian utopia, in which wealth, power, and social influence were widely if not always equitably, distributed to an urban dystopia did not occur without protest. That urban dystopia was one in which ever greater accumulations of wealth, and the inordinate political influence that wealth can obtain, were concentrated in the hands of a small monied elite, i.e., the so-called "robber barons" such as the Vanderbilts, Harrimans, Goulds, Carnegies, Rockefellers, and Morgans. Meanwhile, an increasingly high percentage of Americans were either bereft of political influence, crowded into ugly and dangerous warrens, or both.

The form these protests took, however, suggests a significant shift away from the synergistic balances on which the authentic American dream was premised toward a species of a moral absolutism. What distinguished the Founding Fathers from most later champions of social reform is that they did not have to first attain power in order to wield it. The landed gentry that staged the American Revolution *were* the power elite of colonial America. With few exceptions, those who sought to change America after 1890, apart from members of the corporate plutocracy, were political outsiders. Traditionally, the Gothic imagination has been cautionary rather than radical in its outlook. By subverting whichever half of the dystopian/utopian dialectic threatens to gain ascendancy over the other half, it seeks to adjust imbalances between reason and emotion, femininity and masculinity (in Jungian terms), individualism and a more community-oriented ethic. The radical mind-set, however, does not aim at achieving dynamic equilibrium. Its aim is to subvert and overthrow the dialectic itself, either by smashing its standards or simply by escaping from them into the ether of its own utopian imaginings.

Hofstadter notes that the problem with the various utopian movements that sprang up in America in the late nineteenth and early twentieth centuries is not that they set out to smash standards but that they set impossibly high standards. While there had always been "a struggle against those forces which were too exclusively preoccupied with the organization of economic life and the milking of our natural resources to give much thought to the human costs" (Hofstadter 18), the realignment of wealth and power that overtook America between the end of the Civil War and the Great Depression resulted in a situation in which a dysenfranchised multitude was increasingly constrained to either serve the new corporate elite or take refuge in paranoid myths and utopian fantasies. This multitude included farmers, the laboring poor (comprised largely of first-generation immigrants), and the professional classes, i.e., lawyers, clerics, academics, artists, and intellectuals who felt excluded from participation in America's new plutocracy.

Either directly or indirectly, these paranoid myths and utopian fantasies, which served as substitutes for significant participation in the political process, gave symbolic expression to the traumas unleashed by America's new economic order. For many, that new order was perceived in Gothic terms as a monstrosity, a corporate Leviathan in comparison with which the threat to democracy posed by Dickens's burlesque Gothic Ebenezer Scrooge seemed almost benign. If one of the unanswered questions first posed by Charles Brockden Brown concerned capitalism's capacity to transcend its own inherent greed and rapacity, i.e., can democracy and capitalism coexist, the political and economic dispossession of Jefferson's "sturdy yeoman" and the ruthlessness of industrial monopolies and corporations seemed to supply a resounding answer in the negative.

Often, Gothic narratives that dealt with the abuses of these informal power structures offered simplistic explanations and impossible solutions to sophisticated socioeconomic problems. In doing so, they arguably diminished the status of the Gothic imagination among America's intelligentsia. However, they also provided a cathartic release, a psycho-social mechanism whereby popular tensions that might otherwise have sought more destructive outlets were channeled into harmless forms of entertainment. Conversely, one might argue that such entertainment aggravated society's problems—debasing and demoralizing their audiences while at the same time dissipating the public's outrage and frustration rather than directing it toward the discovery of realistic solutions. Do Gothic arts harm or benefit society? That philosophical question has been debated from the age of Plato and Aristotle to the present. In addition to scholarly books, essays, monologues, fictional literature, and other traditional venues for the venting of political Gothic fears and hopes, newer forms of artistic expression provided by radio, film, and pulp fiction have arguably supplied generations of beleaguered citizens, rich in the trappings but poor in the substance of democracy, with temporary relief from their frustrations and anxieties.

Appropriately enough, the first phalanx of protest against late-nineteenth-century corporate capitalism came from Southern and Midwestern farmers disgruntled with industrialization, including the industrialization of farming itself. According to what Hofstadter refers to as the "agrarian myth," independent farmers were the first American patriots, responsible for the victorious revolution against British imperialists. This myth was powerful, writes Hofstadter, because in the first half of the nineteenth century the United States consisted largely of literate and politically enfranchised farmers, i.e., Jefferson's sturdy yeoman (Hofstadter 29). By the 1890s this same class of patriots found itself in a fight for its economic survival. However, by that time a great many farmers were not just politically disenfranchised, they were intellectually impoverished as well. Therefore, the political movement they founded, known as Populism, pandered to the fears and prejudices of a quasi-illiterate constituency at best. Not unlike the conservative movement of the 1950s, Populism was anti-Semitic, xenophobic, jingoistic, and conspiratorial in its perception of the world. Its principle villains, however, were Wall Street stockbrokers, bankers, and corporate capitalists.

Ironically, one of America's most successful corporate capitalists, Henry Ford, would eventually emerge from Populist ranks. Indeed, in many ways Populism represented the first political thrust of what is referred to in these pages as covert fascism. "There was a widespread Populist idea," writes Hofstadter, "that all American history since the Civil War could be understood as a sustained conspiracy of the international money power" (Hofstadter 70). Just as conservative

Republican extremists of the 1930s and 1950s foresaw dire consequences arising from the liberal Democratic policies of Franklin D. Roosevelt and John F. Kennedy, seen by these conservatives as dupes of international Jewish communism, Populists in the 1890s and early decades of the twentieth century predicted an impending apocalypse emanating from a close alliance between Washington and Wall Street. The fear of this impending apocalypse found imaginative expression in Ignatius Donnelly's political Gothic novel *Caesar's Column.*

Just as Aristotle's aesthetics in the *Poetics* are best understood as a response to those of Plato in the *Republic,* Donnelly's dystopian fantasy serves as a companion piece to a roughly contemporary specimen of utopian literature, Edward Bellamy's *Looking Backward.* "*Caesar's Column,*" was arrived at, writes Hofstadter, "by standing Bellamy on its head" (Hofstadter 67). Similarly to the peaceful escape from corporate America's air-conditioned anthills portrayed by Charles Reich in the 1960s, Bellamy's utopia, set in the year 2000, envisions a nonviolent transition to a socialistic America purged of economic competition and warfare by the elimination of capitalism. Donnelly's dystopia, set in 1988, envisions a capitalistic totalitarianism. It is a world governed by plutocratic leaders and their political minions who employ a fleet of "Demons," i.e., dirigibles carrying gas bombs designed for use against insurrectionist farmers. These farmers, degraded by a long period of economic and political abuse from sturdy yeoman into bloodthirsty peasants, form a revolutionary army known as the Brotherhood of Destruction that initiates a prolonged American Reign of Terror. Ultimately this dissident brotherhood succeeds in overthrowing the established order (Hofstadter 68–69).

Expanding on what he would later call "the paranoid style in American politics," Hofstadter contextualizes Donnelly's conspiratorial fantasy by pointing out that Jefferson believed in a Federalist conspiracy to reestablish a monarchy, Federalists believed in a Jeffersonian conspiracy to subvert Christianity, Pre–Civil War parties such as the Know-Nothings and the Anti-Masonic movements were founded on conspiracy theories, America's entry into WWI was seen by some as a conspiracy of bankers and arms manufacturers, and Cold War conservatives viewed the entirety of post-WWII American history as a communist conspiracy engineered by leftists sympathetic to the Kremlin (Hofstadter 72). Historical commentary such as this, though perfectly warranted, has helped to create a matrix of opinion that goes a long way toward explaining the predisposition of later historians to dismiss conspiracy theories arising out of the 1960s and the literary and cinematic narratives they have inspired, such as Oliver Stone's *JFK* and *Nixon*. It is important to note, however, that while Hofstadter is theoretically willing to acknowledge that conspiracies do occasionally occur, the overwhelming impression with which his readers are left is that conspiracy theories are the province of ignorant and politically unsophisticated paranoiacs.

The fallacy he attributes to Populists is their fixation on the personal vices of their enemies as opposed to the systemic vices of the social system to which they contribute (Hofstadter 73). This is exactly the criticism leveled against Oliver Stone by critics such as Alexander Cockburn and Patrick Daniel Moynihan (see Cockburn's "J.F.K and JFK" and Moynihan's "The Paranoid Style" in Stone and Sklar's anthology of journalistic film criticism entitled *JFK: The Book of the Film*). Such criticism is premised on a stubborn faith in American history as a closed Newtonian system impervious to outside influences. The Gothic imagination, of course, sees life itself as a more or less continuous intrusion from outside upon our carefully constructed rationalist belief systems. Moreover, there are those, such as conspiriologist Peter Dale Scott (see his *Deep Politics and the Death of JFK*) who offer a systemic rather than—to coin a term—an "intrusionist" interpretation of the Kennedy conspiracy.

The Progressive movement, whose policies led ultimately to Franklin Roosevelt's New Deal, inherited Populism's distrust of big business and plutocracy, though not its conspiratorial mentality. Based in New England, with its historical ties to the precepts of democratic idealism, however, this movement attracted well-educated, highly literate members of the professional classes. These classes, similarly to Midwestern and Southern farmers who comprised the core of discontent around which the Populist movement was formed, were either co-opted or excluded by the new monied aristocracy. Hofstadter's thesis is that the primary appeal of the Progressive movement was to those who felt shut out from democratic participation and status within the larger community rather than to those who were economically deprived. Such individuals suffered from a sense of disempowerment that accompanied the political ascendancy of corporate America in the closing decades of the nineteenth century (Hofstadter 135). The Progressive movement's most illustrious political spokesmen were Theodore Roosevelt and Woodrow Wilson.

While the ethos of Populism tracks back to the frontier values of Jacksonian democracy and ahead to those of LBJ's constituency, that of the Progressives embraced the intellectualism and aestheticism of Jeffersonian democracy and, in doing so, anticipated the resurgence of the authentic American dream inspired by JFK. "They tended to look to New England's history for literary, cultural, and political models and for examples of moral idealism. Their conception of statecraft was set by the high example of the Founding Fathers" (Hofstadter 140).

Ultimately, these strange political bedfellows formed an alliance against their common foe, corporate capitalism. This alliance led to the creation of a Farm Federation Bureau that worked in tandem with the federal government and various banking associations to induce farmers to adopt a more businesslike outlook. Consequently, a two-tiered economic system resulting in a disparity between rich and poor within the farming community, comparable to that found between labor and capital in urban centers, was eventually established (Hofstadter 28). Meanwhile, the legislation of labor and anti-trust laws, the establishment of labor unions, the creation of the Federal Reserve Board (a measure designed to regulate and discipline the banking community, or else place it in the driver's seat, depending on one's political perspective), the extension of the franchise to women, and the internationalist concept of "collective security"—enshrined initially in Wilson's League of Nations, and later in the United Nations—corrected somewhat the imbalances between democracy and state-sponsored capitalism that had developed during the last half of the nineteenth century. Though the nature of farming changed and the "agrarian myth" was laid to rest, the farm community itself prospered economically. Moreover, the most blatant abuses of the corporate business community were ameliorated and the world was once more made safe for capitalism and militarism, if not for democratic idealism.

The War of Horror

Then came the Great War (1914–1918). At this distance in time, with sensibilities blunted by subsequent political atrocities, it is difficult to register the magnitude of that Gothic bloodletting. In part, the trauma it provoked was a result of the genocidal new technologies it utilized. For the first time, the world was forced to acknowledge the dark side of science (Mary Shelley's Gothic theme) which it had previously viewed as a trustworthy tool of human progress. Aerial warfare, chemical warfare, and trench warfare were among the concepts introduced by this conflict. Flame-throwers, machine guns, mustard gas, and barbed-wire barricades were among the "improvements" in human slaughter it unleashed. The figures, which can be verified by consulting any number of history texts, are staggering. It has been estimated that on an average day, approximately five thousand lives were lost, over two thousand more than were sacrificed in the terrorist attacks on New York City's Twin Towers, the Pentagon, and the plane crash near Pittsburgh, Pennsylvania. At Verdun in 1916, six hundred thousand lives were ended in four months. At the Somme, the British and the French lost another six hundred thousand men, while five hundred thousand Germans were slaughtered. By 1918, an entire generation was erased in France! Ironically, improvements in medical science and prosthetics spared the lives of thousands who, in previous wars, would have died of their wounds. These mutilated survivors were then sent home to live out their lives as unwelcome reminders of a killing spree that those who brought it about were subsequently unable to explain. In the absence of any more rational explanation for these events, Freud concluded: "Homo homini lupus," "Man is a wolf to man" (as quoted in Van Doren 294), an insight that would later inform Curt Siodmak's most memorable contribution to the gallery of archetypal monsters conjured by pop culture in response to the horrors of war, *The Wolf Man*. Many of those who managed to escape grievous bodily harm were nevertheless injured, as the following reminiscence—devastating in its understatement attests: "'Most men, I suppose, have a Paleolithic savage somewhere in them.... I have anyway,' wrote a gentle English scholar about his experiences in the trenches" (Garraty and Gay 992).

The impact of the Great War, which shattered European culture, was less so to American culture. Our entry did not occur until 1917. Casualties, though large, were comparatively light (approximately 115,000 Americans died), and the conflict itself was, of course, waged on foreign soil. Consequently, the war was popularly perceived as a heroic, if unnecessary, adventure. President Woodrow Wilson justified our involvement by misrepresenting WWI as a fight "for democracy ... for the right of those who submit to authority to have a voice in their own government, for the rights and liberties of small nations...and for such a concert of free peoples as shall bring peace and safety to all nations, and make the world itself at last free" (Nevins and Commager 395).

Although there were surely better ways of fostering an American commitment to global community than by lashing a pacifist nation into an anti-German war frenzy, Wilson's primary objective—to stress the concept of collective security implicit in the Enlightenment conception of human brotherhood—was commendable. President Kennedy, many years later, sought to forge a comparable alliance, i.e., the Alliance for Progress, with Europe and Latin America that would promote democracy by establishing a foreign policy based on a respect for national sovereignty and international cooperation. Wilson called his program the New Freedom and pinned its hopes for success on the creation of an international League of Nations. Much of America disapproved. Unable to transcend the parochialism of its isolationist heritage, the country rejected Wilson's idealistic agenda in favor of economic conservatism and an "adamantine stubbornness" toward the defeated Axis powers that helped to make a second world war inevitable (Nevins and Commager 405). As a result, the war to end all wars became, in effect, the catalyst for a century of unending warfare.

European war trauma found its way into American popular culture primarily through the cinema, a comparatively new medium. Filmmakers, writers, directors, and actors were among those who immigrated to America from England and other European countries during the first half of the twentieth century. They did so in search of economic and political opportunity as well as sanctuary from Nazi persecution. Many of them, such as studio heads Carl Lammele and his son, Carl Lammele Jr., writers John Balderson, R. C. Sheriff, and Curt Siodmak, directors James Whale, Paul Leni, and Edgar Ulmer, and actors Lon Chaney, his son Lon Chaney Jr., Boris Karloff, Bela Lugosi, and Basil Rathbone formed an expatriate colony in Southern California. Hollywood's Universal film studio, in particular, mythologized the horrors of the Great War by concocting war-related entertainments rooted in the traditions of European Gothic literature and folklore. These entertainments stressed the themes of mutilation and disfigurement that armed conflict had forced upon a civilization in denial of its own recent past (see David J. Skal's *The Monster Show: A Cultural History of Horror*).

Silent films of the 1920s, such as *The Cabinet of Dr. Caligari* (1920) and *Nosferatu*, set an early standard. Subsequent to the advent of the cinematic sound track in 1926 and 1927, many of these same Gothic narratives would be recycled in sound and/or colorized versions. Indeed, it was the "talkies," as sound pictures were later called, that transformed film viewing into a national pastime. By 1929 between eighty and one hundred million persons went to see the movies each week (Nevins and Commager 412). By 1946, Hollywood's best year according to film historian Thomas Schatz, annual profits soared to $122 million (Schatz 298). Commenting on *J'Accuse* (1937), an antiwar film by French filmmaker Abel Gance, David Skal writes of the connection between early Gothic cinema and the Great War:

> For his unnerving final sequence ... Gance ... created a nightmarish montage of all the ruined faces that had been haunting the world's cinemas for the past fifteen years in the guise of 'horror entertainment.' The actual men are nameless, but they could easily be the living models for the masks worn by Lon Chaney, Boris Karloff, Lionel Atwill, and the others. (Skal 205–6).

Universal Studio produced two primary cycles of horror films. These films were important for several reasons: They not only formed the economic backbone of Universal Pictures and established the Hollywood careers of numerous character actors, directors, producers, makeup artists, and scriptwriters, but they also created a Gothic franchise unlike that enjoyed by any other Hollywood studio. Moreover, based on their earning power, which has been temporarily eclipsed from time to time but never extinguished, they achieved a popularity that suggests an archetypal appeal. Finally, these particular films would provide templates for future remakes, imitations, and parodies. Three in particular have special relevance to the political Gothic genre: English director James Whale's two films based on Mary Shelley's classic novel about mad science (*Frankenstein* and *The Bride of Frankenstein*) and Edgar G. Ulmer's loosely adapted film version of Poe's *The Black Cat*. Many of the others, however, are also pertinent. *Dracula,* for example, which launched the film career of Hungarian actor Bela Lugosi and was the first American horror film premised on an authentically supernatural plot, can easily be read as a political parable. The central European legend of the vampire received its most sophisticated literary setting in Bram Stoker's 1897 novel, *Dracula*. In America, the 1890s were a time of Populist upheaval over the evils of capitalism. In Europe, that same upheaval had received its strongest impetus from the *Communist Manifesto* of Karl Marx. Commenting on the Gothic component in Marxist thought, Mark Edmundson observes:

Marx's favorite Gothic trope is vampirism. He writes that British industry, vampire-like, lives by sucking blood, and children's blood at that. On another occasion, the bourgeoisie is said to have become a hoary vampire that sucks out the peasant's blood and brains and "throws them into the alchemist's cauldron of capital." For Marx, as Chris Baldick says, capital is accumulated, or dead, labor; the capitalist preys on the living, turning their energy and life force into inert property, just as the vampire takes living blood and uses it to perpetuate his death in life. (Edmundson 19)

Similarly, the Gothic films of James Whale can be understood as parables of postwar trauma. The bandaged figures of Boris Karloff in *The Mummy* and Claude Reins in *The Invisible Man,* for instance, must have seemed uncomfortably familiar to the post–WWI audiences that flocked to see them. Whale's Frankenstein films are autobiographical in that they draw their emotional and imaginative force from his firsthand experience of trench warfare. Referring to a Universal film based on the best-selling novel of the Great War by Erich Maria Remarque, *All Quiet on the Western Front,* David Skal calls attention to the image of a disembodied pair of hands gripping a barbed-wire fence seconds after their owner is blown to pieces, noting its similarity to the disembodied hands grafted unto the body of Boris Karloff in Whale's two most celebrated Gothic films (Skal 128). He goes on to observe that, "Since the village sequences were shot on the same outdoor sets as *All Quiet on the Western Front,* no doubt audience members experienced a certain level of déjà vu, whether or not they consciously equated *Frankenstein* with the celebrated war picture" (Skal 136). It was by means of intertextual quotations and oblique references such as these, rather than by any more direct method, that Whale established a connection between the horror of war and the war of horror.

In a BBC film distributed by Universal entitled *Gods and Monsters* (1999), American pop celebrity Brendan Fraser and award-winning Shakespearean actor Ian McKellen collaborate in a fictionalized portrayal of James Whale's later years in Hollywood. Based on a novel by Christopher Bram (*The Father of Frankenstein*), *Gods and Monsters* was adapted by Bill Condon into a sensitive screenplay that is at once a powerful coming-of-age story and an intriguing evocation of Gothic film history, as well as a contemporary exploration of the alienation experienced by America's homosexual subculture. As the film opens, Clayton Boone—beach bum, ex-Marine, and odd-job man—is en route to Whale's modest California residence, where he has been employed to do yard work. Whale, who has long since retired from filmmaking, has recently suffered a stroke that has left him susceptible to seizures characterized by temporary paralysis and alarming brainstorms characterized by vivid olfactory and visual hallucinations. Consequently, he is increasingly constrained to relive traumatic and long suppressed experiences from earlier days. These include episodes from his poverty-stricken childhood in a Northern England industrial slum, horrific images from his time in the trenches of WWI, and vignettes from his heyday as an influential director of Hollywood movies.

Informed by his doctor that his mental deterioration is irreversible, Whale concocts a desperate scheme whereby he hopes to induce his homophobic young caretaker to resolve his medical dilemma by provoking him to commit murder. He invites Boone to model for him, pretending to sketch his portrait, a task that his mental condition has made impossible. Whale, haunted by wartime images of a young lieutenant's agonizing death and subsequent display on the barbed-wire barricade in no-man's-land, is overwhelmed by remorse. Later, in a series of surrealistic dream sequences, Boone, transformed into a facsimile of Whale's famous monster, leads Whale back to the trenches where he is temporarily reunited with his long deceased comrades in arms, including the hapless lieutenant for whose fate he blames himself. Boone, meanwhile, conceals a different, but equally debilitating, war-time sorrow in that he was discharged from the Marine Corps during the Korean War for medical reasons unrelated to military service, a circumstance that he regards as a humiliating mark against his manhood.

In the course of their encounter, these two alienated Gothic heroes discover commonalities of background and shared vulnerabilities that allow each to transcend former fears and misconceptions. Whale discovers in Boone a substitute son in need of the support and protection denied to him by his own father—a support and protection that he, in turn, is guilty of having denied the trusting young lieutenant who now haunts his memory. The visionary presence of this silent ghost from Whale's past signals the ambiguity of madness itself, a favorite Gothic motif. To the Gothic imagination, madness can serve as a mode of transcendence. Other modes of Gothic transcendence include artistic afflatus, trance states induced by the contemplation of sublime nature, sexual rapture, redemptive love, narcotic or psychedelic visions, religious mysticism, humor, and—under certain circumstances—even suicide. In the words of British author Rider-Haggard, "In madness is much wisdom, and in wisdom is much madness" (Rider-Haggard 27). In states of Gothic madness, however they may be induced, the doors of perception swing open to reveal vistas beyond the limits of consensus reality. Boone, meanwhile, finds in Whale a substitute parent whose devastating war experiences and compassionate regard confer an acceptance that he was never accorded by his drunken biological father. Both men had been conditioned by economic and political circumstances beyond their control to see themselves as social misfits, not unlike the creature portrayed by Boris Karloff in Whale's Gothic films. In the company of one another, however, both men learn to transcend their past traumas. Ultimately, in what is presented as a sad but courageous act of self-affirmation, Whale cheats destiny by taking his own life.

In the brief epilogue that follows (not included in Bram's book) Boone is seen years later with a wife and young son for whom he produces the original sketch of the Frankenstein monster, first presented to him by Whale on the evening of his suicide. By means of this unpretentious domestic tableau and the symbolic legacy that Boone confers upon his own son, we recognize that Clayton Boone has safely negotiated the difficult rite of passage from adolescence to adulthood. He thereby achieves an authentic transcendence of his own. That he has been able to do so is, in part, owing to an ephemeral but significant friendship between an anguished young heterosexual and an ailing and lonely Hollywood recluse, who happened also to have been homosexual. In the final scene we see Boone, as he wanders out into a back alley to depose of the household trash, lurching through a downpour, whimsically aping the awkward gait and menacing mannerisms of Whale's classic film monster. By means of these poignant gestures, Brendan Fraser manages to convey the fact that Boone's childlike nature has remained intact. Undoubtedly, the effectiveness of his portrayal throughout is enhanced by Carter Burwell's superb film score, which provides a compelling blend of pathos and grotesquerie.

To the covertly fascist mentality, politics is merely the extension of war by other means. To the Gothic mentality, however, it is a means whereby the dialectical process experienced in *Gods and Monsters* between Boone and Whale, i.e., a process characterized by reconciliation through empathy and compromise, is promoted as a primary tenet of social exchange and democratic governance. Democracy is defined, in effect, by the opportunity to engage in a vital and potentially transformative exchange of views. In Condon's cinematic parable of war trauma, and the human capacity to transcend it, the potential synergy of opposites essential to the authentic American dream is role-modeled by its two Gothic protagonists. Implicit in Condon's narrative is a realization that the breakdown of dialogue, typically occasioned by an incapacity to overcome mutual insecurities and resentments (Mark Edmundson's "dead-end Gothic"), receives its most complete political expression in the insensate violence of warfare. The antiwar narratives of author Christopher Bram and filmmaker Bill Condon, therefore suggest that, whereas fascism embraces violence as an honorable and legitimate means of furthering one's political agenda, democratic idealism views it as a defeat. If the first casualty of war is truth, Condon's Gothic perspective on the American experience of WWI implies that its second casualty is democracy itself. Where there is no vital exchange of views, there can be no democracy; and on a battlefield, the only exchange possible is an exchange of hostilities.

Edgar G. Ulmer's film adaptation of *The Black Cat* (1934), though less familiar than Whale's Gothic entertainments, is no less pertinent to the connection between Hollywood Gothic and war trauma. A compelling exploration of human sexual perversion and lust for vengeance, *The Black Cat,* according to Ulmer's widow, was more than just a studio assignment, it was a personal obsession. Commenting on the nature of that obsession, Gothic film historian David Skal points out that unresolved trauma concerning WWI is central to Ulmer's conception (Skal 177–78). The plot concerns a deadly reunion between Vitus Wedegast, a vengeful psychiatrist played by Lugosi, and Hjalmar Poelzig, a sadistic architect and satanist played by Karloff. The setting is a Bauhaus-style residence situated on the site of a once great battlefield of the First World War. The Bauhaus, probably the most celebrated and influential art school of the early twentieth century, was closed by Hitler's Gestapo in 1933. Poelzig's converted fortress, characterized by Werdegast as "a masterpiece of construction built on a masterpiece of destruction," therefore serves as an architectural trope of both its creator's divided psyche and the Gothic contradictions that define modernity itself. The aboveground portion, with its clean lines, sparse furnishings, and geometric designs often realized in glass, is a monument to postwar modernism (see Edmundson 113). Its self-conscious commitment to objectivity and rational transparency is belied, however, by its dark subterranean levels comprising a labyrinth of structures originally designed to house weaponry and munitions.

That subterranean domain has since been transformed by Poelzig into a grim exercise in human taxidermy, a demented museum in which the attractive and perfectly preserved bodies of his former wives are encased in glass. During a chilling scene in which the diabolical Poelzig proudly escorts Werdegast on a guided tour of his underground necropolis, Poelzig asks, "Are we any the less victims of war than those whose bodies were torn asunder.... Are we not both the living dead?" The obvious rejoinder to his rhetorical question is that they are indeed both victims of the psychic toll taken on their entire generation by the horror of war, as is James Whale in *Gods and Monsters*. Arguably, the animated cadavers that populate Gothic films and pulp fictions of the 1920s and 1930s, e.g., robots, mummies, zombies, and vampires, are mythic archetypes of the spiritual condition in which Poelzig and Werdegast find themselves, as are the barren and blighted landscapes that these two Gothic hero-villains inhabit.

One of the preserved females in Poelzig's atrocity exhibit proves to be the former fiancée of Werdegast, a rival in love whom Poelzig had disposed of by betraying him to the enemy. Detained for fifteen years in an infamous war prison, a sentence he was not expected to survive, Werdegast has nevertheless returned to wreak vengeance on his treacherous former comrade. His scheme is disrupted by the advent of two young American honeymooners, played by David Manners and Jacqueline Wells. They, along with their accidental traveling companion, Werdegast, are constrained to seek shelter from Poelzig when their tour bus overturns in a severe storm. The sinister Poelzig, intent on adding to his collection of female specimens, is induced by Werdegast to enter into a game of chess with the young girl's freedom at stake, a wager to which he agrees but has no intention of honoring. At the film's climax, Werdegast, on the point of skinning Poelzig alive, sacrifices his own life to save the honeymooners. These two almost allegorical representatives of naïve love, renewal, and outraged innocence flee the fortress which is then destroyed in a warlike demolition similar to the one that claims Frankenstein's castle in the earlier Gothic films of James Whale.

As with *Gods and Monsters*, the film's message is appreciably enhanced by its musical score, a classical-pastiche of appropriately chosen selections of Gothic music from Bach, Beethoven, Liszt, Schubert, Chopin, Schumann, Brahms, and Tchaikovsky.

The Black Cat's antiwar theme, religious iconoclasm, and exploration of psychosexual abuse (daring for its time) aroused

Hollywood censors and other guardians of public morality. Consequently, Ulmer's film generated the kind of controversy later associated with films such as *Silence of the Lambs* and *JFK*. Though its connection to Poe's original short story is tenuous at best, both narratives deal with philosophical, psychological, and broadly political forms of Gothic denial. Moreover, Ulmer's film helped to establish a visual vocabulary of cinematic effects and images that would later come to define the Gothic in film, as did all previous and subsequent contributions to the Universal horror cycles. That vocabulary includes stormy weather, indirect lighting sources, stark contrasts of light and shade, long corridors, winding stairways, vertiginous or distorted camera angles and perspectives, billowing curtains, oceanic imagery, and abrupt shifts from long shots to close-ups. It also helped to subvert America's consensus understanding of WWI as an honorable and heroic adventure undertaken on behalf of universal peace and freedom. President Wilson's intentions, however noble, led to a tragic and horrendous outcome. As we are about to discover, Gothic perspectives on America's experience in the twentieth century suggest that dystopian means adopted in the service of utopian ends invariably produce results that are...horrific.

"It Has Happened Here"

Film continued to play a crucial role in exploring America's unaddressed traumas and apprehensions, though it was not the only art medium to do so, nor was war and the rumor of war their only source. Organized crime, political espionage, persistently high levels of immigration, economic depression, a growing disparity between rich and poor, union strikes, urban blight, the increasing menace of science, a continuing dependence on technology, the anonymity and anomie of metropolitan lifestyles, and widespread unemployment, as well as the rise of ominous foreign dictatorships were among the worrying social realities that marked life in America during the interim period between the two world wars, roughly equivalent to the decade of the 1930s. In the previous decade, "Government withdrew from business, but business moved in and shaped most government policies" (Nevins and Commager 406). This period of "normalcy" was an era of unabashed isolationism and materialism during which the civic virtues practiced by Jefferson and the global idealism preached by Wilson were forgotten. As the Gothic imagination warns, however, the cost of such forgetfulness is frequently high. In this instance, it set the stage for the disastrous stock market crash of 1929 and the Great Depression that followed. These events, in turn, led to the election of Franklin D. Roosevelt and the innovative policies of the New Deal. Though to some these policies seemed revolutionary and hostile to capitalism, in point of fact, America had once again discovered a champion of the authentic American dream, someone who, at a time of great crisis, sought to restore the synergistic balance between capitalism and democracy that the era of normalcy had conceded to business interests. In retrospect, this period was also a golden age of pulp fiction, radio drama, and comic books. In varying ways, each of these pop-culture art mediums rushed in where law-enforcement and investigative journalism feared to tread. Writing of this era, pulp fiction historian Don Hutchison remarks, "It is ironic that the most galvanic era in American popular culture was not that of the two Great Wars but the decade of the Great Depression when the popular arts were fired with creative optimism" (Hutchison 2).

Anxiety, not optimism, was the dominant mood of the country. Given this circumstance, the popularity of pulp fiction strongly suggests that its principle function was to fill a political void. Absent a plethora of official heroes capable of providing real-life solutions to America's most pressing social problems, monthly and bimonthly magazines furnished unofficial ones cheaply and in abundance. They could be purchased at the nearest newsstand for only a dime. Often pulp heroes such as Doc Savage, Batman, Spiderman, Superman, The Phantom Detective, Nick Carter, The Whisperer, all men who blazed a trail of justice using vigilante methods, were also staples of dramatic radio and comic books. The escapist nature of pulp culture and the emotional needs from which it arose are addressed by Hutchison, who asserts that, "During the 'roaring twenties' and early thirties in America, organized crime went unchecked.... The average man felt helpless. When The Shadow entered the scene in 1931, that same average guy was in the mood for instant justice. The Shadow meted it out with blazing .45s and chilling laughter" (Hutchison 219).

America's best known criminal organization in the 1930s was the Mafia, sometimes inaccurately referred to as the Syndicate, the Mob, or Murder Incorporated (all of which are synonyms for a federation of criminal organizations that included the mafia but was not limited to it). Ironically, the etymology of the term *mafia* can be traced to Sicily where, in the Middle Ages, it signified "disdain for anything foreign." By the nineteenth century, it was interpreted as an anagram for *Morte Alla Francia Italia Anela* ("Death to France is Italy's Cry"), an Italian patriotic slogan (see C. Wilson's *A Criminal History of Mankind* 541). Whatever its origins, its very existence in America was officially denied by J. Edgar Hoover, the F.B.I's most sinister and influential director—a circumstance that helps to explain why The Shadow and not Mr. Hoover was America's premier crime-fighter throughout the 1930s. Indeed, the Shadow, the Black Bat, the Avenger, and Dick Benson (the leader of "Justice Incorporated") had remarkably little competition from official quarters until the 1960s when John and Robert Kennedy made the harassment of organized crime a high priority.

The Shadow magazine, authored by journalist and part-time magician Walter Brown Gibson, under the pen name of Maxwell Grant and published by Street & Smith, first hit the newsstands in April of 1931. Its last issue, no. 325, appeared in 1949. Concurrently, the radio drama version, which opened with its famous signature line, "Who knows what evil lurks in the hearts of men? The Shadow knows!" (followed by a distinctly maniacal peal of laughter), premiered in 1930 on CBS and enjoyed an unbroken weekly run until 1954. There was also a Smith & Street comic book series, developed later by other comic book companies including DC, Dark Horse, and Archie Comics, as well as one Saturday matinee serial with Victor Jory in the title role and seven feature length films, including a slick, sadly underrated version starring Alec Baldwin. Commenting on the distinction between the magazine and radio versions, Hutchison notes that plots dealing with werewolves, ghouls, haunted houses, and "other trappings of the Gothic spook story" were common in pulp magazines (Hutchison 28).

The Shadow was released by Universal Pictures in 1994. Though unable to attract either critical acclaim or a large viewing audience, it nevertheless provided stylish Gothic entertainment spiced with tongue-in-cheek humor, opulent period costumes and settings, visually compelling special effects, and memorable performances from a cast of Hollywood celebrities and character actors including Ian McKellen as the comically absentminded scientist Rinehardt Lane, Jonathan Winters as Police Commissioner Weston, Penelope Ann Miller as the Shadow's paramour and Professor Lane's daughter, Margot Lane, and John Lone as the villainous Shiwan Khan. The plot, which seems prescient in light of the terrorist attacks of 9/11/01, is a pastiche garnered from the long-running magazine and radio series. It concerns an attempt by a sinister descendent of Genghis Khan to gain world domination through threatening to detonate an atomic bomb in New York City. In a plot device reminiscent of the zombie/slave scientists in another pulp series, *Terrence X. O'Leary's War Birds* (see Hutchison 203), Reinhardt Lane, oblivious to the ethical and political implications of his work, assembles a nuclear device while in a trance-like state induced by the nefarious Khan. This plot is anachronistic in that the atomic bomb would not be developed until the mid-1940s, though a similar device was actually anticipated in the *Operator #5* pulp fiction saga (see Hutchison 110). Nevertheless, film director Russell Mulcahy's pulp fiction revival is historically accurate in its underlying attitude of contempt for the ethical irresponsibility of modern science, a mood that gained considerable impetus from the First World War.

It also reflects a once prevalent fear of the "Yellow Peril" captured in pulp fiction thrillers with titles such as *The Coming of the Mongol Hordes* and *Corpse Calvary of the Yellow Vulture*. This pervasive and racially charged xenophobia was lashed to a fever pitch by newspaper moguls such as William Randolph Hearst. Indeed, pulp literature in the first half of the twentieth century drew heavily on this theme. "No matter what the depths of ignorance and paranoia it sprang from," writes Hutchison, "the menace of the Yellow Peril certainly added thrills and chills to literally thousands of motion pictures, plays, books, magazines and even comics" (Hutchison 233). Though Hollywood made some attempt to balance public perception with films that portrayed Asians in a more favorable light, as in its film adaptations of Earl Derr Bigger's popular *Charlie Chan* detective stories, it perpetuated the cultural stereotype of oriental villainy in others. The 1940 Saturday matinee serial based on *The Shadow* features an oriental crime lord known as the Black Tiger. Since the days of Populism, the alleged peril posed by European and Asian immigrants has been a leitmotif of American covert fascism. It continues to be of central concern to right-wing demagogues such as Pat Buchanan and his disgruntled blue-collar, fundamentalist Christian constituency.

A theme common to the melodramas of pulp fiction is *enantiodromia*, i.e., the *doppelgänger* theme in Gothic arts. The psychological genesis of Walter Gibson's evocative title was explained in the opening lines of the very first radio broadcast of *The Shadow* on October 31, 1930: "The Shadow of the law is ever present and cannot be violated with impunity.... The Shadow knows" (Tollin 4). In other words, our positive self cannot be indefinitely deceived or suppressed. Conversely, our negative self cannot and must not be eradicated. These twin aspects of our divided human psyche shadow one another. When seen in this light, the seemingly naïve estimation of evil's potency, later intoned at the beginning of each episode—"crime does not pay"— becomes a valid and sophisticated insight into the essential duality of the human condition. According to this insight, the enemy within is, in reality, the loyal opposition. We inadvertently hasten our own demise when we surrender to it unconditionally or seek its absolute destruction. Indeed, in Jungian psychology, the shadow is presented as a universal archetype that must be integrated into our consciousness if we are to achieve, within ourselves and our community, the synergy of oppositional forces that Jung terms "self-actualization." Commenting on the role played by the shadow in analytical psychology, Edward C. Whitmont observes:

> The existence of, or necessity for a shadow is a general human archetypal fact, since the process of ego formation—the clash between collectivity and individually—is a general human pattern. The shadow is projected in two forms: individually, in the shape of the people to whom we ascribe all the evil; and collectively, in its most general form, as the Enemy, the personification of evil. Its mythological representations are the devil, archenemy, tempter, fiend or double; or the dark or evil one of a pair of brothers or sisters.... Recognition of the shadow can bring about very marked effects on the conscious personality.... It takes nerve not to flinch from or be crushed by the sight of one's shadow, and it takes courage to accept responsibility for one's inferior self. (Whitmont 163)

The Shadow's interior double, or alter ego, in Gibson's pulp fiction saga is Lamont Cranston that "mild-mannered man-about-town," a public persona that he has adopted in order to conceal his true identity as the Master Avenger. As the story unfolds, we learn that Cranston harbors an undisclosed sorrow rooted in a secret past that he is eager to hide, a trait frequently encountered in Gothic heroes. Cranston had, at an earlier point in his life, spent several years in the Orient, first as a dreaded drug lord known as the "Butcher of Lhasa," and later as an adept of occult arts under the tutelage of a mysterious Tibetan monk—the Tolku—by whom he was weaned from a life of vicious cruelty and sensual self-indulgence and transformed into a committed crusader against crime and injustice. Shiwan Khan, also a former student of the Tolku, was "not turned so easily," to cite his own characterization. Khan, Cranston's unregenerate double, ultimately murders the Tolku. He acknowledges his inverted alter ego, Cranston, as a kindred spirit and his own equal. The shared identity between them is further attested by a nightmare in which Cranston stands before a bathroom mirror peeling away the flesh from his own face until that of his arch enemy, Shiwan Khan, stands revealed. One's shadow is a fitting symbol of the discarded or unrecognized self that, according to Jung, is an inescapable constituent of the human psyche. Chamisso's 1813 fantasy *Peter Schlemihl,* the prototype for all subsequent works based on the *doppelgänger* theme, suggests that the results of losing one's shadow can be catastrophic.

Another comparatively recent feature length film based on a pulp fiction hero to have explored this theme is the 1989 Warner Brothers release *Batman,* starring Michael Keaton as the winged avenger. In its climatic confrontation between Batman and his *doppelgänger* in the belfry of a Gotham City cathedral, the Joker, referring to an earlier confrontation that resulted in his permanent disfigurement, a grotesque, clownlike grin, says to his opponent, "You made me," to which Batman responds, "You made me first"—a reference to the fact that The Joker as a young man (a.k.a. Jack Napier) had murdered his parents. Both are correct in that the humanity of these two well-matched supermen has been sacrificed in their pursuit of moral absolutism. One of the striking parallels between Bruce Wayne and Lamont Cranston is that both are, in varying degrees, emotionally stunted by their obsessive quest for moral perfection, much as Napier is destroyed by his vengeful *idée fixe.* Similarly to Nathaniel Hawthorne's Gothic antihero in the well-known literary parable cited in chapter 3, Wayne and Cranston are men of adamant, i.e., alienated loners who shun socially accepted opportunities to engage in dialogue and normal human interaction. This recurrent Gothic trait suggests that radical idealism, defined as a failure to achieve synergistic balance between Gothic/transcendent or dystopian/utopian impulses, leads to alienation and, ultimately, to Jungian *enantiodromia.* The core insight offered by American Gothic arts is that a compulsion to achieve personal or political perfection, and the corresponding determination to root out imperfections in one's enemy that often accompanies it, are likely to unleash a destructive monster within that is oblivious to its own intolerance.

A similar identity of opposites exits between Obe-Wan Kenobe and Darth Vadar from *Star Wars,* Indiana Jones and his archeological counterpart Belloq from *Indiana Jones and Raiders of the Lost Ark,*

Batman and the Joker, David Dunn and Mr. Glass from *Unbreakable*, Professor Xavier and Magnato from *X-Men*, Count Dracula and Professor Van Helsing, Dr. Who and The Master, Frankenstein and Praetorius from *The Bride of Frankenstein*, and many other cinematic icons based upon or appropriated from literary models such as Dr. Jekyll and Mr. Hyde, Sherlock Holmes and Professor Moriarty, and Jane Eyre and Bertha Mason. The message typically conveyed by these Gothic dualisms is that we are sane, individually or collectively, to the extent to which we have assimilated and balanced our internal contradictions. Conversely, to the extent that we have denied them or projected them onto others, we are not.

The setting for *Batman*, clearly modeled on modern New York City, is a claustrophobic nightmare of organized crime, official corruption, overpopulation, architectural enormity, and urban squalor. Indeed, the metropolis of film director Russel Mulcahy's pulp cinema fantasy, *The Shadow*, is a realistic recreation of New York City as it might actually have appeared in the 1930s, whereas Tim Burton's Gotham City is its mythic duplicate, i.e., an architectural *doppelgänger* of that same metropolis. Burton's *film noir* masterpiece features a vibrant performance by Jack Nicholson as the hero's nihilistic, sardonically witty villain, the Joker. It also provides biting social satire on the violence, corruption, and commercial greed of a consumer culture that has lost its democratic compass. For example, having laced common household products with a chemical that reproduces his own disfigurement ("the new, improved Smiley!"), The Joker stages a series of televised commercials that savagely lampoon the inanity of modern advertising. Later, he organizes a parade in order to ensnare Batman and bribe public support with a twenty million dollar handout. In a grim bacchanal, eerily reminiscent of the Nazi gas chambers, he and his henchmen disperse money to the frenzied crowd. The gold lust of this gathering is soon punished, however, as remote-controlled inflatable clowns attached to parade floats discharge a deadly fume that instantly transforms the revelers of Gotham City into a panic-stricken mob. In pulp fiction stories, featuring titles such as *The Werewolf of Wall Street*, the Populist and Progressive distrust of corporate America and Wall Street lives on.

Though *Batman* is much darker in mood than *The Shadow*, its deeply conflicted protagonists have much in common. Similarly to the Shadow, Batman hides his private persona behind a public mask. By day he is Bruce Wayne, a charming, fabulously wealthy socialite seemingly devoted to a hedonistic lifestyle. By night, however, he is the "winged vigilante," a fearless champion of civic virtue serving on the frontline of the struggle for law, justice, and the American way. Commenting on the connection between the affluence of pulp fiction heroes and the widespread poverty and unemployment of the Depression era in which they were spawned, Hutchison notes that wealth was a prerequisite for pulp heroes (Hutchison 210). Such fantasy figures allowed anxiety-ridden fans, faced with the harsh realities of crime and poverty, to experience vicariously the pleasures of retribution and financial security.

Arguably, the appeal of the villains in Gothic melodrama and pulp fiction—an appeal that often rivals that of their virtuous counterparts—is attributable not only to their infectious vitality but to the fact that they sometimes do the work of heroes. That is to say, they sometimes do the work we secretly wish our heroes to undertake, even though, in doing so, they must violate professed codes of political correctness and decency. For instance, a pervasive cultural fear of "the plutocracy of science" is transformed by pulp fiction anti-hero Doctor Death into a reactionary political program that would have appealed to Populist fanatics in the nineteenth century, German Nazis in the twentieth century, or Muslim fundamentalists in the twenty-first century. It calls for scientists to cease work, the wheels of industry to stop, the destruction of the United States Patent office, and the emptying of the cities in order to restore America to an agrarian lifestyle (Hutchison 226–27). In another episode of the *Dr. Death* pulp fiction serial, President Roosevelt himself joins a conspiratorial organization known as the "Secret Twelve" devoted to thwarting Doctor Death's atavistic agenda.

In lurid episodes such as these, one can glimpse the emergent moral relativism of a nation increasingly frustrated by the apparent impotence of policies and institutions premised on democratic idealism. My point is not that most Americans consciously endorsed the reactionary schemes of Dr. Death, but that his covert methods, and those of other less sinister pulp heroes, resonated to a subconscious national mood in favor of certain ends regardless of the illegality of the means used to achieve them. If undesired social and political trends cannot be stemmed by acting within the limits of the law, perhaps they should be thwarted by less scrupulous methods. This subliminal message from pulp fiction would later find political expression in the covertly fascist ideology of Alan Dulles, Dean Acheson, and other proponents of America's shadow government. The *enantiodromia* implicit in America's Cold War ideology and the "invisible government" it spawned were, in short, prefigured by the vigilante indulgences of pulp hero-villains from the Shadow to James Bond.

In fact, the stylishly brutal antics of Agent 007 were explicitly anticipated by James Christopher, the pulp fiction hero of the *Operator #5* stories that ran to forty-eight issues from 1934 to 1939. Commenting on the paranoid, often conspiratorial, scenarios on which this series was based, Hutchison calls attention to the savage hordes, actual enemy nations such as Germany and Japan, aliens from space, and creatures burrowing up from the center of the earth that "plunged America's Secret Service Ace into one paranoid fantasy after another" (Hutchison 98). Nevertheless, the Hollywood horror of *The Black Cat* and pulp-fiction paranoia of *Operator #5*, though they may have exercised a stronger hold on the popular mind, were neither the most enduring nor the most significant contributions to political Gothic arts of the 1930s and 1940s. Certainly, they were not the most realistic narratives to emerge from America's political Gothic counterculture. For a time, however, the radio voice of *The Shadow* belonged to a filmmaker whose cinematic exploration of American economic and political culture in *Citizen Kane* stands as a landmark in the annals of Gothic realism.

Orson Welles, the twenty-four-year-old "boy wonder," arrived in Hollywood in 1941, riding the crest of international publicity accorded his 1938 Mercury Theater of the Air radio adaptation of *The War of the Worlds* by H. G. Wells. This program, heard by millions of listeners, simulated a live news broadcast of an alleged invasion from Mars. It obviously touched a sensitive nerve. Though the predominant mood of the country at the time was isolationist, the widespread hysteria provoked by Welles's broadcast suggests that underlying this mood of political and psychological denial was a subconscious awareness that America was indeed menaced by the threat of Hitlerism. It also suggests that there may well have been an uneasy awareness that certain powerful sectors of public opinion were by no means antagonistic to that threat, despite the fact that his Nazi experiment clearly violated virtually every recognized precept of democratic idealism. Indeed, it is now a well established fact that a significant coterie of American icons and corporate industrialists were sympathetic to Hitler, including Charles Lindbergh, Henry Ford, and William Randolph Hearst. These same men were violently opposed to President Roosevelt's New Deal, which they regarded as implicitly socialistic, if not blatantly pro-Soviet. Clearly, Welles's live radio broadcast crystallized America's political Gothic fears of subversion from within and without.

At a time of unprecedented economic crisis and widespread public trauma, Americans had elected another president willing to implement a positive definition of freedom by using the resources of the federal government, in this case to relieve distress caused by massive unemployment and the unbalanced pro-business policies that brought it about. During the decades of the 1920s and 1930s, Republican politicians conspired with conservative businessmen to transform a government of the people into a partisan power elite. Franklin Delano Roosevelt's New Deal, which was perceived as a radical revolution by its enemies, was in reality a conservative restoration. Similarly to Jefferson and Wilson before him, Roosevelt sought to restore the balance and synergy essential to a free society and to "protect against violence from the left or from the right, the essentials of American democracy" (Nevins and Commager 419–20). In short, Roosevelt's New Deal policies were informed by the liberal precepts of the authentic American dream.

One of Roosevelt's programs aimed at putting Americans back to work was the Federal Theater Project (FTP)—a division of the Works Progress Administration, or WPA—headed by Ms. Hallie Flanagan. Even before the notorious *War of the Worlds* broadcast, Welles had achieved a certain degree of notoriety with his production of *The Cradle Will Rock,* a politically provocative musical by composer/pianist Marc Blitzstein that was subsidized by the FTP. The House Committee on Un-American Activities in Washington was particularly anxious to thwart this production. "The Blitzstein operetta," writes one Welles biographer, "was supposed to have all the dynamite of Beaumarchais's *Marriage of Figaro,* which was supposed to have touched off the French Revolution" (Callow 295). When federal funding for Blitzstein's pro-labor musical was cut, just prior to its scheduled premier, the cast and crew went ahead in defiance of both the labor unions that had ironically ordered a work stoppage and the would-be political censors in Washington. In subsequent years, Touchstone Pictures turned the entire cause célèbre into an entertaining film directed by Tim Robbins entitled *Cradle Will Rock.* The iconoclastic Welles, convincingly portrayed by actor Angus Macfadyen, rides the tumultuous political currents of his time like an experienced surfer. Toward the conclusion of the film, a cabal of pro-fascist, anti–New Deal moguls including Nelson Rockefeller and Hearst are shown hatching a plot to promote abstract art as a means of discouraging creativity unfavorable to their capitalist agenda in future. Welles himself is presented as being ideologically neutral, i.e., neither pro fascist nor pro-communist, a point to which we will return in reference to his political Gothic masterpiece, *Citizen Kane*.

Suspected by right-wing factions within the government of harboring communist infiltrators, which to an extent it may have done, the FTP itself became the target in 1938 of the infamous House Committee on Un-American Activities, headed by archconservative Texas Democrat Martin Dies. Earlier, Chairman Dies had turned his sites on international banking interests, now he was investigating alleged communists. "Common to both conceptions," writes one New Deal historian "was the conviction that the crises of the thirties had been caused by conspiratorial elements whose suppression would quickly restore the nation to 'a normal condition'" (Leuchtenburg 280). Interestingly, in a possible preview of events that would transpire again during the 1950s and early 1960s, unwarranted fears of left-wing conspiracy within the government may well have provoked a counter conspiracy from the right.

Just as some thirty years later, according to Oliver Stone, President Kennedy may have been murdered by a Cold War establishment primed by a decade of right-wing paranoia, some modern conspiriologists suspect that in 1933 a group of prominent Americans in the Morgan and Du Pont financial empires may have concocted an elaborate coup d'état against the first Franklin Delano Roosevelt administration. One obvious difference is that this earlier "cabal of millionaire bankers and industrialists" did not have access to the resources and expertise of an invisible government trained in "black operations," as did America's covertly fascist conspirators during the Cold War era. Accordingly, their plot was exposed by Major General Smedley Darlington Butler, a retired commandant of the U.S. Marines (see Vankin and Whalen 337–42). It was against this paranoid backdrop of conspiracy and counter conspiracy that Sinclair Lewis's dystopian novel *It Can't Happen Here* and Orson Welles's cinematic portrait of W. R. Hearst, *Citizen Kane*, were conceived. Arguably, they are the most important artistic achievements of the political Gothic imagination to emerge from the late 1930s and early 1940s.

"It was not that he was afraid of the authorities," writes Sinclair Lewis in defense of his unlikely hero, Doremus Jessup, "He simply did not believe that this comic tyranny could endure. *It can't happen here*, said even Doremus—even now" (Sinclair Lewis 132). Doremus Jessup, editor of the Fort Beulah, VT, *Daily Informer*, is the Jeffersonian spokesperson for the authentic American dream in Lewis's 1935 novel about the coming of fascism to America. According to this dystopian exercise in alternative history, dire consequences arise when Berzelius "Buzz" Windrip, a right-wing demagogue, is elected president. The new president's name reveals his character: Berzelius combines "berserk" and "zealous" while Windrip suggests "windy" and "drip," a reference, perhaps, to his homespun, highly emotive style of oratory. The pseudo-democratic Windrip proceeds to transform America into a fascist state modeled on Nazi Germany. The Washington Irving-like dismay and cultural dislocation that Jessup experiences stems from his outspoken commitment to republicanism, a commitment that results in his local reputation as a clever but unreliable crackpot. As the novel opens, the Fort Beulah Rotary Club is playing host to retired Brigadier General Herbert Y. Edgeways. In an enthusiastically received speech, the general laments the selfishness of citizens who have turned their back on responsible businessmen attempting to restore prosperity and accuses organized labor of being communistic. He advises the young to set aside ethical scruples and pin their faith instead on America's wealth and military prowess. For General Edgeways, might makes right and the exercise of power is its own justification (S. Lewis 21).

Most of Fort Beulah's prominent citizens agree. Louis Rotenstern, for instance, who advocates white supremacy, opines that all foreigners, "Kikes just as much as the Wops and Hunkies and Chinks," should be excluded (S. Lewis 23). Mrs. Gimmitch, an avid member of the Daughters of the American Revolution, is similarly approving, as is Mr. Francis Tasborough, president and owner of the Tasborough & Scarlett Granite Quarry, who asks Jessup why he is afraid of the word fascism, and suggests that it might not be so bad for a strong man like Hitler to restore America's efficiency and prosperity. Jessup, who regards Thomas Jefferson as his model American and keeps a set of his complete works in his study states his view that to cure the failings of democracy by resorting to the evils of fascism is "funny therapeutics" (S. Lewis 29).

As Lewis's Gothic scenario unfolds, American industry is nationalized and labor unions are disbanded, the two-party system is abolished, the Bill of Rights and the Constitution are suspended (for their own protection, of course), liberal arts education is abandoned in favor of a purely vocational curriculum, the law courts become a travesty of justice, intellectuals are imprisoned or exiled, freedom of the press disappears except for the Hearst newspapers favorable to Windrip, and the right of lawful assembly is dealt with by Windrip's Storm Troopers, known as "Minute Men." Eventually the systematic "elimination of the Negroes" and other less-than-100-percent Americans begins in earnest, and concentration camps are established—though their existence is routinely denied by government officials and the journalistic community.

For the most part, these radical changes are condoned, as they were in Nazi Germany, on the grounds that unemployment has virtually disappeared under the new administration (S. Lewis 143). Windrip's chief political opponents are Walt Trowbridge and Franklin Delano Roosevelt. Trowbridge is described as an honest man, a possible Republican candidate for the presidency, and a realist who shuns Windrip's utopian rhetoric and extreme right-wing politics. Roosevelt heads a splinter party, i.e., the Jeffersonian Party. His chief failing is that, like Trowbridge, he appeals to the integrity and reason of American voters rather than to their tribal instincts. Eventually, Jessup joins the N.U., or New Underground, a counterrevolutionary movement started by Trowbridge. He's betrayed and imprisoned. Windrip is driven into exile by his own party, his fascist successors are eventually overthrown, and the concentration camp in which Jessup is being held prisoner is liberated.

During the 1930s, the synergistic balance sought by proponents of democratic idealism was threatened by radical polarization. The pro-Hitler extreme right, which represented the graver danger according to Lewis, was threatening to transform America's covert fascism into an overt imitation of Nazi utopianism, while the pro-Stalinist extreme left was equally intent on subverting the authentic American dream in favor of a Soviet-style utopia of the proletariat. Psychologically, the most compelling feature of Lewis's political Gothic fantasy is the transformation of Jessup from a politically disengaged skeptic, uncertain of his own commitment to the American experiment, into a firm adherent whose changed outlook is ratified by political activism. In the course of that transformation, Lewis defines and affirms the essentials of democratic idealism in relation to competing ideologies.

In chapter 13, Jessup recites a sardonic litany of the abuses of power and wealth that have been committed in the name of patriotism and idealism, citing Marat, Danton, Robespierre, Lenin, Trotsky, and William Randolph Hearst as wealthy and powerful demagogues who lent credence to political causes that promised utopia but delivered dystopia.

He then ventures more deeply into his own American heart of darkness by questioning the validity of a Civil War that pitted brother against brother while capitalists such as the Rockefellers, the Morgans, the Astors, and the Vanderbilts remained safely behind battle lines to profit from the general slaughter. Finally, he goes on to question the very necessity of the American experiment itself, wondering if "the most vigorous and boldest idealists have been the worst enemies of human progress instead of its greatest creators" (S. Lewis 108–11).

As the atrocities of the new administration mount and ideological lines are sharply drawn, Jessup realizes that the middle way advocated by Jefferson—the way of the authentic American dream—is indeed his way. An ongoing debate as to the merits and demerits of avoiding ideological extremes in favor of synergistic balance with a longtime friend, Karl Pascal, climaxes in chapter 20. Pascal is a worker at the stone quarry and a radical proponent of Marxism. In the early days of America's new fascist experiment, Pascal responded to Jessup's glum prognostications by pointing out that the advent of Windrip's American fascism was a turn of events ideally suited to his left-wing hopes for the ultimate triumph of communism (S. Lewis 103). In a heated exchange, Jessup articulates the distinction between the extreme ends of the political spectrum, right as well as left, and his own liberal heritage of democratic idealism. He accuses Pascal of slavish devotion to Russia and to an ideology of egalitarianism that repudiates both the individualism and the civic-mindedness of Jefferson's democratic idealism.

When Pascal asks why Jessup, who clearly deplores many facets of contemporary American culture, has refused to make common cause with the political left, Jessup replies that he is a middle-class intellectual, not a member of the proletariat. He insists that just because actors, teachers, nurses, and musicians are no better paid than stagehands and electricians, it does not follow that their political interests are identical. "It isn't what you earn but how you spend it that fixes your class— whether you prefer bigger funeral services or more books. I'm tired of apologizing for not having a dirty neck" (S. Lewis 185). Pascal confidently predicts that Jessup will finally be forced to side with the communists, but Jessup insists that he will always reject murder as a way of argument, a position that he regards as the touchstone of a true liberal. Later in the novel, when he is invited to join a vigilante group of his fellow prisoners, including Pascal, intent on murdering a new inmate, i.e. a former top official in Windrip's hated regime, Jessup declines. Pascal can't believe that, after all they've been through, Jessup continues to abide by Jeffersonian principles. Jessup, however, assures him that he still does not believe in assassination as an effective means of fighting despotism (284).

The turning point for Jessup comes when his own son, an apologist for America's new fascism with an eye toward a political appointment, visits his father in order to dissuade him from his whimsical advocacy of liberal democracy. When confronted with the fact that his own brother-in-law has fallen victim to Windrip's gangster tactics, his son objects that while he abhors the necessity of violence, "you can't make an omelet without breaking eggs." His father explodes at the application of this cliché to Windrip's political atrocities, emphatically asserting that men's souls and blood are not eggshells for tyrants to break. His son replies lamely that the political means should be forgiven if the ends bring about a rejuvenated nation. Doremus again vehemently disagrees, citing Romain Rolland to the effect that "a country that tolerates evil means—evil manners, standards of ethics—for a generation, will be so poisoned that it never will have any good end" (S. Lewis 212–13). Lewis's principled denunciation of his son's newly adopted creed of expediency and opportunism was repeated in *Citizen Kane*, a 1941 political Gothic film masterpiece by Herman J. Mankiewitz and Orson Welles loosely based on the life of American tycoon William Randolph Hearst.

Citizen Kane is a modern morality play. Its kaleidoscopic plot unfolds as an unsolved Gothic mystery. In a vain attempt to resolve the conflicts and contradictions of a life that in many ways mirrored the conflicts and contradictions of America in the early decades of the twentieth century, an explanation for Kane's now famous dying word, "Rosebud," is sought retrospectively in a series of journalistic interviews. As is often the case in Gothic storytelling, the mysteriousness turns out to be greater than the mystery. We eventually learn that Rosebud is the name of a sled that, for Cane, represents the human love and acceptance he lost in early childhood and devoted a misspent life to recapturing. In real life, there is some evidence to suggest that it was a perverse term of endearment applied by Hearst to his mistress and longtime companion Marion Davies. "The Gothic-thriller atmosphere and the Rosebud gimmickry (though fun)," writes Pauline Kael, one of America's premier film critics, "are such obvious penny-dreadful popular theatrics that they're not so very different from the fake mysteries that Hearst's *American Weekly* used to whip up—the haunted castles and the curses fulfilled" (Kael 237). In other words, they belong to the melodramatic genre of pulp fiction and pulp journalism that flourished during the 1930s. Kael, who finds the sentimentality and ersatz-Freudianism of the Rosebud device distasteful, goes so far as to characterize *Citizen Kane* as "almost a Gothic comedy." However, the intentions of Mankiewitz and Welles were anything but burlesque.

On a technical plane, the Gothic origins of Gregg Tolland's compelling cinematography is well established. Tolland's mentor was German cinematographer and director Karl Freund, whose film credits include the original sound version of *Dracula* as well as the 1932 horror film classic *The Mummy,* starring Boris Karloff. Freund, in turn, derived his visual sensibilities from the silent horror and science fiction fantasy films of the 1920s, such as Fritz Lang's *Metropolis*—in which modern labor is represented as a hypnotized mob of mindless zombies, stripped by their capitalist masters of all human will and dignity—Robert Wiene's *The Cabinet of Dr. Caligari*—another allegory of mindless murder, frequently referenced to the mindless murder of WWI and the first film to link the Gothic with German Expressionist art—and F. W. Murnau's *Nosferatu*—the earliest cinematic rendering of Bram Stoker's literary saga of Count Dracula.

Tolland's use of stark black-and-white photography, cathedral-like shafts of light, menacing shadows, spacious, vaulted interiors, winding stairwells, the *doppelgänger*-like imagery of the famous Hall of Mirrors sequence, the spatial and temporal disorientation achieved through visual montage, the somber resonance of deep focus, high aperture photography, and the mythic stature imparted to its protagonists by a low camera placement that transforms mere mortals into mythic giants are all part of the brooding Gothic atmosphere of *Citizen Kane.* Welles, whose own Gothic credentials are attested by his many dramatic and cinematic forays into to Gothic literature including Curt Siodmak's *Donovan's Brain,* Shakespearean tragedies such as *Hamlet,* Joseph Conrad's *The Heart of Darkness,* and Charlotte Brontë's *Jane Eyre,* obviously shared Tolland's affinity for the romantic sensibilities of German cinema and contributed many Gothic effects of his own devising, aural as well as visual. Indeed, many critics have pointed to the stunning audio effects in *Citizen Kane* derived from Welles's experiences in radio. Another aural dimension was added by the film score of Bernard Hermann, a Julliard graduate who worked closely with Welles on several other projects including *The War of the Worlds* and *Jane Eyre.* His only opera is based on another Gothic classic, Emily Brontë's *Wuthering Heights*. He also composed film scores for the Cold War science fiction fantasy *The Day the Earth Stood Still* and Hitchcock's psychological Gothic thriller *Psycho*. His music for *Citizen Kane* was later adapted into a concert suite entitled *Welles Raises Kane* (Tony Thomas 186–94).

On a narrative plane, Kane himself is a prime example of the Gothic hero-villain. Proud, sardonic, unconventional, irreverent, uniquely gifted, and alienated, he stalks through the film like a grotesque monster, destroying everything and everyone with whom he comes into contact. Kane, an obvious variation on Cain, is at once an American Faust who wagers his soul on power and wealth, an American Dorian Gray whose decadence and boundless self-indulgence corrupt his soul, and an American Jekyll and Hyde who experiences an involuntary reversal into the opposite as his youthful idealism on behalf of the people mutates into a sadistic need to dominate literally everyone who drifts within his ever-widening orbit of influence. A fascinating Gothic sidelight on the saga of *Citizen Kane* is the *doppelgänger* relationship between Welles and Hearst that Mankiewicz weaves into his screenplay. This becomes the subject of *RKO 281*, a Golden Globe–winning television film about the making of *Citizen Cane* starring Liev Schreiber as Welles, John Malkovich as Mankiewicz, and James Cromwell as Hearst.

In their differing spheres, Welles and Hearst were equally precocious, egotistical, emotionally crippled, ruthless, and at once hugely successful and hugely frustrated in their careers. Hearst had amassed a fortune at an early age, whereas the youthful Welles amassed a comparable artistic cachet. Hearst controlled and dominated a journalistic empire, while Welles controlled and dominated all those who came within the domain of his theatrical and cinematic projects. Kane, though not Hearst, was incapable of loving or inspiring love in those around him, i.e., according to the screenplay, he gave only on his terms, which according to him were the only terms anyone knew, while Welles was similarly barren in his personal relationships. Hearst/Kane was suspected of having betrayed, bribed, bullied, blackmailed, and even murdered his way to prominence, while Welles certainly bullied and betrayed others, including his friend and dramatic cohort, Mankiewicz. Hearst/Kane began as a millionaire who became a formidable force in politics but ended as an impotent, largely forgotten man, whereas Welles began as a "boy wonder," who reached the pinnacle of success with his very first film (*Citizen Kane*) and ended as an impotent, largely neglected Hollywood celebrity.

These striking parallels form the basis of John Logan's incisive screenplay for *RKO 281*, the identification number assigned by the RKO Studio to *Citizen Kane*. At a dramatic high point, Hearst is confronted with his imminent bankruptcy by his mistress, Marion Davies. He repels her vulgar but sincere attempt to penetrate his carapace of psychological denial, telling her, "I will not have this in my house," to which she replies, "I'm only trying to understand, Pops" (her favorite term of endearment). Hearst abruptly cuts her short, exclaiming "No you're not! You want to condemn me like everyone else, to point your finger at the pathetic old man grown lunatic with his spending, trapped in his ridiculous castle, still fighting old battles that he will never win." He concludes with the following pathetic confession: "There *is* nothing to understand, only this: I am a man who could have been great.... but was not" (*RKO 281*). This shattering self-admission is also a moment of transcendent self-realization. It would have served Welles and Hearst equally as an epitaph. Politically, however, these two men were complementary opposites rather than mirror images of one another.

While there is persuasive reason to suspect that Welles's distaste for the covert fascism of Hearst had more to do with his interest in artistic freedom of expression than with a deep and principled respect for Jeffersonian democracy, he nevertheless strikes an idealistic pose (in Logan's screenplay) in defense of his film to a board of New York investors on the point of yielding to pressure from Hearst to block the film's release. Welles/Logan, with understated eloquence, reminds these investors that *Citizen Kane* and the legacy he hopes to leave behind are harmless, a mere dream, unlike the brutal realities that constitute the legacy of his adversary, William Randolph Hearst. However, says Welles, on this occasion, they have been given a rare and timely opportunity to let the artistic dream prevail over the brutal reality by allowing freedom to prevail over the corruption of inordinate wealth and influence. In other words, Welles pleads his case for the release of *Citizen Kane* on behalf of the authentic American dream:

> Today a man from Germany invaded Greece. He's already swallowed Poland, Denmark, Norway, and Belgium.... Everywhere this man goes, he crushes the life and freedoms of his subjects. He sows yellow stars on their lapels. He makes them corpses. In this country we still have our views. We can argue with him. We can say and we can be heard because we are, for the moment, free....

Will you send a message across America that one man can take away our voices? (RKO 281)

In 1941, the very year in which *Citizen Kane* was finally released, Hollywood writer Curt Siodmak completed the Universal Studio's quartet of archetypal Gothic monsters with his screenplay for *The Wolf Man,* a role made famous by actor Lon Chaney Jr. In his 1997 autobiography, *Wolf Man's Maker: Memoirs of a Hollywood Writer,* written three years before his death, Siodmak wrote, "To believe in myth, is, for me, an abrogation of rationality." Ironically, he goes on to boast of having "added one of the three ghosts to American lore." The remaining two, according to Siodmak, are Frankenstein's creature and Count Dracula. In this same book, Siodmak reveals another intriguing coincidence between himself and Welles, his [Siodmak's] visit to the real Xanadu of Citizen Kane: "Americans do not like to mention death. People 'pass away,' a circumvention of the word *dying.* I could not find a second word for death in any other language. When I visited the publisher William Randolph Hearst in his castle in San Simeon in 1937, I was instructed never to mention the word death in his presence, as if he could ban that final human outcome by ignoring it" (Siodmak, *Wolf Man's Maker* 440–41). This documented evidence of denial is perhaps a more revealing clue as to the mainspring of Hearst's private and public motivations than the meaning of Kane's famous valediction, "Rosebud."

A third intersection between Welles and Siodmak is provided by the fact that Welles's most famous radio broadcast, apart from *The Shadow* series and *The War of the Worlds,* was an adaptation of Siodmak's Gothic science fiction novel, *Donovan's Brain.* Its plot concerns the mesmerizing will of a disembodied criminal financier who reverses the role of physician and patient by exerting telepathic control over the scientist who would turn his living brain into a lab experiment. This familiar tale, which spawned at least two film versions as well as a radio adaptation, explores the recurrent Gothic themes of the divided self and the danger of *enantiodromia* to which it is exposed. At the moment of crisis, the scientist/protagonist exclaims, "I, mute witness of the scene, wanted to cry out.... But I had no mouth to make myself heard. I was nothing but a brain in a vessel" (Siodmak 134). The philosophical problem of the mind/body split between consciousness—conceived as the ghost in the machine—and body—conceived as a supposedly inert and mindless machine of nature—has occupied thinkers since at least the time of Newton and Descartes. Indeed, a radical separation of mind and matter is the starting point of the Newtonian paradigm, sometimes also referred to as the Cartesian paradigm after the seventeenth-century mathematician and scientist René Descartes (see Morris Berman, *The Reenchantment of the World*, chapter I, "The Birth of Modern Scientific Consciousness"). Conversely, the inseparable unity of mind and matter and the synergistic balance between them is a central concern of the philosophical Gothic imagination.

Donovan's Brain is also a political parable. Written in 1942 at the height of the Second World War, an expatriate Austrian Jew who came to America seeking refuge from Nazi persecution tells of a charismatic personality devoid of recognizable human characteristics and capable of inducing others to commit murder. Such a plot must have had an obvious resonance with Hitler's Germany for its author. Siodmak's most enduring and popular Gothic achievement, the screenplay for *The Wolf Man*, certainly did. The correct German title of memoirs, inaccurately translated as *Wolf Man's Maker* is *Under the Wolf People* (*Unter den Wolfsmenschen*), an explicit allusion to the fascist inhabitants of Nazi Germany. In several interviews and written statements, Siodmak made clear the connection between his seemingly authentic folktale and his Gothic political dilemma. For example, in a passage from his obituary notice in the *New York Times*, quoted from a magazine interview, Siodmak says, "I am the Wolf Man. I was forced into a fate I didn't want: to be a Jew in Germany. I would not have chosen that as my fate. The swastika represents the moon. When the moon comes up, the man doesn't want to murder, but he knows he cannot escape it, the Wolf Man destiny" (Martin, Sunday Obituaries, *New York Times*, 11/19/2000).

As with the other films discussed in this section, the mythic atmosphere of *The Wolf Man* is greatly enhanced by its musical score. The same could be said of all the second cycle of Universal Studio's horror films that spanned the Second World War, including *The Son of Frankenstein* and *The Tower of London*, both filmed in 1939. The scores for all three films were the result of a musical collaboration between composers Hans J. Salter and Frank Skinner. In the case of *The Wolf Man*, the Universal's music director, Charles Previn, also made a contribution. Salter, a European-trained student of Alban Berg—one of the Austrian masters of musical Expressionism—drew freely upon a tradition of Gothic musical symbolism that was used by nineteenth-century Romantics such as Liszt and Saint-Saëns. Coincidentally, it was Saint-Saëns who composed the signature music used to introduce *The*

Shadow in the radio melodrama. The famous three-note leitmotif in Salter's score that announces the presence of the Wolf Man, for example, outlines the interval of a tri-tone, or augmented fourth. This disturbing interval has been known for centuries as the *diabolus in musica* ("the devil in music"). From the Middle Ages on, its use was prohibited by the Church owing to its dissonant nature. This prohibition, of course, made it ideal as a musical device suggestive of things otherworldly and diabolical, which is precisely why it figures prominently in *Dance macabre*—a programmatic depiction by French composer Camille Saint-Saëns of the dead rising from their graves, the lurid and sulfurous opening of the *Faust Symphony* by Franz Liszt, and, of course, the film score to The *Wolf Man* by Salter, Skinner, and Previn. An orchestral recreation of the lost scores for *The Son of Frankenstein* and *The Wolf Man* has been recorded on the Marco Polo label by Moscow Symphony Orchestra, DDD 8.223747.

As Gothic artists such as Welles, Lewis, and Siodmak labored at home, American soldiers and civilians approached the end of a titanic struggle on behalf of democracy abroad. Though most Americans were blissfully ignorant of their implications at the time, apocalyptic events transpired in the Japanese cities of Hiroshima and Nagasaki that would inaugurate a new Cold War on the very heels of the previous conflict. According to certain Gothic narratives, the tragic and unforeseen outcome of these events would be the triumph of a covert government-within-the-government, an occult, i.e., hidden, priesthood of official secrets known as the intelligence community—in a word, Truman's "American Gestapo." This covert government was established without public debate, foreknowledge, or consent by some of the very Nazis that thousands of courageous young Americans had recently given their lives to defeat. Created in response to an inflated estimate of the threat posed by Soviet Communism, this shadowy but formidable offspring of official paranoia would be committed to achieving ostensibly justifiable ends by dishonorable, often criminal, means. Romain Rolland predicted that any country that tolerated evil for a generation would bring about its own destruction (see S. Lewis, *It Can't Happen Here* 213). Arguably the questionable means employed by the CIA and similar organizations would poison America's political waters for more than a generation.

When he signed the National Security Act of 1947, thereby creating a plethora of secret governmental agencies such as the Central Intelligence Agency, Army Intelligence, the Defense Intelligence

Agency, and the Office of Naval Intelligence, President Truman along with Allen Dulles and his brother, John Foster Dulles (the two Eisenhower appointees who came to power shortly after Truman), instituted and nurtured a network of legally sanctioned criminal conspiracies. These organizations were licensed to operate within a constitutional government historically committed to public disclosure and the rule of law. In Gothic terms, by summoning into existence this two-faced bureaucratic monster, these men invoked a danger to the *Constitution,* a danger from the right that was arguably clearer and certainly more present than the left-wing danger of Soviet and Chinese Communism it was intended to thwart. This situation raised the level of tension within American political consciousness, caused by the uneasy coexistence of idealism and covert fascism, to the level of an insupportable moral dilemma. Commenting on the *doppelgänger* relationship of the Dulles brothers, conspiriologist Jim Marrs cites the following passage from a book by Thomas B. Ross and David Wise entitled *The Invisible Government,* "Uniquely, they embodied the dualism—and indeed the moral dilemma—of United States foreign policy since World War II.... Foster Dulles reflected the American ethic; the world as we would like it to be. While he took this position, his brother was free to deal with nastier realities.... He was, as Allen Dulles once put it, able to 'fight fire with fire' (as quoted in Marrs 184). In other words, John Foster Dulles spoke on behalf of the very democratic ideals, e.g., sovereignty and the rule of international law, that his brother Allen actively sought to undermine. To appreciate the Gothic significance of this dilemma, one has only to consider that a large number of Gothic plots climax at the point at which the protagonist realizes he or she is no longer in control or that the enemy without has somehow gained entrance to the protagonist's stronghold. The catastrophe in the Frankenstein legend, for instance, is reached when the mad scientist realizes he is at the mercy of that which he has created. Dr. Jekyll's moment of truth comes when he is compelled to admit that he can no longer suppress Mr. Hyde. *The Wolf Man,* as portrayed by Lon Chaney Jr., is a pathetic figure precisely because he can neither understand nor prevent the transformation by which he is periodically overtaken.

Similarly, the unfolding plot of America's Gothic history reached its catastrophe when our elected and appointed officials decided to compromise the Jeffersonian ideal, along with their own moral judgment, in favor of embracing the expertise of Nazi officers to whom they turned for advice and assistance at the end of World War II. Determined to fight communist fire with fascist fire, they sought the services of a Nazi intelligence apparatus known as the Gehlen Organization, which subsequently formed the basis of the FIA, or West German Federal Intelligence Agency (see Wise and Ross 133–35). At that moment, like the German student in Washington Irving's Gothic parable of the French Revolution, these men consented to sleep with the enemy. In the words of assassination researcher Dick Russell: "If the Communist Chinese could master the art of 'brainwashing' our POWs in Korea, the CIA's MK-ULTRA and ARTICHOKE programs would seek to go one better via hypnosis and drugs. If the Soviet KGB could maintain 'Department 13' for political assassinations, the CIA would adopt a less superstitious, more elegant title: 'Executive Action' ... little by little, Jekyll was becoming Hyde" (Russell 69). As Doremus Jessup might have expressed it, "They agreed to break as many eggs as necessary, by whatever means were deemed politically expedient, to make an omelet suited to their ideological palates." In doing so, according to Gothic artists such as Oliver Stone, they involved their country in a Faustian bargain that imperiled its very soul.

Are those who embrace such a Gothic perspective on the American experience guilty of the same 20/20 hindsight, or "presentism" as McPherson calls it, of which I have accused the critics of America's founding? Perhaps, but had Americans taken seriously the utopian example set by Jefferson and Adams, it is unlikely that someone of Truman's limited intellectual horizon, whatever his other merits, would have achieved the presidency in the first place. In that hypothetical case, he—and the rest of us—would have been spared the Mephistophelean temptation to sanction the willful annihilation of civilian populations or to authorize the CIA's pursuit of an un-Constitutional mandate that, according to its detractors, turned against the very democracy it was intended to serve. More importantly, America and the world might have been spared the divisiveness, nuclear paranoia, and disillusionment brought about by two decades of seemingly unremitting diplomatic and military conflict, propaganda warfare, political assassination, and public scandal. In yielding to the Faustian bargain by which America was beset between 1945 and 1947, Truman and the Dulles brothers set an ethical precedent that will forever qualify America's claim to have occupied the moral high ground in either the Second World War or the Cold War that succeeded it.

From the countercultural perspective of the Gothic imagination, only Faustian hubris and the dark denial that accompanies it can adequately explain America's tragic journey from Hiroshima to Dallas. Truman, the Dulles brothers, and other responsible agents of the government were undoubtedly burdened by the necessity of making momentous decisions during an uncertain and dangerous time in our history. Nevertheless, the course they chose was radically inconsistent with the tenets of democratic idealism they were sworn to uphold. This is particularly so in light of the historical context in which their decisions were made. The use of nuclear weapons on the innocent and the infirm was approved at a time when young men were valiantly dying to stop Hitler from doing to innocent and infirm Jews, over a period of years, what Truman proposed to do to the equally innocent Japanese citizens of Hiroshima and Nagasaki in a matter of seconds. Ultimately, "the greatest generation" fought and died to oppose precisely the kinds of state-sponsored terrorism, pseudo-science, and deliberate deception that their own government would soon be practicing at home and abroad in the name of anti-Communism.

Admittedly, there is a comic tinge to the notion of give'em-Hell Harry, Truman's popular nickname, fraternizing with the likes of Mephistopheles. The image of Truman, a folksy icon of Americana, in Faust's Gothic study seems as incongruous as that of Goethe behind the wheel of a Missouri farm tractor. Conversely, President-elect Buzz Windrip was, to all outward appearance a simple, homespun character whose Americanized version of *Mein Kampf,* entitled *Zero Hour,* invoked the Trumanesque language of the Common Man. Indeed, in Sinclair Lewis's prophetic novel it is the apparent incongruity between Windrip's down-home demeanor and the brutality of his political agenda that forestalls opposition until it is too late for reasoned criticism to make a difference.

Truman's good intentions ended by paving a one-way road to Hell down which his country would soon travel at breakneck speed. By acting on those intentions, Truman formalized a long-standing ideological split between adherents to the principles of democratic idealism and those of covert fascism. This split lacked formal status prior to 1947, though it existed from the very outset of the American experiment. However, the fact that it enjoyed no official status is crucial to an understanding of the distinction between America in the pre–and post–World War II eras. Regardless of how often or willfully certain individuals and institutions might have twisted the Constitution to covertly fascist purposes previously, fascist precepts and practices had never before been officially sanctioned by the federal government. All that changed when Truman imprudently accommodated right-wing adversaries of America's democratic heritage by providing them with an institutional base of operation from within the very stronghold of American power—a seemingly unassailable position from which to subvert the authentic American dream. Throughout the period of the Cold War, America's Gothic *doppelganger,* i.e., a government of, by, and for the military-industrial complex, would circumvent or violate democratic standards of law and order in ways that not even the overheated imagination of Ignatius Donnelly dared envision and that Jefferson, were he alive to bear witness, would not have hesitated to condemn as treasonable. In the next and final chapter we will consider the Gothic implications of America's Faustian bargain in relation to a modern filmmaker whose cinematic narratives speak to the suspicion, shared by millions, that on November 22, 1963 *It*—meaning the ascendancy of covert fascism over Constitutional democracy—did, in fact, happen to America.

Discussion Topics and Questions

1. Discuss the effect on the Gothic imagination produced by the disappearance of the "agrarian myth" and the rise of corporate capitalism.
2. How do WWI and WWII relate to the Gothic mythology of the two Universal horror film cycles?
3. What social and political realities did pulp Gothic mirror, what was the psychological basis of its appeal, and what ethical values did it promote?
4. What do the political-Gothic masterpieces of Sinclair Lewis and Orson Welles have in common and how do they differ?
5. How were political events that transpired during the Truman and Eisenhower administrations anticipated by the Gothic mythologies developed earlier in the century in film, pulp fiction, and literature?

5 Chronicles of Redemption

The political Gothic imagination explores perverse power relationships, dialectical inequalities within our system of constitutional checks and balances, hidden histories, and the conspiratorial mechanisms whereby officially sanctioned versions of history, i.e., consensus histories, are shaped and rendered plausible. As a narrative genre, the political Gothic may function almost independently of other Gothic genres. Conversely, it may seek to achieve a blend of political, philosophical, psychological, and supernatural perspectives, as does the complex cinematic mythos of Oliver Stone's complementary pairing, *JFK* and *Nixon*. Whereas *JFK* seems a comparatively straightforward exercise in *cinéma vérité*, a docudrama that presents an alleged hidden history of the Cold War era, it is also a self-conscious exploration of what academic philosophy refers to as the epistemological question, i.e., an examination of the meaning and nature of truth itself. Moreover, Stone's film furnishes a compelling study of the psychological price exacted from authentic Gothic heroes who confront disturbing truths that most of us prefer to either ignore or deny. *Nixon,* meanwhile, is an almost classic instance of the interior drama on which psychological Gothic narrative thrives. Nevertheless, for much of its imagery and characterization it draws upon prototypes derived from literary and cinematic horror. These prototypes suggest the supernatural Gothic in ways that provide an archetypal dimension to Stone's portrayal of Richard M. Nixon as a half-crazed tyrant caught in the snares of his obsessive need to destroy his political "enemies," exorcise personal demons from his troubled past, and gain political mastery over the sinister forces of covert fascism that have lifted him to national prominence. The literary, journalistic, and cinematic antecedents of Stone's sophisticated and richly textured blend of Gothic genres are many.

In 1962, Fletcher Knebel and Charles W. Bailey II wrote a political thriller entitled *Seven Days in May* that was subsequently turned into a critically acclaimed film starring Burt Lancaster as the treasonous General Scott, Kirk Douglas as Colonel Jiggs, the thankless informer responsible for exposing Scott's planned coup, and Frederick March as the Kennedy-style President Jordan Lyman. John Frankenheimer, who also worked on *The Manchurian Candidate,* and screenwriter Rod Serling of *Twilight Zone* fame, collaborated on *Seven Days in May. The Manchurian Candidate*, adapted from another literary Cold War thriller, is premised on the ability of governments to create, á la Frankenstein, a programmed assassin. As attested by John Marks (see *In Search of the Manchurian Candidate: The CIA and Mind Control*), this capability is one that was being developed by the CIA's MK-ULTRA program at the very time Hollywood's cautionary Cold War parable was in production. Frankenheimer's film was informed by canons of political correctness that prevailed during the McCarthy era. Consequently, the sinister conspirators it features are communists from the Far East. The fictional plot of *Conspiracy Theory,* a more recent cinematic foray into the realm of the political Gothic, explores a similar premise, though the post–Warren Commission climate of opinion in America rendered it unnecessary for Hollywood to identify the origin of those who are seeking to program Jerry Fletcher—a likable patsy portrayed by Mel Gibson—as emanating from any point further east than Langley, Virginia.

Conversely, *Seven Days in May* envisions a planned military *coup d'état* provoked by the decision of a liberal president to ratify a controversial peace treaty with the Soviets at the height of the Cold War. The dénouement of the novel includes the following short speech from a general loyal to his constitutional oath: "I did a lot of putting two and two together on the way over here, Senator, People always say it can't happen here, and I'm one of those people. But all of a sudden I figured out I was wrong. Given the right circumstances, it can happen anywhere. and don't quote me in the Senate, but the military has been riding awful high-wide-and-handsome in this country ever since World War II" (Knebel and Bailey II 311). This sentiment was forcefully, if somewhat belatedly, expressed by another prominent military man, President Dwight D. Eisenhower in his Farewell Address to the Nation on January 1, 1961: "The conjunction of an immense military establishment and a large arms industry is new in the American experience....We must never let the weight of this combination endanger our liberties or democratic processes. We should take nothing for granted" (Stone and Sklar 1).

Documentary footage of Eisenhower's televised address comprises the opening segment of *JFK,* Oliver Stone's recreation of the Cold War at its most perilous hour. In it, Stone complies with Eisenhower's advice to take nothing at face value with regard to the events of that period. Interestingly, John F. Kennedy himself had offered to vacate the White House during the filming of *Seven Days in May*, predicting that the scenario it developed was one that could happen to him if another fiasco similar to the Bay of Pigs incident were to occur during his administration (Frankenheimer, director's commentary, DVD). Kennedy was, of course, referring to the unsuccessful, CIA-engineered invasion of Castro's Cuba in 1961. From the standpoint of America's shadow government, a similar disaster did, in fact, occur the following year when the Cuban missile crisis resulted in a pledge from Kennedy to Soviet Premier Khrushchev. In essence, Kennedy assured the Soviets that America would never again invade Cuba provided the Russian-supplied nuclear warheads were dismantled and permanently removed from that island. In Dallas on November 22, 1963, according to Oliver Stone, America's shadow government implemented the coup that President Kennedy anticipated in response to such a pledge.

What distinguishes Stone's efforts from those of the other entirely fictional films mentioned above is that he uses actual people and events as a springboard for historical speculation, or revision, as some would prefer to call it, thereby polluting time-honored distinctions between fact and fiction, history and romance, art and propaganda. These distinctions, however, are neither so pure nor so time-honored as Stone's detractors would have us believe. Walpole's *The Castle of Otranto*, English fiction's first neo-Gothic novel, was originally presented as a true story. A short time later, MacPherson's *The Poems of Ossian*, another Gothic literary hoax passed off as the product of an antique Celtic bard, incited the intelligentsia on both sides of the Atlantic to heated controversy over its authenticity. To cite a more recent example, Whitley Streiber's 1987 best-selling novel *Communion*, which allegedly chronicles its author's encounters with an alien intelligence, is either an artful literary hoax or an astounding confirmation of Hamlet's Gothic assertion that there are indeed more things in heaven and earth than are dreamt of by scientists wedded to consensus understandings of the cosmos.

Stone's own defense against the charge of historical distortion vacillates, somewhat disingenuously, between the claim that he is a mythmaker not an historian, and the countercharge that his critics are inconsistent in signaling out *JFK* and *Nixon* while ignoring other dramas that are at least as flagrant in their distortion of history, such as Peter Shaffer's *Amadeus*—an historically questionable account of the alleged murder of Mozart. Nevertheless, Stone's arguments are essentially valid. In the manner of Shakespeare, Walter Scott, Charles Brockden Brown, and Nathaniel Hawthorne, he uses history as artistic raw material from which to fashion a modern political mythology, though his literary predecessors typically softened their criticisms of contemporary events by distancing them in time and/or geographical setting. Similarly, the harsh invective directed at Stone's work by lawyers, journalists, and historians such as Robert G. Blakey, George Wills, Anthony Lewis, George Lardner Jr., Gerald Posner, Stephen Ambrose, and many others, suggests levels of denial and disingenousness that run far deeper than any to be found in Stone's forthright, if not entirely convincing, rebuttals. Not unlike the assassins in the film's mythic reenactment of the Dallas conspiracy, Stone's character assassins often shoot from protective cover at their moving target—attacking his continually evolving perspective from so many angles as to render an effective response impossible.

Apart from Frankenheimer's successful Cold War fantasies and the more generic historical influence of silent filmmakers such as Sergei Eisenstein and D. W. Griffith, at least two modern Hollywood practitioners of the political Gothic influenced and anticipated Stone's work. In his commentary, included in the *Special Edition Director's Cut* of *JFK*, he refers specifically to Frank Capra and Orson Welles in this regard. Alluding to the essential "harshness of vision" that informed Capra's films during the 1930s, he takes pointed exception to the standard criticism of Capra as a purveyor of patriotic sentiment grounded in an idealized perception of America. Many critics were quick to compare Stone/Costner's portrayal of Jim Garrison, the New Orleans District Attorney who brought the only prosecution in the murder of President Kennedy, to Jefferson Smith, played by James Stewart in Capra's 1939 classic *Mr. Smith Goes to Washington:* "According to one such critic, Stone also made this comparison. 'The D.A.,' Stone said, was.... someone who undertakes to investigate something that had been covered up. He makes mistakes. He has many frustrations. He has few successes. He is reviled, ridiculed, and the case he brings to trial crashes....Capra's movie is a declaration of principles in the face of murderous odds. 'Lost causes,' as Mr. Capra says, 'are the only causes worth fighting for.'" Thus, according to Frank Beaver, 'JFK resulted in a different kind of Stone film—one with more bathos than edge, a cause movie rather than a caustic one'" (Mackey-Kallis 37). The ahistorical nature of such criticism fails to take into account Capra's impact on his journalistic contemporaries. Similarly to *JFK*, *Mr. Smith* touched a popular nerve while managing to reduce pundits, diplomats, and politicians to a condition bordering on hysteria. Writing of this phenomenon in his autobiography, Capra comments wryly, "I took the worst shellacking of my professional life. Shifts of hopping-mad Washington press correspondents belittled, berated, scorned, vilified, and ripped me open from stem to stern as a villainous Hollywood traducer" (Capra 283).

One Democratic senator proclaimed that *Mr. Smith* was "exactly the kind of picture that dictators of totalitarian governments would like to have their subjects believe exists in a democracy" (Capra 287). Ironically, one of the film's most illustrious critics was none other than the American Ambassador in London, Joseph P. Kennedy, who upon viewing the film phoned a top executive at Columbia Pictures to complain that, in criticizing democracy, it furnished America's enemies with a propaganda weapon (Capra 289). Kennedy went on to urge that the film be withdrawn from Columbia's European market. Columbia's Harry Cohn responded that *Mr. Smith* was a "shot in the arm for all the Joes in the world that resent being bought and sold and pushed around by all the Hitlers in the world" (Capra 289). Obviously, Capra's vision of America seemed far less warm, fuzzy, and inoffensive to the guardians of truth in his own day than it does to their modern counterparts. Today's champions of consensus history have been similarly assertive in their denunciation of Stone's *JFK* as a dangerous attack on democracy itself. Often they have employed the very arguments used by critics of Capra's film in 1939.

In a scene reminiscent of the democratic letter campaign in Capra's film, Garrison/Costner, during his closing argument to the jury, holds up a handful of letters containing small cash donations. According to Garrison, these letters from ordinary men and women throughout America who wish to support his legal crusade attest to the people's hunger for truth and justice with regard to the murder of their president. In an impassioned appeal to the jury—and by extension, the viewing audience—Garrison/Costner refers to the Kennedy assassination as America's darkest moment and exhorts his audience in the following terms to uphold the authentic American dream: "Do not forget the young President who forfeited his life. Show the world this is still a government *of* the people, *for* the people, and *by* the people. (Stone and Sklar 178–79). Garrison's stirring tribute to the authentic American dream, which might have come directly out of Capra's earlier film, invokes the language of Thomas Jefferson as well as Jefferson Smith. In an earlier scene deleted from the final cut, Garrison's assistant, Numa Bertell, reads aloud from one of the thousands of letters Garrison later refers to in his closing argument: "Dear Mr. Garrison, God bless you for having the courage to go after the murderers of President Kennedy.... We have four kids and not an extra lot of money but we enclose a contribution to help with your work." Bertell comments, "That's what it's about, boss. For every lousy article in the press there's a hundred of these" (Stone and Sklar 95). Dramatizing the difference, not only between Garrison and his detractors but between the age of Capra and that of Stone, Bill Broussard, another, far more cynical assistant who would later betray Garrison, sarcastically reminds Bertell that Garrison's opponents are not corresponding (Stone and Sklar 95).

The most obvious and telling difference between Mr. Smith in Washington and Mr. Garrison in New Orleans is that, in the end, the former prevailed over the forces of greed, anomie, and corruption arrayed against him, whereas the latter did not. According to an arithmetic of the human spirit difficult to calculate, suggests Stone, that difference measures the defeat sustained by democratic idealism during a Cold War supposedly fought in its defense. Advocates of covert fascism have always accused their opponents of gross sentimentality. This charge was raised by critics of Dickens's appeal to human decency in *A Christmas Carol* and by critics of Capra's imaginative gloss on that appeal in *It's a Wonderful Life*. Similarly, it is raised by critics of Stone's insistence that anti-Communism and pro-capitalism together do not necessarily equal American patriotism. Indeed, according to Stone, the highly combustible chemistry of that Cold War formula may have destroyed the authentic American dream.

In the same DVD commentary on *JFK* in which Stone expresses his affinity for Capra, he asserts, "Orson Welles should have made this film. He had the right kind of jigsaw mind." Although Garrison's impassioned plea on behalf of the truth as our most prized possession would seem to imply an infallible judgment, Garrison's Platonic idealism (and by extension that of Oliver Stone) implies no such thing. On the contrary, one of the obvious points of similarity between Stone and Welles is the way in which both filmmakers encode the allusiveness and complexity of truth into the very structure of their Gothic narratives. That structure consists of a kaleidoscope of episodes that are discontinuous in time, style, setting, and technique. These disjunctive episodes include actual documentary footage, pseudo-documentary footage, the use of surrealistic montage, rapid-fire time shifts, and confrontations between human perspectives that are mutually exclusive. By these disorienting means, Welles and Stone recreate the confusing welter of impressions that anyone who would gain so much as a fleeting glimpse of the truth must confront and master. In doing so, they pay homage to the impenetrable mystery of life that lies at the core of the philosophical Gothic paradigm.

Indeed, both *Citizen Kane* and *JFK* project a postmodernist conception of truth as something that is unknowable, or at least unverifiable. Both plots present their audiences with mysteries that are not only unsolved but unsolvable. The meaning of Kane's final utterance, "Rosebud," is rejected as a key to a definitive understanding of his character and motivations. Similarly, Garrison fails in his quest to define the exact parameters of the conspiracy that claimed Kennedy's life or to bring those responsible for it to justice. In the words of Susan Mackey-Kallis, "In many ways it [*JFK*] is .... the most sophisticated and complicated of Stone's films, taking as its theoretical polemic the search for 'truth' with the realization that there is no single, ultimately knowable truth about the Kennedy assassination" (Mackey-Kallis 38). The truth about the Kennedy assassination, as David Ferrie—a complex and grotesque character unconvincingly portrayed by Joe Pesci—emphatically asserts is "a mystery wrapped in a riddle inside an enigma" (Stone and Sklar 93). Indeed, the painful paradox of the Gothic hero is that he or she is driven by a moral imperative to seek truth in a world in which such a quest is destined to fail.

Gothic heroes from legend and classical literature, e.g., Robin Hood and Hamlet, to more recent examples such as Stone's Jim Garrison and John F. Kennedy himself, are restless characters whose idealistic quest for enlightenment and justice is conditioned by a realization that the price they must pay, even for partial success, will be inordinately high. That is why, in Gothic terms, success is measured not so much by achievement as by authenticity of purpose. Norman Mailer once spoke of John Kennedy as "an outlaw sheriff." With that inspired characterization, he captured an aspect of the Kennedy myth that speaks to the charge of uncritical hero-worship so often leveled against Oliver Stone and other alleged Camelot loyalists. Many of those who dismiss Stone's countercultural perspective on the Cold War era would maintain that

Kennedy's ambiguous political record and his well-publicized sexual exploits suggest that he was neither different from nor better than his immediate successors, Lyndon Johnson and Richard Nixon. Stone, of course, rejects this view, insisting that Kennedy's principled advocacy of democratic idealism, his intellectual distinction, and his growing disenchantment with the Pentagon, the CIA, organized crime, and big business not only set him on a collision course with Eisenhower's covertly fascist military-industrial complex, but set him far above those who would follow.

In assessing the question of Kennedy's character from Stone's perspective it is important to realize that Stone is a melodramatist, as are all exponents of the Gothic imagination. Melodrama is an unfairly maligned artistic genre that speaks the operatic language of dream and myth, as opposed to that of psychological realism (see *One Half of Robertson Davies* 143–60). Hyperbole is Stone's element and in some instances the modern-day classicists who object to his work are, one suspects, offended as much by the melodramatic manner in which his message is delivered as by the message itself. Accordingly, Stone paints the world as he experiences it, not in terms of subtle, finely drawn distinctions, but in boldly romantic, sharply defined contrasts and vivid emotions. Based on his other films, however, one suspects that, like Kennedy himself, Stone is an idealist without illusions, well aware of human complexity and ambiguity, i.e., the shadow side of the human condition. As Mackey-Kallis astutely observes, several of Stone's characters recognize that "growth requires a balancing of opposites, an acknowledgement of the human capacity not only to love but also to hate and destroy" (Mackey-Kallis 123). Indeed, in commenting on some of the minor characters in *JFK* from the seedier side of life in Dallas, Stone invokes the complex moral and psychological vision of Dostoevsky, claiming "There is redemption in everything, even in crime" (DVD commentary). The crime of high treason and its damning or redemptive effect on all of us is the subject matter of *JFK*.

Paradoxically, *JFK* is not about Kennedy in the sense that *Nixon* is about Nixon. Neither is it fundamentally about Jim Garrison. Its focus is the political climate within which Kennedy functioned and the matrix of opinion and emotion that coalesced to bring about his death. Garrison is merely the dramatic vehicle used to explore that matrix. Consequently, a psychologically nuanced portrait of either Kennedy or Garrison would have blurred Stone's essential insight, which is that the "dark side of

Camelot" pales by comparison with the darkness that engulfed it. Stone's frequently noted idée fixe with the decade of the 1960s suggests that his therapeutic quest for redemption from past traumas is being figuratively and literally projected upon a culture that shares his Gothic obsession as well as his need to transcend it.

The extent to which the Kennedy of history and myth will eventually merge or diverge is an issue that can only be resolved in the long councils of time. For Stone, and those who share his Gothic outlook, however, the issue is moot. Kennedy was, to them, a modern Robin of Locksley, an Earl's son who renounced the comforts of wealth and privilege to champion the cause of social justice. His stirring summons to excellence seemed to embrace and encourage America's disenfranchised, i.e., its youth, its artists, its intellectuals, its immigrants—the very classes and types who had participated in the original American experiment and who, according to Hoftstadter, were subsequently excluded from a sense of participation by the rise of America's plutocracy (see Hofstadter on the Mugwumps and the "status revolution," 135). All Americans were once again invited to the banquet, summoned to participate in an American renaissance of art and learning as they had been two centuries earlier by the Founding Fathers. Henry Fairlie, one of Kennedy's most severe, if fair-minded critics, called this summons the "politics of expectation" (see Fairlie, *The Kennedy Promise*).

Whether warranted or not, the devastating sense of loss occasioned by Kennedy's death, the sense of having been suddenly and violently deprived of an historic opportunity, evicted almost from the stream of time itself, has haunted an entire generation. Stone is a courageous and eloquent spokesperson for that lost generation, but he is not its only spokesperson. Chris Carter's *X-Files* television series offers an alternative conspiratorial mythology to that of Stone in which the infamous Cigarette-Smoking Man, a sinister, all-powerful representative of America's shadow government, is identified as the assassin of both JFK and MLK (see *Musings of a Cigarette-Smoking Man*). The persistent yearning, in the wake of Kennedy's murder, to recapture a better, more hopeful time is poignantly expressed in a brief dream sequence from the prologue to one of the "Lone Gunman" episodes of the *X-Files*. The protagonists are an oddly assorted trio of computer nerds, Byers, Frohike, and Langly, who write and publish their own conspiracy newsletter entitled *The Lone Gunman*—an ironic reference to the Warren Commission's baseline conclusion that one lone assassin,

Lee Harvey Oswald, murdered President Kennedy. The dream sequence, narrated by Byers, depicts a well-dressed young man about to enter a lovely suburban home, where he is enthusiastically greeted by his adoring family. The narration reads:

> My name is John Fitzgerald Byers. I was named after the thirty-fifth president, and I keep having this beautiful dream. In that dream the events of November 22, 1963 never happened. In it, my president was never assassinated. Other things are different too, in my dream. My country is hopeful and young again, young in spirit. My fellow citizens trust their government, never once having been betrayed by it. My government is truly of the people, by the people, and for the people. All my hopes for my country and for myself, all are fulfilled. I have everything a person could want. I have a family and love. Everything that counts for anything in life, I have it. (*Three of a Kind*)

At this point, the setting abruptly shifts to a barren desert in which the disoriented Byers stands alone and disconsolate, as the voice-over continues, "But the dream ends the same way every time...I lose it all."

Cited out of context, the outstanding feature of this vignette is, perhaps, its overt sentimentality. This feature is mitigated, however, by the authenticity of Byers's quest for truth and by the many sacrifices he and his cohorts have made on its behalf, as depicted in earlier episodes. Moreover, the unabashed emotionalism of Byers's melodramatic dream language, in this instance, becomes a metaphor of the very openness and freedom of expression that are impossible in a post-Kennedy world presided over by covert government. Temporal displacement and the obsessive need to relive past traumas are recurrent Gothic themes. Both figure conspicuously in Byers's dream sequence. They signal either an insurmountable cycle of grief leading to despair or a transcendent impulse to attain redemption through achieving continuity and closure with the past. In *X-Files* episodes such as "Three of a Kind," "Musings of a Cigarette-Smoking Man," and "Operation Paper Clip," Carter fictionalizes documented government programs, e.g., CIA's MK-ULTRA and the FBI's COINTELPRO to assassinate heads of state, experiment "scientifically" on unwitting civilian populations, and provide safe haven for Nazi war criminals.

Libra is a political Gothic novel, first published in 1988, that explores the allure of secrets and the predicament in which a patriotic young Marine by the name of Lee Harvey Oswald is landed by succumbing to their seductive power. It provides yet another variation on the theme of conspiracy explored by Oliver Stone. As in *JFK,* Oswald is seen by Don DeLillo, *Libra*'s author, as an innocent patsy manipulated by CIA conspirators. The tragic twist in DeLillo's alternative to the consensus history of these events is that the original, comparatively benign, conspiracy itself becomes a tool in the hands of a more sinister faction of covert operators garnered from organized crime, the CIA, and the Cuban exile community. The initial plan called for a bogus assassination attempt on Kennedy that would galvanize public support for another Bay–of–Pigs style invasion of Cuba, thereby sabotaging Kennedy's conciliatory policy toward Castro following the Cuban missile crisis. This possibility, along with several others, is a topic of discussion among Garrison's team of investigators in Stone's screenplay as well (see Stone and Sklar 134). DeLillo, Stone, and others who have agonized over these events seem preoccupied by the inconclusiveness of the Kennedy saga and the lack of closure that it imposes. In the absence of a more substantive explanation, they are forced to conclude that the veiled nature of hidden history, i.e., the seductiveness of esoteric knowledge, is itself a motivating factor to those who illicitly conspire to alter the course of human events. That there is a world inside the world, a conclusion gleaned from his infatuation with communist ideology, is one that the youthful Lee Harvey Oswald finds intoxicating.

The Gothic imagination seeks to uncover the secret wellsprings of human action, which is why so many Gothic narratives, including *Citizen Kane, JFK,* and *Nixon* puzzle over the obscure motivations of their protagonists and villains. Often, owing primarily to Sigmund Freud, these motivations are sought in the repressed experiences of early childhood. (For a particularly interesting discussion of Freud's influence on the Gothic imagination see Mark Edmundson's *Nightmare on Main Street*). Kane's craving for love and acceptance is therefore traced to "Rosebud" and all the childhood memories associated with it. Similarly, in Oliver Stone's *Nixon,* which is in many respects a modern retelling of *Citizen Kane*—the man gains the world only to lose his soul—Richard Nixon's pathetic attempt to substitute power for love is tracked to the losses and humiliations of his childhood. Indeed, Stone makes extensive use of many Wellesian devices throughout *Nixon,* such as audio and visual montage, documentary news footage, and an episodic structure replete with disorienting time shifts. DeLillo's *Libra* furnishes another instance of the "Freudian fallacy," i.e., an attempt to reduce complex psychological events to simple causes, often having to do with alleged sexual traumas in early childhood. In an extended trope of power and secrecy, the opening chapter explains Oswald's later attraction to the hidden, subterranean world of espionage with reference to his childhood predilection for riding the subways of New York City: "He was riding just to ride. The noise had a power and a human force. The dark had a power.... Never again in his short life, never in the world, would he feel the inner power, rising to a shriek, this secret force of the soul in the tunnels under New York" (DeLillo 13).

The 1973 film *Executive Action* starring Burt Lancaster, Robert Ryan, and Will Greer was the first major motion picture based on the Kennedy assassination. It was adapted from a book co-authored by Mark Lane, whose groundbreaking *Rush to Judgment* (1966) was the first best-selling nonfiction critique of the Warren Commission, and Donald Freed, who would later contribute a fictionalized exploration of the RFK assassination. The film's director, David Miller, also relied on well-known assassination researchers Penn Jones Jr. and David Lifton for detail and historical background. *Executive Action* is premised on a plot hatched by the CIA and funded by extreme right-wing Texas oil baron H. L. Hunt, once characterized as the richest man in America. Five political incentives to murder Kennedy are cited in this conspiratorial scenario: Fear of a liberal Kennedy dynasty; fear that Kennedy would disengage from Vietnam; fear that he would encourage rather than resist the civil rights movement ("the Black revolution"); fear that his Nuclear Test Ban Treaty signaled a policy of appeasement toward the Soviet Union; and fear that Kennedy's anti-business stance (as evidenced by his confrontation with U.S. Steel) would result in the elimination of the lucrative oil-depletion allowance. A sixth Malthusian motivation, darkly hinted at by one of the architects of the conspiracy, is a covertly fascist plan to use perpetual global war as a means of population control. Once again, the substance of Lane's scenario, though downplayed, is also considered in *JFK*. In retrospect, the most interesting feature of this comparatively plodding docudrama is its use of news footage of Kennedy speeches in which he articulates his commitment to democratic idealism. Music, costumes, characterization, and scene selection, though realistic up to a point, seem, on the whole, better suited to a Hollywood Western than a political Gothic thriller.

Two cinematic retellings of the Robin Hood legend, Kevin Reynold's *Robin Hood: Prince of Thieves* and Robert Young's *Herne's Son*, neither of which garnered critical acclaim, deal, as does *JFK*, with the fate of a heroic leader who defies a corrupt government in order to serve the cause of justice for all. Both contain words that those who share Stone's sense of deprivation might subconsciously apply to Mailer's outlaw sheriff, John F. Kennedy: In the more recent of the two, Azeem—Robin Hood's Muslim sidekick played by Morgan Freeman—consoles his self-accusatory friend following a murderous attack on their forest retreat: "I once heard a wise man say, 'There are no perfect men in this world, only perfect intentions'" (*Robin Hood: Prince of Thieves*). In *Herne's Son,* which takes place several years subsequent to the capture and execution of England's prince of thieves, an embittered and still grieving John Little is asked to explain his belief in the fallen hero. He replies, "The fire burned bright in him, and for a while it warmed us all. Now he's gone and the fire went with him. It's all over." "No," says Robert of Locksley, "nothing's forgotten. Nothing is ever forgotten" (*Herne's Son*). The flame that fired Oliver Stone's youthful idealism was extinguished, though not forgotten, by the brutal murder of John F. Kennedy. For Stone, as for many others, the world has seemed a much darker and colder place ever since.

At the peroration of his final address to the jury in *JFK,* Garrison proclaims "We have all become Hamlets in our country—children of a slain father-leader whose killers still possess the throne. The ghost of John Kennedy confronts us with the secret murder at the heart of the American dream" (Stone and Sklar 176). This interesting comparison, which became the focus of a journalistic broadside, reminds us that *JFK* is a ghost story as well as a political thriller. Stone's troubling narrative speaks of an America haunted by a guilty awareness of subversion and betrayal. "Foul deeds will rise," says Hamlet, "Though all the earth o'erwhelm them, to men's eyes" (Act I Scene II). The secret murder that both Hamlet and Garrison investigate carries the weight that burdened Brockden Brown and Hawthorne, i.e., the Oedipal murder of a father/king, but also the curse of Cain/Kane, ("the primal eldest curse ... A brother's murder," *Hamlet,* Act III Scene III). Small wonder that those who surround Hamlet prefer to bury the past, dissociate themselves from Hamlet's "unprevailing woe" and rationalize his behavior. It also comes as no surprise to Stone's defenders that "the media's strange rage for silence in this matter presents us with a textbook case of denial, disassociation, and double-think" (Oglesby 267). Essentially, the question that divides Stone from his critics is the same as that which divides Hamlet from his critics at Elsinore: Whose version of reality is delusional?

Is the ghost of Hamlet's father real; and if not, is Hamlet's obsession with avenging his father's death symptomatic of clinical paranoia? Brockden Brown's Wieland was prompted to commit murder by just such a disembodied voice. The tormenting apparition was similarly vivid and the injunction it delivered proved just as ruinous. Throughout the drama, Shakespeare toys with the ambiguity between Hamlet's feigned madness and behavior that suggests genuine lunacy. The guards on the watchtower see the ghost in the first act, as does Hamlet, but only Hamlet speaks to it. Later, in his mother's bedroom, Gertrude sees and hears nothing, while Hamlet, who will shortly commit his first murder, is driven to distraction by the visionary specter. In Gothic narratives, madness is often presented as being in the eye of the beholder. For example, is Fox Mulder, in the *X-Files* television series, truly paranoid, as many of his more conventional colleagues suspect, or is his apparent paranoia a mark of superior insight and intellect?

Gothic heroes often seem eccentric, restless, and obsessed, if not clinically unbalanced, to those around them. The "madness" of the heroine in Gilman's "The Yellow Wallpaper," however, is precisely what enables her to recognize the psychological double bind in which she has been placed by her husband. From his vantage point, of course, the tyrannical motives to which she attributes his actions are delusional. Stone's conspiratorial version of reality raises similarly disturbing doubts and questions. If his outlook is sound, then it is the officially sanctioned version of recent American history, i.e., consensus history, that is unsound. Similarly to Stone, both Hamlet and Garrison feel that the times are out of joint. They are burdened by "the cursed spite that ever they were born to set it right." In other words, both characters share a daunting sense of responsibility to set the public record straight and confront sinister forces that have conspired to change history. Ultimately, they share a disturbing intuition that the legitimacy of the state has been fatally compromised, despite comforting reassurances of continuity and normalcy tendered by their leaders, i.e., King Claudius and President Johnson. According to Stone, the death of Kennedy changed America and the world forever (Stone and Sklar 183). Stone perceives Kennedy's assassination as a point of impact that prompted an ever-expanding ripple effect. In *Hamlet,* Shakespeare gives pointed expression to Stone's contention that such deeds ultimately transform society:

> The cease of majesty dies not alone, but, like a gulf doth draw what's near it
> with it; it is a massy wheel, fix'd on the summit of the highest mount, to whose

huge spokes ten thousand lesser things are mortis' and adjoin'd; which when it falls, each small annexment, petty consequence, attends the boisterous ruin. Never alone did the king sigh, but with a general groan. (*Hamlet* Act II Scene III)

In testimony given before Chief Justice Earl Warren, Oswald's murderer Jack Ruby, in fear for his life, pleaded to be removed from Dallas to Washington where he could tell the whole truth, asserting that a new form of government was taking over the country (Oglesby, *The JFK Assassination* 272). Stone/Garrison's primary insight concerning the effects of Kennedy's murder is that Ruby was accurate in his prediction. This new form of government, according to Garrison, proved to be an old and infamous form of government, the very form of government, indeed, that he and thousands of others fought to overcome in World War II. In a passage from his summation speech to the jury that was partially cut from the final version of the film, Garrison warns that fascism in America will assume the guise of national security. There will be no goose-stepping soldiers in the streets and no concentration camps, other than the "clever concentration camps of the mind" fashioned by journalists. He claims that America has arrived at a juncture in history, comparable to Germany in the 1930s, that is unrecognized as such because fascism in our country has assumed the benign form of liberal democracy (Stone and Sklar 177).

Clearly, if Garrison was right, the "hippies" of the sixties who took to the streets carrying protest signs denouncing "Amerika,"—a Teutonic misspelling intended to suggest that current policies were more in keeping with the precepts of Hitler than Jefferson—were not far wrong. The critical barrage leveled against Garrison's assertion that the Kennedy assassination has turned Americans into Hamlet figures grieving the loss of a slain father-leader came from the pen of Alexander Cockburn (see Stone and Sklar 379–83). As it happens, the Stone/Garrison analogy to *Hamlet* was lifted from an afterword written by historian Carl Oglesby to one of Garrison's two books on the assassination. Ironically, Cockburn finds a "fascist yearning" in Oglesby's analogy. Oglesby hotly denies this charge, pointing out that what he and most Americans yearn for is a democratic openness in government that has absolutely nothing to do with fascism. As for the charge that those who share his Gothic perspective are guilty of idolizing Kennedy, Oglesby reminds us that Hamlet's father was no more a moral paragon than was Kennedy himself. Indeed, he was cut off in the blossom of his sin. Quoting from

Hamlet, Oglesby confirms that far from seeking to escape the harsher realities of politics, as Cockburn suggests, those who subscribe to a conspiratorial reading of Kennedy's death carry a special burden: "The bumper sticker of the Dealey Plaza revisionist movement reads 'The time is out of joint. O cursed spite, that ever I was born to set it right'" (Oglesby, *The JFK Assassination* 300).

Stone's cinematic narratives offer a cathartic mythology that respects evidence rejected out of prejudice and entertains speculation concerning the present and future status of our democracy that adherents of consensus histories dare not confront. Ultimately, as film critic Roger Ebert affirms, "*JFK* accurately reflects our national state of mind since November 22, 1963. We feel that the whole truth has not been told." Stone's film, insists Ebert, is not about the factual accuracy of Jim Garrison's case. "It is about Garrison's obsession....The assassination of John F. Kennedy will obsess history as it has obsessed those whose lives were directly touched" writes Ebert. He concludes that, like other subversive narratives of the political Gothic imagination, "*JFK* is a brilliant reflection of our unease and paranoia, our restless dissatisfaction. On that level it is completely factual" (Ebert 234–38).

Lewis in Nixonland

Adlai Stevenson, twice Democratic contender for the presidency during the Cold War era and Ambassador to the United Nations under Kennedy, once referred to Richard M. Nixon's interior landscape as "Nixonland." He characterized it as "a land of slander and scare, of sly innuendo, of poison pen and anonymous phone call and bustling, pushing, shoving—the land of smash and grab and anything to win" (Summers 136). Nixonland was in many respects Sinclair Lewis's imagined land of American fascism made real. In examining Stone's screenplay for *Nixon,* we will simultaneously consider the salient aspects of Nixon's personal and political legacy that parallel the coming of American fascism as depicted by Sinclair Lewis in *It Can't Happen Here.* Nixon's distrust of reason, for example, was attested by his own irrational behavior, which was noted and commented upon by advocates and adversaries alike. Author Anthony Summers has compiled an extensive list of primary sources close to Nixon who doubted his sanity. For instance, Henry Kissinger, Nixon's Machiavellian secretary of state, claimed that "Nixon seemed driven by his demons." Media news anchor Walter Cronkite, once voted the most trusted man in America, said that

Nixon "actually seemed unbalanced." According to Kenneth O'Donnell, John Kennedy's special advisor, "JFK never trusted his [Nixon's] mental stability." *Newsweek*'s John Lindsay regarded Nixon as a "walking box of short circuits," and Robert Green, senior editor of *Newsday,* once referred to Nixon's "Hamlet-like moments" (Summers 95). In one such tragic/comic moment from Stone's screenplay, the unhinged president invites his alarmed secretary of state to kneel with him in prayer. Alluding to this scene, Gothic cultural historian Mark Edmundson writes: "Nixon—to me anyway—simply *was* a Gothic hero-villain, very light on the hero....When the mad bomber of Cambodia gets on his knees late at night in a haunted White House and begins talking to the portraits of former presidents, we are with Monk Lewis and Horace Walpole" (Edmundson 22).

Edmundson's allusion to Nixon's Gothic penchant for conversing with works of art refers to a climactic moment in Stone's screenplay when the distraught president, realizing that congressional exposure of his crimes in connection with the Watergate burglary has left him with no viable alternative to resignation, apostrophizes the portrait of his former nemesis, John F. Kennedy. Padding over to the portrait in slippers very late at night and looking up he muses aloud, "When they look at you, they see what they want to be. When they look at me, they see what they are" (Rivele, Wilkinson, and Stone 303). Stone's fictional dialogue envisions a transcendent, if farfetched, moment of self-realization on Nixon's part that simultaneously gives expression to Stone's perception of Kennedy and Nixon as personifications of America's essential Gothic dilemma, i.e., its ongoing struggle to balance its utopian and dystopian tendencies. Fundamentally, Stone conceives of Nixon as Kennedy's *doppelganger,* his Jungian shadow. At one point, Watergate burglar, and former CIA operative E. Howard Hunt characterizes Nixon as "the darkness reaching out for the darkness" (263). In Stone's incarnational mythology, therefore, the excess of Nixon's demonic and unreasoning paranoia is presented as a dark mirror image of Kennedy's democratic restraint and reasonableness. In other words, Stone perceives these two men as projections, on a wide historical screen, of the deep divisions within American political consciousness. The psychodrama in which they are engaged is continually reenacted on a smaller scale within each of us. Their struggle for synergy defines the American experience from a Gothic point of view.

Edmundson's "the mad bomber of Cambodia" epithet suggests yet another strand in Stone's polyphonically textured parable. Among his closest circle of advisers, Nixon was known as "the mad monk" (one more coincidental link to Matthew Lewis—known as "Monk" Lewis— an eighteenth-century English novelist whose best-known work, entitled *The Monk,* is a literary landmark in the Gothic revival of that era). Nixon's Gothic nickname originated in a Hamlet-like strategy decision on Nixon's part to affect madness, to put on an antic disposition in order to confound and intimidate his enemies. Referring to the so-called Eastern Establishment, Kissinger tells Nixon that the communists respect only strength, and they will only negotiate if they fear the madman Richard Nixon. At which point, Nixon smiles darkly (191). A short while later, Nixon echoes Kissinger's grasp of realpolitik, affirming a view founded on years of red baiting, that the best way to gain the enemy's cooperation is to convey a predisposition for unpredictable violence (195). Based on several statements made by Stone subsequent to the release of his film, it seems probable that his understanding of Nixon in relation to both Kennedy and the Cold War establishment evolved over time. Expecting "demonization," critics who scoffed at Stone's earlier "idealization" of Jim Garrison and John F. Kennedy were pleasantly surprised to discover a sympathetic portrayal of Kennedy's chief political rival. Far from being the caricature anticipated by Stone's critics, the Richard Nixon of Stone's imagining is insecure, needy, bemused, and at times even anguished by his own personal and political dilemmas.

At the heart of his anguish, suggests Stone, lay a dark suspicion that he, no less than his immediate predecessors, was at the mercy of sinister and uncontrollable forces. Clearly, Stone's Nixon is haunted by the ghost of Kennedy, as evidenced by, among other things, his obsessive contention that he has nothing in common with his deceased predecessor. When his wife, Pat claims that her love for him is inadequate to compensate for the disapproval of his political adversaries, Nixon objects, asserting that, unlike Kennedy, he does not crave public approval. Later that same night he asks his young Cuban valet Manolo if he had cried when Kennedy was killed and, if so, why. Manolo admits that he did cry, but can offer no explanation other than that Kennedy somehow made him "see the stars." In an uncharacteristic moment of candor and self doubt, Nixon silently ponders the inspirational qualities of his former adversary (217). Later, when he confronts a small cluster of incredulous, bleary-eyed adolescents protesting the Vietnam War during an impromptu late-night visit to the Lincoln Memorial, he tells them that neither he nor the Vietnamese want the conflict to continue. An earnest young woman replies that someone certainly does. Realizing the chilling implications of this tacit admission that even the commander and chief is powerless to oppose a military-industrial system bent on war, she asks Nixon why, in that case, he should wish to be president. He nervously replies that there is more at stake than his own personal desire for peace or hers. The commentary of the screenplay at this point reads, *"The nausea of the Beast makes him reel"* (221). In humanizing moments such as these, we catch a glimpse of Nixon that differs from the mechanical, untrustworthy public figure with whom most of us are familiar. At such moments, Stone's Gothic villain seems to be reaching tentatively for the light. The question, of course, is whether the humanity with which Nixon is endowed by Stone and Hopkins belongs to Nixon or to them.

The "Beast," alluded to above, is another supernatural Gothic motif, comparable to the ghost of Oswald in *JFK,* a visual code that Stone contemplated but ultimately discarded. In the working script, however, he periodically calls for a brief image that will recur throughout the film, an image of evil identified as "the Beast" (40). What he evidently had in mind was a sequence of bestial or reptilian images that would be flashed on the screen in the manner of a subliminal message whenever Nixon was confronted by or reminded of the covert fascism that conspired to promote Vietnam and destroy Kennedy. It was to have occurred, for example, when he discussed his political prospects with a group of Texas oilmen and Cubans just prior to Kennedy's assassination (157). It is mentioned again when Nixon refers to the Bay of Pigs in a meeting with his political aide H. R. Haldeman (181)—who came to regard all such references as veiled allusions to the Kennedy assassination (50)—and again on the occasion of his visit to the office of CIA Director Richard Helms (208). Indeed, the entire sequence, i.e., scenes sixty-six through sixty-eight, involving Nixon and Director of Central Intelligence (DCI) Helms vividly illustrates Stone's method of using the conventions of supernatural Gothic to underscore his political Gothic message. When Nixon first arrives at Langley, he passes the Orwellian seal of the CIA— "You shall know the truth and the truth shall make you free"— a Biblical citation that eerily echoes the Nazi motto posted on the entrance to the concentration camps: "Work shall make you free." Indeed, the almost savage irony of this false tribute to honesty and openness is apparent when considered with reference to the authentic American dream.

Jefferson made an informed public the cornerstone of democracy. For the CIA, an organization premised on deception and secrecy, to embrace such a motto carries a corollary implication that its true purpose is to enslave—to create, in the name of national security, a gulag of the mind that requires no barbed wire and within which dismay and confusion are the only guard dogs necessary.

When Nixon enters Helms' office by a "secret door," the viewer is subconsciously made aware that the forces of covert fascism are, in effect, an occult, i.e., hidden, priesthood whose power derives from its status as the keeper of state secrets. When Helms spots Nixon, he extends a welcoming hand and offers what the screenplay refers to as a "reptilian" smile. Throughout their conversation Helms occupies himself with his award-winning collection of orchids—a symbol of tropical decadence—that exude the sweet decay of death. As he bends to examine them, placing himself at eye level with the camera, his eye sockets turn completely black. In that instant, the dark abyss of America's cryptocracy is fleetingly revealed for what it truly is, a zombie-like monster from the annals of Gothic horror. In this chilling scene, Helms asks Nixon if he appreciates flowers. Nixon states emphatically that he does not, claiming that they remind him of death. He then informs Helms that there are, however, things in life more dreadful even than death, such as evil (212)—an observation that, once again, seems uncharacteristic of Nixon, though not of Stone.

Later in the screenplay, during a discussion of who would be most effective at obstructing the FBI investigation of the Watergate burglary, Nixon nominates Helms, who can scare anyone (114). The identification of the CIA with the Beast is made even more explicit in the final line of dialogue between Nixon and Helms in which Helms quotes a famous passage from William Butler Yeats' Gothic poem, *The Second Coming*: "What rough beast in its hour come round at last/Slouches toward Bethlehem to be born," concluding with the observation that, "Yes, this country stands at such a juncture" (Rivele, Wilkinson, and Stone 212). This allusion to Yeats was perhaps inspired as much by *Slouching Towards Bethlehem*, a well-known collection of essays on America in the 1960s by New York journalist and author Joan Didion as by the original poem that furnished the title of her book.

When the topic turns to covert operations and President Kennedy, Nixon tenses, suddenly sensing the presence of the Beast. Helms comments that Kennedy threatened to smash the CIA. In response,

Helms receives the President's personal assurance that the Agency under Nixon's watch is secure, suggesting in the same breath that a communistic Cuba would be a small price to pay for stabilizing the balance of world power. When Helms menacingly reminds Nixon that President Kennedy shared this conviction, Nixon suddenly envisions Kennedy with his head blown off in Dallas and himself laid out in a coffin (211). According to Garrison, in Stone's screenplay, the murder of Kennedy reduced the president to the status of a mere public relations officer for the military-industrial-intelligence complex. Confronted by Helms and the sinister forces he represents, Nixon clearly realizes that the power of the presidency is slight compared with that of the Beast. Reflecting on the young women with whom he spoke at the Lincoln Memorial, Nixon muses to Haldeman, "She understood something it's taken me twenty-five **** [expletive deleted] years in politics to understand. The CIA, the Mafia, the Wall Street bastards.... 'The Beast.' A nineteen-year-old kid. She understands the nature of 'the Beast" (222). Just as the dark side of Camelot diminishes to almost zero, in Stone's estimation, against the backdrop of America's covert fascism, Nixon's darkness is mitigated by the abyss that opens before us in the presence of Helms. The reason for this is obvious: While, for Stone, the dualism of Nixon and Kennedy symbolize a potential synergy between America's dystopian and utopian dialectic, the covert fascism of men like FBI Director Hoover, DCI Richard Helms, and crime lord Johnny Roselli threaten to destroy the very dialectic on which that synergy depends.

In Nixonland, as Stone clearly demonstrates, respect for human rights is replaced by brute strength, just as integrity and openness are replaced by an accepted code of behavior premised on lies and covert operations. In response to the release of the *Pentagon Papers* by Daniel Ellsberg, Nixon expresses his admiration for the terrorist tactics of the Nazis, suggesting that those responsible for news leaks within his administration should be intimidated as members of indigenous resistance movements in German-occupied countries were intimidated by Nazi threats of arbitrary execution. In 1970, something very like this Nazi policy was implemented at Kent State University in Ohio, when, as shown in the film, a phalanx of National Guardsman opened fire on students and professors assembled on the campus lawn, killing four of them. In the film, as these events unfold on television, Nixon fumes at the spectacle of rioting guardsmen advancing on unarmed civilians, contemptuously referring to student dissidents as "bums" and asserting that these so-called flower children should be taken to the woodshed (193). Responding to Nixon's panegyric on Nazi war crimes, presidential aide, Chuck Colson replies, "Just whisper the word to me sir, and I'll shoot Ellsberg myself" (106).

From the "dirty tricks" campaign of Dwight Chapin to the oval office audience granted a delegation of hard hats who physically assaulted law-abiding antiwar protesters on Wall Street, the Nixon administration embraced and encouraged brown shirt tactics, deception, forgery, slander, stonewalling, burglary, arson, bribery, and illegal surveillance as legitimate political tactics. Did Nixon's political opponents do likewise? Yes, though to a significantly lesser degree. However, from the standpoint of democratic idealism, acceptable ends do not justify unacceptable means. Discussing this very point in the film, Nixon aide John Ehrlichman tells his cohort Bob Haldeman that Nixon is wrong in his assertion that Presidents Truman, Kennedy, and Johnson were guilty of using the same vicious methods that erupted into the Watergate scandal. He points out that none of Nixon's immediate predecessors would have dared forge a cable, as E. Howard Hunt did, implicating President Kennedy in the CIA-sponsored assassination of South Vietnamese President Diem. He goes on to question Haldeman concerning Nixon's evident dread whenever mention is made of the 1961 invasion of Cuba at the Bay of Pigs (259–60). Clearly, there is no room in Nixonland for constructive dissent. Democratic belief in the value of dialogue, according to Nixon's covertly fascist mind-set, is a left-wing fallacy. For Nixon, as one journalist points out, politics is war and one's political adversaries are viewed not as the loyal opposition but as the enemy (138).

Stone's Nixon sincerely believes that law and justice are unrelated, not just in practice but in principle. In *JFK*, Garrison, as he recounts the suspicious circumstances of Oswald's arrest, reminds the jury that Dr. Best, Himmler's right-hand man in the Gestapo, believed that as long as the police carry out the will of the government they serve, they are acting legally (Stone and Sklar 174). Similarly, when Haldeman tries to warn the president that by attempting to head off an FBI investigation he may be guilty of obstructing justice, Nixon replies that his decision is dictated by considerations of "national security." When Haldeman inquires as to the relevance of this doctrine to the situation at hand, he is told peremptorily that national security is involved whenever the president says it is (Rivele, Wilkinson, and Stone 115). Nixon's concise expression of the fascist leadership principle and its corollary belief in legally infallible government by an elite group was a cornerstone of Nazism (Ebenstein, Ebenstein, and Fogelman 73). Inevitably, one is reminded of Garrison's warning that national security is a concept as easily invoked in defense of fascism as democracy (Stone and Sklar 117). It is revealing in this regard that the president appeared on national television to announce his determination to learn the truth about Watergate no matter who was involved during the very period in which he and his people were desperately conspiring to obstruct justice (Rivele, Wilkinson, and Stone 268).

Racism, another cardinal tenet of both German fascism and its American counterpart as envisioned by Sinclair Lewis, is an obvious component of Nixon's outlook. This is attested by his many derogatory allusions to Jews and "niggers" in the Watergate tapes. At one point in Stone's screenplay, Nixon's Attorney General John Mitchell says of Henry Kissinger, "The Jewboy's a Harvard whore with the morals of an eel—sells himself to the highest bidder." Seemingly indifferent to Mitchell's racial slur, Nixon commends Mitchell for his political savvy (149). Later, as he is constrained to listen to a sampling of his own racial slurs recorded on the White House tapes, a Nixon in denial vehemently protests that he never made those comments about Jews (292). In the opinion of some, Nixon's most flagrant expression of racism was his decision to widen an inherently racist war in Southeast Asia with his secret bombing campaigns in Laos and his infamous Cambodian "incursion" (more Orwellian language)—an event that provoked the Kent State massacre and led directly to the killing fields of Cambodia.

Nixon's disregard of constitutional and international law, as manifested in this flagrant violation of Cambodian neutrality and congressional intent, was originally listed as an impeachable offense on an indictment drafted by Congress, but later dropped because, as Nixon boasted to General Haig, the president can bomb whoever he wants (283). Similarly, the surprise Christmas bombing of Hanoi aroused the ire of the international political and journalistic community. Reporting these events, Stone makes use of documentary footage with a B.B.C. voiceover to the effect that the Nixon administration, in launching the most brutal bombing campaign in American history, has resorted to a Stone Age tactic worthy of a crazed tyrant (236). Credited in later years with having ended a war he did not begin, it has become politically correct in certain quarters to view the "rehabilitated" Nixon as more sinned against than sinning. Such flagrant revisionism fails to take into account the fact that the Eisenhower/Nixon administration pursued a policy with regard to the Geneva Accords of 1954 that made war in Vietnam inevitable. Moreover, Nixon's efforts to sabotage Johnson's peace initiative in 1968 for reasons of partisan political expediency may have prolonged that war unnecessarily. Countless American combatants as well as Asians, to say nothing of the young patriots murdered at Kent State and Jackson State for protesting an unjust war, paid with their lives for Nixon's pointless pursuit of a policy that promised "peace with honor" and ended in a chaotic flight from Saigon that delivered neither peace nor honor.

　　Though he ran for office as a staunch exponent of law and order, Nixon's covertly fascist domestic policy was consistent with that of his renegade foreign policy. Indeed, it was in the domestic arena that Nixon's contempt for democracy and his use of totalitarian tactics were most damaging to his administration. His efforts to obstruct justice in the Watergate affair extended from simple lack of cooperation and the payment of hush money to a contemplated Frankenheimer-style coup in which the military would be used to thwart Congress (see footnote, 297). Fortunately, the military was uncooperative. Stone's screenplay abounds in allusions to Lincoln and the Civil War. Clearly, Nixon saw the liberal counterculture, comprised largely of John F. Kennedy's alienated constituency and the antiwar movement it spawned, as a latter-day Confederacy—with himself cast in the role of stalwart Abe Lincoln fighting to preserve the Union. In another Hamlet-like moment of Gothic introspection, Nixon soliloquizes on death as he stares up at a portrait of Lincoln. Who helped them both to power—God or death—asks Nixon rhetorically (184).

　　In his memoirs, Nixon evinces a seemingly inexhaustible capacity for denial: "If I could be hounded from office because of a political scandal like Watergate," he writes, "the whole American system of government would be undermined and changed. I never for a moment," Nixon reflects with a self-complacence reminiscent of the Nazi war criminals prosecuted at Nuremberg, "believed that any of the charges against me were legally impeachable" (Summers 466). Stone vividly dramatizes the psychotic split implicit in Nixon's perception of himself as an innocent defender of the American way at the very time he is actively engaged in subverting constitutional authority. As Nixon and his discomfited secretary of state, Henry Kissinger, kneel together in prayer,

Nixon suddenly sobs out his sense of unmerited persecution. With a theatrical hypocrisy equal to that of Mr. Pecksniff, Nixon calls upon God to save America from its enemies, i.e., all those who disapprove of his conduct in office. Anticipating the revisionists who would later come to his defense, he recites a highly selective version of his resume according to which he brought peace in our time to a slavering horde of pinko liberals whose hatred of him epitomizes the ingratitude of a politically depraved Eastern establishment (Rivele, Wilkinson, and Stone 301-02). The climax of Nixon's Alice-in-Wonderland inversion of the issues raised by the overt Civil War of the 1860s and the covert civil war of the 1960s is dramatized in Stone's portrayal of the 1968 Republican National Convention. Nixon's Lincolnesque pledge to heal the wounds of war by bringing a divided nation together is interspersed with scenes of Gestapo-like police riots in Chicago, FBI attacks on Native American militants at Wounded Knee, and shots of George Wallace whipping a right-wing crowd of white supremacists into a frenzy. Against this totalitarian backdrop, Nixon's populist appeal to a "silent majority" in favor of war and the suppression of political dissent assumes the distinct aura of a party rally at Nuremberg.

Distrust of reason, denial of basic human equality, adherence to a code of behavior based on lies and violence, espousal of government by an elite group, racism, opposition to international law, and the use of totalitarian tactics: these were the political precepts of Nixonland. They are also the political precepts of the fascism that Sinclair Lewis foresaw as a plausible outcome of the political turmoil by which twentieth-century America was engulfed (see chapter 3 in *Today's ISIMS* by Ebenstein, Ebenstein, and Fogelman). Despite the obvious differences between Nixonland and Nazi Germany, the following passage relating to fascism from Ebenstein's standard political science textbook should give Americans pause: "As long as the people did not make any trouble politically and did not interfere with the rule of the dictator and his henchmen, they could often lead their own lives relatively freely" (73). Cold War America did not have a dictator, of course; even Nixon was eventually compelled to abide by the rule of law. It did, however have a covert intelligence establishment based on Nazi protocols, a right-wing creed that justified immoral means in pursuit of allegedly moral ends, and a fervent belief that "only a small minority of the population ... is capable of understanding what is best for the entire community" (72).

In effect, Nixon attempted to resist "the Beast" by duplicating the very sins that summoned it into existence—the original sins of America's Cold War fall from grace. He chose to fight communist evil with fascist evil, to defend a public code based on law, dialogue, and an open political process by adopting a private code premised on crime, intolerance, and secrecy. "Funny therapeutics," as Doremus Jessup might have said. The Gothic split between democratic idealism and covert fascism embraced by Nixon and the Cold War establishment he represented is explicitly denounced by Jefferson: "To say, in excuse, that gratitude is never to enter into the motives of national conduct, is to revive a principle which has been buried for centuries with its kindred principles of the lawfulness of assassination, poison, perjury &c.... *I know but one code of morality for men, whether acting singly or collectively*" (as quoted in Padover 37, italics mine).

The disparity between Jefferson's democratic idealism and America's subsequent Faustian bargain is clearly expounded in Robert Bolt's 1960 drama *A Man for All Seasons* concerning Sir Thomas More's principled protest against Henry VIII's politically expedient marriage to Ann Boleyn. Though set in Tudor England, it clearly addresses ethical and political dilemmas posed by the times in which it was written. When More's son-in-law, Roper, a Protestant fanatic cut from the same mold as later fundamentalist fanatics, angrily asks More whether he would give the Devil benefit of the law, More replies heatedly, "Yes, what would you do? Cut a great road through the law to get after the Devil?" Roper responds, "I'd cut down every law in Europe to do that." "Oh," says the aroused and indignant More, "And when the last law was down, and the Devil turned round on you—where would you hide, Roper, the laws all being flat? This country's planted thick with laws from coast to coast with man's laws, not God's—and if you cut them down—and you're just the man to do it—d'you really think you could stand upright in the winds that would blow then? Yes, I'd give the Devil benefit of the law, for my own safety's sake" (Bolt 38).

To the extent that both Kennedy and Nixon struggled against the Beast and lost, Stone's portrayal of the latter as the dark alter ego of the former is justified. However, to the extent that Nixon's code differed from that of the Beast in degree only, Stone's moral vision is perhaps blurred by his use of this *doppelgänger* motif. The tragedy of President Nixon is that he was a man who defined himself in terms of his enemies rather than his ideals. Like Roper, he had few scruples when it came to upholding the law, and when the Devil turned on him—as it inevitably will, according to the Gothic imagination—he had nowhere to hide. Nixon was a typical American in many ways. Similarly to a great many other Americans, he endorsed an inauthentic version of the American dream that confuses *ex*cess with *suc*cess and power with privilege. As he once proclaimed to Kissinger, his conception of geopolitics envisioned a world linked by enlightened self-interest and motivated by fear (Rivele, Wilkinson, and Stone 196). Ultimately, Nixon's American dream was about seizing and maintaining an advantage by whatever means, fair or foul. As Jim Garrison says to his wife Elizabeth in *JFK*, however, American democracy is fundamentally not about gaining the upper hand. It is, as John F. Kennedy suggested, about acknowledging a mutuality of interest that is mindful of our shared needs and our shared mortality (Stone and Sklar 140).

Indeed, the authentic American dream is about letting go—of property, security, wealth, privilege, power, celebrity, influence, and life itself if need be—in order to advance the cause of justice. It is not, as the warped ethic of Nixonland maintained, about holding on to those advantages at any cost, including the triumph of injustice. During the Kennedy years, Americans were called upon to uphold a faith in the ultimate vindication of right over might. Kennedy's tragedy, and ours, is that at the time of his death he seemed to be moving the nation toward a post–Cold War conception of the American experience that transcended the blinkered perspective of Nixonland. Indeed, this nascent conception may well have enabled him to transcend his own all too frequent surrender to the ethics of Nixonland, sometimes referred to as *The Dark Side of Camelot* (the title of a book on the subject of Kennedy's frailties by Seymour M. Hersh). What many of Kennedy's admirers and detractors alike seem not to realize is that his dark, shadow side—which undoubtedly existed—was an essential component of the Kennedy promise. The point is not that both he and Nixon possessed a dark side. According to the political Gothic imagination we all do, as Jung affirmed. The point is that unlike Nixon, Kennedy demonstrated a capacity to rise above the limitations that so often hamper the hero-villains of Gothic fiction to become an authentic hero, i.e., one whose unique advantages are justified and redeemed in the service of others. That is why, as Stone's Nixon correctly observes, in Kennedy we saw ourselves not as we are, but as we might be.

As the end of the Camelot era approached—which to many seemed only a beginning—the pampered patrician and zealous cold warrior ready to pay any price and bear any burden to defend the cause of liberty was finally subordinate to the Kennedy who made us see the stars. Having at last tamed his own Cold War demons and emerged from beneath his father's shadow to become a mature statesman of imposing stature, he seemed to have attained within himself a synergy between a romantic need for self-assertion and a classical restraint imposed by his highly cultivated sense of historical perspective. Kennedy's pragmatism, which he defined as idealism without illusions, had finally reconciled republican and frontier conceptions of America, capitalism's dream and democracy's dream, in a way that, had he lived, might truly have benefited his country and the world. In 1963, the presidency was still a fulcrum of immense power. In an America unbalanced by the alliance of capitalism and covert fascism, Kennedy was the first and, in many ways, the last Cold War president to use that fulcrum on behalf of democratic idealism. By doing so, however, he became, as Oliver Stone's Mr. X maintains, a threat to the national security structure (Stone and Sklar 113). Moreover, his inherited wealth enabled him to largely skirt the polluted swamp of the American political process in which Nixon had been totally submerged from the outset of his career. By late 1963, Kennedy seemed intent on replenishing the forests of national and international law that had been leveled by the cold winds of a Cold War, winds that in all probability claimed his life. "President Kennedy was a work in progress when he was killed," writes historian Carl Oglesby. "It is a great loss that we never got to see the finished product, but it was also a kind of national disaster that he chose to treat the White House as a finishing school" (Oglesby, *The JFK Assassination* 302).

Images of the Beast

Though it was not included in the finished version of the film, in the uncut version the ghost of Lee Harvey Oswald, played by method actor Gary Oldman (the Count Dracula of Francis Ford Coppola's film re-make of the vampire legend) takes the stand to address Garrison's jury on his own behalf. In an impromptu speech of heartfelt intensity, Oswald/Oldman passionately proclaims his innocence along with his undying love for his country, his young wife, and his family. Though personally moved by Oldman's Gothic improvisation, Stone realized that it was discordant with the note of documentary realism established throughout *JFK*. He abandoned it, accordingly. That Stone's Gothic imagination is predisposed to such flights of supernatural fancy, however, is clearly evidenced in the working script of his second conspiratorial film, *Nixon*. Apart from the hidden histories, perverse power relationships, and conspiratorial agendas developed in *Nixon*, Stone makes ample use of supernatural Gothic conventions: We first encounter Stone's hero-villain alone in the White House Lincoln Sitting Room, which is compared to a tomb, besieged by Gothic weather (Rivele, Wilkinson, and Stone 88). Nixon, himself sits in shadow silhouetted by an open fire. As the stage directions explain, he hates the light (91). Incongruously, the air-conditioning is running full-blast. It is upon precisely such extreme contrasts and incongruities of imagery that the supernatural Gothic thrives. Darkness, within the context of the Gothic imagination, is a symbolic state of mind as well as a physical reality, as are the light and warmth Nixon seeks from his solitary hearth. Hearth-fire itself is an ambiguous emblem of enlightenment, human warmth, companionship, and the hard-won containment of a potentially destructive force.

Apropos of Stone's use of Gothic imagery, *Nixon*'s animal imagery comprises a cinematic bestiary of natural and supernatural creatures used to convey a political Gothic message. In a burlesque scene at the Oval Office between Nixon, Kissinger, Haldeman, and Erlichman, Nixon, who has been unsuccessfully coaxing a pet dog to accept a biscuit, turns the air blue with undeleted expletives, complaining that after two years the animal is still unresponsive and utterly useless as a public relations asset. Finally, Nixon turns on Kissinger, who has tried repeatedly to channel the conversation toward foreign policy matters, blaming him for the dog's uncooperative demeanor. The astonished Kissinger is completely nonplussed while the amused viewer is left to draw the obvious conclusion: Even man's best friend is understandably ill at ease in the presence of these snarling human beasts (103).

Another, more menacing, use of animal imagery occurs at the Del Mar Racetrack in scenes 47–49. FBI Director Hoover, who is earlier referred to as a lizard, is seated with his homosexual partner, Clyde Tolson, and Johnny Roselli, a mobster suspected of complicity in the JFK assassination. As the horses rush to the finish line, the bandaged front leg of one of the animals snaps, producing a sound like a rifle shot. The jockey is thrown from his mount as Nixon approaches Hoover, hoping for his support in his forthcoming political race against Robert Kennedy. Nixon, Tolson, and Hoover leave the bleachers in order to spare Nixon a politically embarrassing encounter with his former friend from Cuba, Roselli. As they walk in the vicinity of the stables, Nixon complains to Hoover that the 1968 race could be 1960 all over again with Bobby "riding his brother's corpse right into the White House" (177). Tolson helpfully suggests that the former Attorney General should be shot. When Nixon obsequiously lobbies for Hoover's backing, the amused director of an institution that came close to being a state-sponsored secret police force explains that the system can only stand so much abuse. Implying that the Kennedys and Dr. King, who he characterizes as a moral hypocrite, constitute such an abuse, Hoover goes on to assert that the White House has already been inhabited by one radical, presumably JFK, and that in his opinion the country could not survive another.

At this point the stage directions suggest that the increasingly uncomfortable Nixon is once again plagued by vague but disturbing images. His discomfort is underscored aurally by the snorting and heavy breathing of the nearby horses (178). In this episode, the actual or potential violence done to and by animals reinforces the conspiratorial violence that has already been perpetrated against John Kennedy and Martin Luther King and that would shortly be visited upon Robert Kennedy. It is alleged that Hoover harbored a pathological fear of anyone stepping on his shadow, a particularly intriguing neurosis from a Jungian point of view. In the words of Anthony Summers, "That a man with a crippled psyche, capable of great evil, became the trusted symbol of all that was safe and good is a paradox of our time. So too is the fact that, in a tribute after Hoover's death, Chief Justice Warren E. Burger said he had 'epitomized the American dream' while renowned psychiatrists consider that he would have been well suited for high office in Nazi Germany" (Summers 6, 7). Obviously, Warren Burger's version of the American dream was not that of Thomas Jefferson and John Kennedy.

In addition to Stone's Gothic bestiary, *Nixon* features an array of standard Gothic archetypes including ghosts, monsters, zombies, robots, and vampires. In the wake of the so-called "Saturday night massacre" in which Nixon fired top officials rather than comply with a legal ruling to turn over the secret White House tapes to a special prosecutor, a television reporter asks if a government of laws has become a government of one man (Rivele, Wilkinson, and Stone 287). While an anxious America awaits an answer to the reporter's question, Nixon, again alone in the Lincoln Sitting Room, is accosted by the ghost of his long-departed mother. Speaking in the Quaker idiom familiar to his childhood, she asks what has happened to change her once devout son into the beleaguered "crook" he has since become. A distraught Nixon, desperate to avoid a confrontation with his repressed Quaker conscience, pleads with her to remain silent (289). In Nixon's case, this apparition is clearly a projection of his repressed guilt and denial—a denial so severe as to raise legitimate doubts as to the besieged president's mental stability. Ultimately, of course, the Gothic monster that stalks the pages of Stone's screenplay is the Beast of America's government-within-the-government, but at one point this beast is explicitly identified with another classic monster: As presidential aides, Erlichman and Haldeman huddle together in a White House corridor discussing Nixon's obsessive, if veiled, allusions to the Kennedy assassination, i.e., the Bay of Pigs invasion, Haldeman confides to his counterpart that when the CIA went after Castro, the plot was somehow turned against Kennedy. Erlichman responds, "Christ, we created Frankenstein with those **** [expletive deleted] Cubans" (261).

Frequently, Nixon's movements and manner of speaking are described as robotic (117), or else he is likened to a living corpse, i.e., a zombie (118). The political Gothic message that informs such comparisons has to do with Nixon as a "hollow man" consumed by an insatiable lust for power. "Whenever a man has cast a longing eye on offices, a rottenness begins in his conduct," says Jefferson (as quoted in Summers 81). After Nixon lost the presidential race to Kennedy in 1960, his campaign manager Murray Chotiner confidently predicted that he will run again, not from a moral imperative to seek office but, "Because if he's not President Nixon, he's nobody" (Summers 123).

The most elaborate Gothic trope developed in the original screenplay has to do with vampirism. Often, the imagery associated with this motif is blood drenched. "The blood is the life," intones Bram Stoker's literary monster (though his readers know perfectly well that blood is just as often, in fact far more commonly, perceived as an accompaniment of death). In the screenplay of *Nixon*, the ambiguous fluid of life/death flows as freely as in those of *Dracula*. Indeed, the imagery used is often explicitly derived from vampire lore. When Nixon considers opening China, he does so in order to drive a stake through the heart of the alliance between communist China and the Soviet Union (196). Early in the screenplay, as Nixon discusses Cuba with political aide Herb Klein, the stage directions describe a Nixon who is besieged by inner demons in the form of persistent images of violent death. Later, in response to the release of the *Pentagon Papers,* Nixon the Impaler characterizes his anticipated vendetta against antiwar intellectuals as sudden death and vows to get them on the ground, stake them, and twist the stake mercilessly (228). Owing to the discovery of the White House tapes, his deepest secrets are about to be revealed. Realizing this, a sleepless Nixon awakens in the middle of the night to find himself covered in blood. He is rushed to a hospital where he experiences a hallucinatory episode rife with sanguine images of pain and death from his own family history and the history of the violent nation over which he has presided. Taken together, this dark overlay of surrealistic images and motifs suggestive of vampirism transform Stone's nominally realistic docudrama into a compelling horror story. In fact, from Stone's Gothic perspective, the "lyrical" 1960s, so often portrayed as a utopian idyll—a colorful era of rebellion, hedonism, and carefree social experimentation—was, in reality, just such a horrific episode. Oliver Stone's vision of the 1960s suggests a Gothic transformation scene straight out of Hollywood Gothic—a transformation scene in which the United States of America ultimately emerges as the United States of Amerika—a rapacious monster that feeds off the flesh and blood of its own sons and daughters.

It is important to understand that, contrary to what today's conservatives would have us believe, nuclear terrorism and anti-communist belligerency during the Cold War era had far more to do with the breakdown of respect for authority in American society than "liberal permissiveness." In terms of its emotional impact and divisiveness, the paradigm shift that took place during the 1960s, from a Newtonian to a Gothic perspective on the American experience, might almost be characterized as a Second Civil War. Overtly, this generational conflict was fought in homes and on the streets between a youth counterculture traumatized by the ever-present threat of nuclear holocaust and an older generation wedded to a politically obsolete conception of the world formed before the advent of nuclear weapons. Covertly, it was fought behind the scenes, so to speak, between Kennedy and the Cold War establishment itself.

At stake was the world as we know it versus a world in which—if Kennedy's diplomatic and social agenda had prevailed—the Cold War would have been phased out in favor of cooperation and peaceful co-existence with the Soviets—thereby preempting the recent proliferation of nationalistic factions—the Vietnam War would have ended before it truly began, the vigilante regime of an invisible government would have been brought within the purview of the Constitution, Dr. King's vision of the beloved community would have replaced the defacto racial segregation that reigns today, the economic anarchy of what came to be known as corporate globalization (and the breeding ground for terrorism it has spawned) would have been nullified by a commitment to democracy in the workplace and a policy of economic self-determination for third world countries, the social pollution of organized crime would have been stopped before it could be effectively assimilated into the mainstream of the economy, and an authentic intellectual and aesthetic culture, rather than the ersatz consumer culture of McWorld and MTV, would have been nurtured at home and exported abroad. As the enigmatic Mr. X from *JFK* comments, however, that enlightened prospect ended on November 22, 1963. One could plausibly argue that Kennedy's utopian prospect, even had he lived, would have been imperfectly realized. However, one could just as plausibly argue that even an imperfectly realized version of that prospect would be preferable to the political and cultural dystopia we currently inhabit.

In the final analysis, critics who attribute the latter position to wishful thinking are unanswerable. Kennedy's murder saw to that. However, it is significant to note that in at least one instance, the post-mortem attacks on his character can be laid to rest. With regard to the Cuban Missile Crisis, it is the duplicity and susceptibility to panic alleged against Kennedy that is myth and his patient and measured rationality under pressure that is confirmed by the historical record (see *The Kennedy Tapes* ed. by May and Zelikow and Roger Donaldson's film based on it, *Thirteen Days*). The attempt to arouse public support for a timely and conclusive reinvestigation of his assassination was partly defused by well-publicized and often tendentious exposés of the so-called Camelot myth. To an extent, these exposés were justified. However, in this instance, and perhaps others as well, it would appear that the autopsy on Kennedy's much-maligned character was as badly bungled as his fraudulent and misleading medical autopsy.

Discussion Topics and Questions

1. Discuss conspiratorial narratives prior to those of Oliver Stone and the social and political realities they reflect.
2. Consider the Jungian concept of *enantiodromia* in relation to America's Cold War history.
3. To what extent was "Nixonland" the realization of Sinclair Lewis's predictions concerning the coming of fascism?
4. Discuss Stone's conception of Nixon and Kennedy as *doppelänger* images of American political consciousness.
5. Consider possible applications of the political Gothic imagination to the current War on Terror.

Conclusion

Speaking at the National Press Club in 1992 of the transition period between the Kennedy and Johnson administrations and of his then recent film, *JFK,* Oliver Stone defended himself against the charge of distorting history by pointing out that the historical record of America immediately preceding and following the Kennedy assassination is controversial and insufficiently researched. He went on to invoke Jefferson's notion of public discourse as a free marketplace of ideas on behalf of a thorough and honest reexamination of this period, claiming that there is currently no such free marketplace with regard to ideas about the murder of President Kennedy. The Warren Commission's version of what happened, Stone proclaimed, is at least as mythical as his alternative version of events, if not more so. Only when the 1960s have been thoroughly and honestly vetted, he suggested, will it finally be possible to distinguish documentary fact from Gothic fiction concerning this era (Stone and Sklar 403–08). Meanwhile, expressions of the political Gothic imagination, such as *JFK,* will presumably continue to serve as a lightning rod for our unconfirmed fears and suspicions. Such works dare to challenge the consensus view that in the twentieth century, democracy achieved an unqualified victory over totalitarianism with America leading the way (see Charles Van Doren's *A History of Knowledge,* chapter twelve for a concise statement of the consensus point of view).

Commenting on the historical legacy of Stone's work and the Herculean efforts of the assassination research community on which it is based, author Ron Rosenbaum reflects on his youthful immersion in the Warren Commission testimony, remarking that while he didn't come any closer to solving the Kennedy assassination, he did learn more about the America that produced both Kennedy and his assassin (or assassins) than was conveyed by the bland consensus view of America that prevailed until November 1963. He goes on to affirm his belief that the enduring legacy of the research community will be the contribution it has made toward nudging a reluctant nation in the direction of a darker, more nuanced understanding of itself (Stone and Sklar 397). According to Rosenbaum, if we have, for the most part, gained a more sophisticated perspective on the American experience, i.e., a Gothic perspective, the credit belongs ultimately to our stern prophets of gloom and dystopianism. It belongs, that is, to the ravens among us who have steadfastly refused to accept the proud eagle's self-confident boasts, obstinate denials, and transparent rationalizations at face value.

From Charles Brockden Brown's *Edgar Huntly* and Sinclair Lewis's *It Can't Happen Here* to Don DeLillo's *Libra,* the tragic cycle of America's Gothic mythology serves as a shadowy counterpoint to the officially sanctioned narratives of American history. Such narratives are invariably self-congratulatory. In this sense, the Gothic imagination provides a permanent counterculture, a discordant, minor key accompaniment to an idealized America graced by God and crowned with continental brotherhood. America's archetypal Gothic plot details an inward journey toward our own telltale heart of darkness. It compels us to identify and scrutinize those cultural ambiguities, traumas, and inconsistencies that we would prefer to forget, deny, or simply dismiss. Ultimately, it leads to a realization that our most cherished conceptions of ourselves are, at best, only partially justified. At worst, they are dangerously deceptive.

We are a nation premised upon a utopian imperative: "Seek thou a new world untainted by history!" In practice, that imperative is shadowed by an uneasy suspicion of failure and subversion. This Gothic shadow impels us to seek satisfactory alternatives to a dystopian status quo that ignores or spurns our democratic pretensions, at times mocking them with savage irony. The Gothic term in America's urgent dialectic between its Gothic and utopianism selves informs us that the way back, or forward, to John Smith's Arcadian paradise, Jefferson's neoclassical city on the hill, Twain's nostalgic journey down river, Roosevelt's community-oriented New Deal, and Oliver Stone's painful but compelling vision of America's lost Camelot, is blocked by a flaming sword. On its hilt is stamped an injunction, simple to state but difficult to attain, "Know Thyself." Institutionalized slavery and racially motivated hate crimes in a land of freedom and racial equality, massacres of Native Americans justified in the name of Manifest Destiny coexisting with an ethos of tolerance and pacifism, ruthless industrial barons and strike-breaking law enforcement officers in a land of economic opportunity and respect for the common man, organized crime and corporate conspiracies in a country committed to the rule of law and order: These are but a random sampling of the contradictions in American history that define our unresolved Gothic dilemmas. Taken together, they demand a candid admission that who and what we wish to be is often far from who and what we truly are.

Nevertheless, the convoluted road to political enlightenment does not necessarily end in annihilation, nor does it imply a wholesale revision of our idealistic self-conceptions. Instead, it calls for a new personal and collective awareness. At the primary level, such an awareness involves a candid recognition that the enemy within imposes as grave a danger to the authentic American dream as the enemy without. Flag-waving bravado, intellectual and ethical Philistinism, unrestrained commercialism, utopian perfectionism, and yes, even Gothic despair itself are all subjective demons with which we must grapple. Though external enemies do undoubtedly exist, the nature and extent of the threat they pose are difficult to assess when viewed through the distorting prism of our own psychological projections. In short, the obstacles to peaceful coexistence we are apt to attribute to foreign countries with alien political and religious traditions are, in large measure, rationalizations by which we seek to excuse glaring discrepancies between American democracy in theory and practice.

At this level, America's most formidable enemy, according to the Gothic imagination, turns out to be its own all-too-human preference for flattering self-deception over difficult and disturbing truth. Just as, in the Frankenstein fables of James Whale, the ultimate villain is the murderous mob not the vilified creature, the real monsters in life are ultimately the ones we ourselves become under the influence of denial. Indeed, the raven warns that, as it is with our Faustian pursuit of scientific and technological panaceas, so it is with our blindly obsessive pursuit of utopian political agendas. If we indulge a subconscious habit of Jungian projection while continuing to vacillate between a posture of defiant self-congratulation and undiscriminating cynicism, we may expect to change periodically—and often spontaneously—into a distorted mirror image of ourselves. At such times, like the protagonists of Stevenson's *Dr. Jekyll and Mr. Hyde* or Curt Siodmak's *The Wolf Man*, we will become a grotesque example of that which we deplore in others. In short, we will have fallen prey to what Jung termed "a fundamental law of life." *Enantiodromia,* he called it, "the reversal into the opposite." According to this lycanthropic law of human psychology, those who "fail to call the wolf his brother" become the wolf (Jung 238). Often they share the fate of those divided Gothic hero-villains who unconsciously commit acts of self-mutilation, or self-destruction. The price of our redemption from such a fate—our transcendence, to substitute a more secular vocabulary—is clearly itemized by America's prophets of the political Gothic. It amounts to this: We must confront and dispel our ignorance in relation to a history that remains partially hidden and in certain respects significantly misrepresented.

America is a nation that, from its inception, embraced a liberal proposition, intoned in Beethoven's *Ode to Joy,* that all men are brothers, a phrase that should not be read as gender exclusive. It thereby broadened and redefined the concept of nationhood itself. Throughout our turbulent history, we have dramatized troubling dilemmas of heart and mind that have yet to be resolved on a national and global scale. The fate of democratic self-government and perhaps even liberal civilization as we know it may depend on the outcome of our experiment in achieving a synergistic balance of opposites. That is why the success of the American experiment, defined not as political or economic preeminence but as transcendence of its own Gothic dilemmas, is still the world's best hope of achieving what was always the ultimate goal of the authentic American dream—"an aristocracy of everyone" (a phrase borrowed from Benjamin Barber's 1992 book by that title).

It follows that, whatever their aesthetic value or historical accuracy, those arts that define the Gothic imagination are by no means marginal in terms of their cultural significance. On the contrary, they are paramount to an understanding of America's past, present, and possible future. What they teach is that America's well-being depends on an ability to rekindle an allegiance to utopian ideals without ignoring the evils that our national penchant for dissociation, projection, and denial have previously unleashed. We can, of course, choose to abandon our historic commitment to the sisterhood of humanity. Conversely, we can choose to extend the embrace of that commitment to all who would welcome it, probably inciting the opposition of corporate capitalism, an international economic system with a vested interest in resisting economic and political self-determination for underdeveloped nations and social justice in first world nations. That is why, on a global scale, "Liberty, Equality, and Fraternity" remains as vibrant and revolutionary a slogan as when it was first coined.

Our Gothic counterculture also teaches that the only way to dispel collective nightmares is to confront them with private determination of the sort exhibited by that much maligned group of American patriots contemptuously referred to by mainstream journalists as "conspiracy buffs." This derogatory characterization was first applied in connection with a CIA orchestrated smear campaign against critics of the Warren Commission (see William Davy, *Let Justice Be Done* 142). However, as we have seen, conspiracy theories were an integral part of the revolutionary matrix out of which the Gothic revival of the late eighteenth-century emerged. The first modern Gothic novel, Horace Walpole's *The Castle of Otranto,* explores the consequences of a secret political murder. The first American Gothic novel, *Wieland,* explores a secret religious murder, perpetrated by a member of the Bavarian Illuminati, a conspiratorial organization with alleged ties to both the American and French Revolutions of the eighteenth century.

The dangers posed by conspiratorial hysteria are manifest, but so too are the potential benefits of exposing hidden history where it actually exists. In assessing the appropriateness of conspiracy theories to the American dialectic, the issue, therefore, is not whether one espouses a conspiratorial interpretation of events, but whether or not that interpretation deepens or diminishes one's adherence to the principles of democratic idealism upon which our system of government rests. The synergistic balance between utopian and dystopian impulses is what ultimately defines authentic American patriotism. Arguably, the anti-communist extremists of the 1950s and 1960s who lost that synergistic balance adopted a patriotism that was bogus. Their conspiracy theories, of the "better-dead-than-red, none-dare-call-it-treason" variety, placed them at odds with the fundamental tenets of our cultural heritage. This criticism cannot be plausibly urged against the countercultural narratives of Gothic gadflies such as Orson Welles and Oliver Stone.

Had members of the assassination research community heeded the uncritical litany of our mainstream media on behalf of the Warren Commission, the public would know far less about the brutal realities of deep politics during the Cold War era than it currently does, and less also about the questionable role of the Fourth Estate in cloaking those realities. In the more dispassionate perspectives of time, the heroic quest undertaken by responsible private investigators willing to hazard the subterranean labyrinths of Fortress America in quest of its most closely guarded secrets will quite possibly be honored by future generations of Americans, much as the ineffectual but courageous efforts of Munich journalists in the 1920s to expose Hitler's coming holocaust deserve to be honored (see Ron Rosenbaum's *Explaining Hitler,* chapter 3). If so, the writers and filmmakers who followed their lead will share in that honor.

That Holocaust was essentially a German government–sponsored conspiracy against European Jews and Gypsies. To paraphrase William James: If you wish to upset the law that all significant political change is devoid of conspiratorial content, you must not seek to show that no change is without a basis in conspiracy; it is enough if you can prove one single outcome of political importance to have resulted from such a far-flung network. The Nazi Holocaust was precisely such an outcome and those who implemented it constituted precisely such a network. When one considers that members of this same Nazi network, e.g., General Reinhardt Gehlen, were secretly welcomed into the post-WWII American intelligence community and that the same dubious cast of characters who were involved in Watergate were also involved in Operation Mongoose, is it paranoia or prudence to ask if the violent deaths of America's most eloquent and persuasive liberals in the decade of the 1960s was the work of this network?

In light of subsequent developments, the covert assignment of the Gehlen Organization and the Nazi scientists of Operation Paper Clip to create a shadow government in opposition to Soviet Communism forges a possible link between the national security state created in the late 1940s and the tragic events that overtook America during the1960s. This sinister possibility is one that would seem to warrant further investigation, as Chris Carter's *X-Files* episode "Paper Clip," imaginatively suggests. With the exception of a few academic mavericks such as Carl Oglesby, Peter Dale Scott, and John Newman, the covert agendas that motivated America's political murders in the 1960s and what those agendas might imply about Cold War and post–Cold War policy decisions are issues that have yet to be explored responsibly by historians. The current popularity of Gothic arts is no doubt related to this circumstance, just as the official suppression of the truth concerning organized and corporate crime in the 1930s and 1940s was related to the popularity of pulp fiction. As we have seen, "The truth will out," and its more recent variant "The truth is out there," is a Gothic leitmotif that resonates to a national mythos of political transparency and openness. The arts and entertainment industry has embraced possibilities, that officialdom seeks to deny or declines to discuss. That is why the fulminations of film critics and culture warriors such as Michael Medved (see *Hollywood vs. America*) finally ring hollow. Greedy Hollywood moguls do not manufacture the public's appetite for ghouls, urban cannibals, ghosts, prehistoric monsters, vampires, lycanthropes, aliens, angels, or sinister conspiracies, as conservative critics of Hollywood suggest; nor do these moguls encourage a sadistic symbiosis between pandering artists and a depraved popular taste. Indeed, our involvement in the imaginal realms of the Gothic is arguably a healthy sign, if not a sign of good health. What these self-styled conservative critics fail to realize is that the cathartic effects of Hollywood Gothic offer a therapeutic substitute for the kind of open political process and dialectical exchange they advocate in theory but seldom seem willing to endorse in practice. Until such time as that process is realized, we will presumably continue to crave the surrogate truths spawned by the Gothic imagination while concurrently looking for ways to reduce our dependence on its dark mythology. If this premise is correct, the dystopian imagination is an indispensable component of our political and artistic heritage; and America's true conservatives, as it turns out, are its liberal critics of the political and economic status quo.

A nation in denial of its own history is a nation locked into a never-ending cycle of Gothic despair. That is why the ravens among us warn that when the appointed guardians of truth and balanced judgment fail us, i.e., academe, the media, the journalistic community, and the legal establishment, we have indeed descended into a chaotic maelstrom from which we may not emerge. From the perspective of the raven, what is needed is reconciliation between the excessively extroverted, uncritical *praxis* of American democracy as symbolized by the predatory impulses of the bald eagle, and the liberal theory on which that *praxis* is based. The failures of those responsible for promoting such a reconciliation occur when our guardians of truth turn a blind eye to subversions of democratic idealism. In doing so, they intentionally or inadvertently substitute official lies and cover stories for probative history and investigative zeal. It follows from these observations that the fundamental dialectic in the American political experience comprises a pairing of complementary opposites. The one, utopian idealism, tells us where we want to be. The other, dystopian pessimism, keeps us on track. Both are indispensable to the realization of the authentic American dream. Those who would defend the socioeconomic status quo at any cost to our democratic institutions and traditions reject this dialectical compass.

Covert government is currently making news once again. In response to the terrorist attacks of 9/11/01, our country is once more committed to an open-ended conflict against an ill-defined enemy, as it was during the Cold War era. That commitment has revitalized Eisenhower's military-industrial complex and created a shadow government in the event of a catastrophic nuclear or biological strike. The exact makeup of this covert government is unclear, but evidently it does not consist of democratically elected representatives. In the months following the World Trade Center attacks, Americans have listened to government officials and familiar media personalities discuss the expediency of torture as a means of extracting information pertinent to the War on Terror. Torture is clearly a violation of the "human rights"— not specially American rights—guaranteed by the Constitution. America, which is by definition a country that does not condone the practice of torture, is therefore being asked, calmly and soberly, to consider whether it can best protect itself by adopting a practice that negates the ideals on which its very identity is premised. Not too many years ago, equally well-known media personalities placidly discussed the duck-and-cover strategies of a civil defense program premised on the death of forty to eighty million Americans (see Lewis Thomas, *Late Night Thoughts on Listening to Mahler's Ninth Symphony*). A short while later, they helped to propagate the view that it was somehow disloyal for citizens of a nation that prided itself on protecting the weak to protest the brutalization of a small peasant nation by an industrialized superpower. Those who subsequently sought an explanation for the breakdown of authority in American culture in the "permissiveness" of the youth counterculture of the 1960s should have looked instead to the permissiveness and schizophrenia of our government's policies during the Cold War and to the polite treachery of those who sought to legitimize them. Apparently, under pressure from Muslim terrorism, America is currently poised to recycle its schizoid appeal to the values of democratic idealism while practicing those of covert fascism.

Consider the following Gothic prospect: America has been at war with Islamic militants for many years. She has suffered a number of devastating setbacks. Consequently, a backlash against the War on Terrorism has swept a new president into office. This new president is aware that throughout much of the twentieth century American business in alliance with the Pentagon and the intelligence community exploited the wealth of Near Eastern nations at the expense of their indigenous populations and encouraged its most fanatical militants to take up arms against the Soviets. In the early twenty-first century this exploitive brand of corporate capitalism called itself globalization. Much of the rest of the world called it economic terrorism. The newly elected administration views the understandable resentments bred by America's Cold War machinations and subsequent globalization as the basis for the ongoing tolerance of the Pan-Islamic Jihad among moderate Islamics. President X, in her determination to deal with political terrorism at its source through reigning in the economic anarchy of globalization, is perceived by the reinvigorated post–Cold War military-industrial complex and the business community it serves as a threat. Unable to eliminate the enemy abroad, teams of assassins originally activated to murder fundamentalist Muslim radicals decide to train their guns on an alternative, more accessible target at home. A far-fetched scenario? Perhaps, but in light of America's covertly fascist history subsequent to the Second World War, it cannot be readily dismissed. If we are to avoid a reenactment at some point in the foreseeable future of the traumatic scenario that unfolded in Dallas in 1963, we would do well to heed the synergistic wisdom of the eagle and the raven that requires us to think twice before consenting to reanimate America's Cold War Frankenstein.

That wisdom is embodied in the personalities and perceptions of archetypal Americans from Charles Brockden Brown to Oliver Stone and from Thomas Jefferson to John Kennedy. The political Gothic myths they have generated suggest that only by achieving a dynamic equilibrium of opposing tendencies can we hope to survive the terrifying vortex of our own nihilism and turn what for many has become a seemingly interminable nightmare into something that at least approximates the enlightened dream of a just society intimated by the founders and subsequently enjoined by Lincoln and other geniuses of the American spirit. According to the Gothic imagination, renewal can only come from remembrance. Although some of its more controversial chronicles seem plausible, if not infallible, their historical accuracy is a separate issue from that of their validity as myth and prophecy. As with the Biblical prophets of old, our contemporary Gothic prophets are not so much people who tell the future, i.e., things about ourselves that we do not already know. Instead, they are people who tell a truth that many suspect but few have the courage to affirm or the opportunity to verify. Carl Oglesby captures the essence of Gothic prophecy with regard to Oliver Stone's film, *JFK,* when he reminds us that the movie's function is not to resolve a historical conundrum, but to crystallize a paradigm of conspiracy within popular culture that we have already surmised (Oglesby, *The JFK Assassination* 296).

Given the obvious omissions, distortions, and rationalizations with which consensus history abounds, the insights of Gothic history are psychologically compelling whether or not they are factually inerrant. America needs the imagination of her dystopian prophets as well as her utopian visionaries. When, in *Martin Chuzzlewit,* Charles Dickens acknowledges America's capacity to rise like a Phoenix from the ashes of its own failings and vices, that is to transcend its Gothic dilemmas, he is paying homage to the resilience of a dream. Though, for many, faith in that dream has been shaken by unjust wars, brutal assassinations, and official denials, the seeds of our nation's redemption are still present in the example and achievements of her distinguished dreamers. It remains to be seen whether, as Sinclair Lewis feared, America's long tolerance of evil ways and means has so compromised our national character that it will never again have any good end.

As we have seen, the Palladian house of democracy, despite a strong commitment to rationality and social justice on the part of those who designed it, or perhaps because of that commitment, has always been a haunted house. Its well-proportioned façade hides the dystopian specters that lurk within—specters of private and corporate greed, racial and sexual bias, military violence, and institutionally sanctioned criminality. Indeed, according to some exponents of the modern political Gothic imagination, a Cold War establishment whose charter and very nature violated the most fundamental precepts of democracy largely nullified the spirit of American democracy first invoked by Thomas Jefferson and revived periodically by men such as Abraham Lincoln and John F. Kennedy. The circumstances under which that spirit might once again be summoned into existence are difficult to envision. Those who could rehabilitate a Jeffersonian balance between individualism and civic culture are seemingly either dead or in denial, while many who would gladly support such a project are in despair. Perhaps what is needed today is not so much a bogus renaissance of national pride, i.e., the will to triumph, as a quiet but determined patriotism willing and able to confront our past openly and imaginatively.

Gothic perspectives on the American experience provide valuable insight into disturbing and mysterious regions of our national life. They reveal political motivations behind policy decisions and social trends that defy a democratic explanation and offer plausible reasons for seemingly random occurrences that have changed our history and distorted our original intentions as a nation. Ultimately, the political Gothic imagination suggests the influence of an undetected predator in our midst, a shadowy presence that tears at the heart of our current longing for a renewal of constitutional democracy, as its sharp talons have always sought to discredit and damage the idealistic underpinnings of the American experiment. Alone, neither the unreflective eagle nor the prophetic raven is a match for this insatiable cormorant of covert fascism. Perhaps together they could be. Until such time as American society is characterized by a true synergy of idealism and expediency, our Gothic compass will hopefully continue to point in the direction of the authentic American dream.

Works Cited

A.I. Dir. Steven Spielberg. Dreamworks Pictures and Warner Bros. Pictures, 2002.

Amadeus. Dir. Milos Foreman. Republic Pictures, 1984.

Baldwin, Neil. *Henry Ford and the Jews: The Mass Production of Hate.* New York: Public Affairs, 2001.

Balsinger, David, and Sellier, Charles E. Jr. *The Lincoln Conspiracy.* Los Angeles: Schick Sunn, 1977.

Barber, Benjamin R. *An Aristocracy of Everyone: The Politics of Education and the Future of America.* New York: Ballantine Books, 1992.

Barzun, Jacques. *The Jacques Barzun Reader.* New York: Harper Collins Publishers, 2002.

———. *Romanticism and the Modern Ego.* Boston: Little, Brown and Company, 1944.

Batman. Dir. Tim Burton. Warner Bros., 1989.

Bellamy, Edward. *Looking Backward: 2000–1887.* New York: Signet Classic, 2000.

Berman, Morris. *The Reenchantment of the World.* New York: Bantam Books, 1984.

Bierce, Ambrose. *The Collected Writings of Ambrose Bierce.* New York: Citadel Press, 1946.

The Black Cat. Dir. Edgar G. Ulmer. Universal Studios, 1934.

Blake, William. *Songs of Innocence and of Experience.* New York: Oxford University Press, 1967.

Bolt, Robert. *A Man For All Seasons.* New York: Vintage, 1960.

Bram, Christopher. *Father of Frankenstein.* New York: Plume, 1995.

Bride of Frankenstein. Dir. James Whale. Universal Studios, 1935.

Brontë, Charlotte. *Jane Eyre.* 1847. Oxford: Oxford University Press, 1993.

Brown, Charles Brockden. *Edgar Huntly or, Memoirs of a Sleep-Walker.* 1799. New York: Penguin Books, 1988.

———. *Wieland or The Transformation.* 1798. Garden City, New York: Anchor Books, 1973.

Buffy the Vampire Slayer. By Joss Whedon. Perf. Sarah Michelle Gellar. Twentieth Century Fox, 1998.

Burstein, Andrew. *The Inner Jefferson: Portrait of a Grieving Optimist.* Charlottesville: University Press of Virginia, 1995.

The Cabinet of Dr. Caligari. Dir. Robert Wiene. From the Blackhawk Films Collection, 1920.

Callow, Simon. *Orson Welles: The Road to Xanadu.* New York: Penguin Books, 1995.

Capra, Frank. *The Name above the Title: An Autobiography.* New York: Da Capo Press, 1997.

Carroll, Noël. *The Philosophy of Horror or Paradoxes of the Heart.* New York: Routledge, 1990.

Chamisso, Adalbert von. *Peter Schlemihl.* 1813. London: Calder and Boyars, 1957.

Chomsky, Noam. *Secrets, Lies and Democracy.* Tucson: Odonian Press, 1994.

Christophersen, Bill. *The Apparition in the Glass: Charles Brockden Brown's American Gothic.* Athens: The University of Georgia Press, 1993.

Citizen Kane. Dir. Orson Welles. RKO Pictures, Inc., 1941.

Clery, E.J. *The Rise of Supernatural Fiction, 1762–1800.* New York: Cambridge University Press, 1995.

Cockburn, Alexander. "J.F.K. and *JFK.*" *JFK: The Book of the Film.* Oliver Stone and Zachary Sklar. New York: Applause Books, 1992. 379–83.

Conspiracies. A&E. 1996.

Conspiracy Theory. Dir. Richard Donner. Warner Bros., 1997.

Cradle Will Rock. Dir. Tim Robbins. Touchstone Pictures, 1999.

Crane, Stephen. *The Red Badge of Courage & "The Veteran."* New York: Modern Library, 1993.

Crèvecoeur, J. Hector St. John de. *Letters from an American Farmer and Sketches of Eighteenth-Century America.* Edited by Albert E. Stone. New York: Penguin, 1986.

Crichton, Michael. *Jurassic Park.* New York: Ballantine Books, 1990

Cuomo, Mario M. "City on a Hill." Democratic National Convention. San Francisco. 16 July 1984.

———. *Reason to Believe.* New York: Simon & Schuster, 1995.

Davies, Paul. *The Mind of God: The Scientific Basis for a Rational World.* New York: Simon & Schuster, 1992.

Davies, Robertson. "Jung and the Theatre." *One Half of Robertson Davies.* New York: Penguin Books Ltd., 1982.

Davy, William. *Let Justice Be Done: New Light on the Jim Garrison Investigation.* Reston, Virginia: Jordan Publishing, 1999.

DeLillo, Don. *Libra.* New York: Viking, 1988.

Dickens, Charles. *A Christmas Carol.* 1843. London: Chapman & Hall, 1843.

———. *Martin Chuzzlewit.* 1843. New York: Penguin Books, 1984.

———. *The Old Curiosity Shop.* 1841. New York: Oxford University Press, 1987.

———. *A Tale of Two Cities.* 1859. New York: Oxford University Press, 1987.

Didion, Joan. *Slouching Towards Bethlehem.* New York: Farrar, Straus and Giroux, 1968.

Donnelly, Ignatius. *Caesar's Column.* Quoted in Hofstadter, Richard. *The Age of Reform.* New York: Vintage Books, 1955.

Dracula. Dir. Francis Ford Coppola. Columbia Pictures, 1993.

Dracula. Dir. Tod Browning. Universal Studios, 1931.

Dylan, Bob. "It's Alright, Ma (I'm Only Bleeding)." *Bob Dylan: Bringing It All Back Home.* New York: 1965.

Ebenstein, Alan, William Ebenstein, and Edwin Fogelman. *Today's ISMS: Socialism, Capitalism, Fascism, Communism, and Libertarianism.* New Jersey: Prentice-Hall, Inc., 1985.

Ebert, Roger. *The Great Movies.* New York: Broadway Books, 2002.

Edmundson, Mark. *Nightmare on Main Street: Angels, Sadomasochism, and the Culture of Gothic.* Cambridge: Harvard University Press, 1999.

Eisenschiml, Otto. *Why Was Lincoln Murdered?* New York: Grosset & Dunlap, 1937.

Ellis, Joseph J. *American Sphinx: The Character of Thomas Jefferson.* New York: Vintage Books, 1998.

Emerson, Ralph Waldo. "Abraham Lincoln." *The Essential Writings of Ralph Waldo Emerson.* New York: Modern Library, 2000. 829–36.

————. "The American Scholar." *Essential Writings*. 43–62.

————. "The Conduct of Life." *Essential Writings*. 621–62.

————. "The Emancipation Proclamation." *Essential Writings*. 801–08.

————. "Politics." *Essential Writings*. 378–89.

Executive Action. Dir. David Miller. Warner Bros., 1973.

Fadiman, Clifton. Introduction: "Ambrose Bierce: Portrait of a Misanthrope." *The Collected Writings of Ambrose Bierce*. New York: Citadel Press, 1974.

Fairlie, Henry. *The Kennedy Promise*. New York: Dell Publishing Co. Inc., 1972.

Fiedler, Leslie A. *Love and Death in the American Novel*. Normal, IL: Dalkey Archive Press, 1966.

Frankenstein. Dir. James Whale. Universal Studios, 1931.

Garraty, John A., and Peter Gay. *The Columbia History of the World*. New York: Harper & Row Publishers, 1972.

Garrison, Jim. *On the Trail of the Assassins: My Investigation and Prosecution of the Murder of President Kennedy*. New York: Sheridan Square Press, 1988.

Gilman, Charlotte Perkins. "The Yellow Wallpaper." Ed. Joyce Carol Oates. *American Gothic Tales*. 87–102.

Goddu, Teresa A. *Gothic America: Narrative, History, and Nation*. New York: Columbia University Press, 1997.

Gods and Monsters. Dir. Bill Condon. Universal Studios, 1999.

Goethe, Johann Wolfgang von. *Faust*. 1808. Trans. Walter Kaufmann. New York: Anchor Books, 1963.

————. *The Sorrows of Young Werther and Novella*. 1774. Trans. Elizabeth Mayer and Louise Bogan. New York: Vintage Books, 1990.

Haffner, Sebastian. *Defying Hitler: A Memoir*. Trans. Oliver Pretzel. New York: Farrar, Strauss and Giroux, 2000

Hamilton, Edith. *The Greek Way*. New York: W.W. Norton & Company, 1942.

Hanchett, William. *The Lincoln Murder Conspiracies*. Urbana: University of Illinois Press, 1983.

Harris, Thomas. *The Silence of the Lambs*. New York: St. Martin's Paperbacks, 1989.

Harry Potter and the Sorcerer's Stone. Dir. Chris Columbus. Warner Bros., 2001.

Hawthorne, Nathaniel. *The Blithedale Romance*. 1852. Ed. Seymour Gross and Rosalie Murphy. New York: W.W. Norton & Company, 1978.

————. "A Man of Adamant." 1840. *American Gothic Tales*. Ed. Joyce Carol Oates. 45–51.

————. *The Scarlet Letter*. 1850. New York: W.W. Norton, 1961.

————. "Young Goodman Brown." 1837. *American Gothic Tales*. Ed. Joyce Carol Oates. 52–64.

Herne's Son. Dir. Robert Young. Playhouse Video, 1985.

Hersh, Seymour M. *The Dark Side of Camelot*. Boston: Little, Brown and Company, 1997.

Hofstadter, Richard. *The Age of Reform*. New York: Vintage Books, 1955.

Howe, Irving. "Hawthorne: Pastoral and Politics." In *The Blithedale Romance*, by Nathaniel Hawthorne. Norton Critical Edition, eds. Seymour Gross and Rosalie Murphy. New York: W.W. Norton, 1978.

Hutchison, Don. *The Great Pulp Heroes*. Buffalo, N.Y.: Mosaic Press, 1996.

Indiana Jones and the Raiders of the Lost Ark. Dir. Steven Spielberg. Paramount Pictures and Lucasfilm Ltd., 1981.

The Invisible Man. Dir. James Whale. Universal Studios, 1933.

Irving, Washington. *The Complete Tales of Washington Irving*. Ed. Charles Neider. New York: Doubleday & Company, Inc., 1975.

———. "Adventure of the German Student." 1895. *Complete Tales*. 223–227.

———. "The Legend of Sleepy Hollow." 1895. *American Gothic Tales*. Ed. Joyce Carol Oates. 19–44.

———. "Rip Van Winkle." 1895. *Complete Tales*. 1–16.

It's a Wonderful Life. Dir. Frank Capra. Columbia Pictures, 1946.

JFK. Dir. Oliver Stone. Warner Bros. Pictures, 1991.

Johnson, Edgar. *Charles Dickens: His Tragedy and Triumph*. Boston: Little, Brown and Company, 1952.

Jung, C.G. *Modern Man in Search of a Soul*. New York: Harvest, 1933.

Jurassic Park. Dir. Steven Spielberg. Universal Pictures, 1993.

Kael, Pauline. *For Keeps: 30 Years at the Movies*. New York: Plume, 1994.

Kennedy, John Fitzgerald. "Commencement Address at American University in Washington: June 10, 1963." *Public Papers of the Presidents of the United States: John F. Kennedy*. Washington: United States Government Printing Office, 1964. 459–65.

Knebel, Fletcher, and Charles W. Bailey II. *Seven Days in May*. New York: Bantam Books, 1962.

Lane, Mark. *Rush to Judgment*. New York: Fawcett Crest, 1966.

Lasch, Christopher. *The Revolt of the Elites and the Betrayal of Democracy*. New York: W.W. Norton & Company, 1995.

Lasn, Kalle. "USA TM." *Adbusters: Journal of the Mental Environment* 28 (2000): 52–55.

Ledeen, Michael A. *Tocqueville on American Character*. New York: Truman Talley Books, 2000.

Lehman, Karl. *Thomas Jefferson: American Humanist*. Chicago: University of Chicago Press, 1965.

Leuchtenburg, William E. *Franklin D. Roosevelt and the New Deal, 1932–1940*. New York: Harper Torchbooks, 1963.

Lewis, C.S. *A Mind Awake: An Anthology of C.S. Lewis*. Ed. Clyde Kilby. New York: Harcourt Brace Jovanovich, 1968.

Lewis, Matthew. *The Monk*. New York: Oxford University Press, 1998.

Lewis, Sinclair. *It Can't Happen Here*. New York: Signet, 1935.

Mackey-Kallis, Susan. *Oliver Stone's America: "Dreaming the Myth Outward."* Boulder, CO: Westview Press, 1996.

MacPherson, James. *The Poems of Ossian*. Boston: Crosby, Nichols, Lee & Company, 1860.

Magistrale, Tony, and Sidney Poger. *Poe's Children*. New York: Peter Lang, 1999.

The Manchurian Candidate. Dir. John Frankenheimer. MGM Studios, 1962.

Marks, John. *In Search of the Manchurian Candidate: The CIA and Mind Control*. New York: Dell, 1977

Marrs, Jim. *Rule by Secrecy*. New York: Harper Collins, 2000.

Martin, Douglas. "Curt Siodmak Dies at 98; Created Modern 'Wolf Man.'" Obituary. *New York Times*. 19 November 2000: A56.

May, Ernest R., and Philip D. Zelikow. *The Kennedy Tapes: Inside the White House During the Cuban Missile Crisis*. Cambridge, MA: Belknap, 1997.

McPherson, James M. *Abraham Lincoln and the Second American Revolution.* New York: Oxford University Press, 1991.

Medved, Michael. *Hollywood Vs. America: Popular Culture and the War on Traditional Values.* New York: HarperCollins, 1992.

Melville, Herman. *Billy Budd and Other Tales.* 1924. London: Signet Classics, 1998.

———. *Moby Dick.* 1851. Oxford: Oxford University Press, 1998.

———. "The Tartarus of Maids." c. 1850. *American Gothic Tales.* Ed. Joyce Carole Oates. 65–77.

Metropolis. Dir. Fritz Lang. Goodtimes Home Video, 1927.

Miller, Edwin Haviland. *Salem Is My Dwelling Place: A Life of Nathaniel Hawthorne.* Iowa City: University of Iowa Press, 1991.

Moynihan, Patrick Daniel. "The Paranoid Style." *JFK: The Book of the Film.* By Oliver Stone and Zachary Sklar. New York: Applause Books, 1992. 328–31.

Mr. Smith Goes to Washington. Dir. Frank Capra. Columbia Pictures, 1939.

The Mummy. Dir. Karl Freund. Universal Studios, 1932.

Natural Born Killers. Dir. Oliver Stone. Warner Bros., 1994.

Nevins, Allan, and Henry Steele Commager. *A Pocket History of the United States.* New York: Washington Square Press, 1942.

Newell, William H. *Institute in Integrative Studies: Reader on Interdisciplinarity.* Oxford, OH: Miami University Press, 1997.

Nixon. Dir. Oliver Stone. Hollywood Pictures, 1995.

Nosferatu. Dir. F.W. Murnau. Film Preservation Associates, 1991.

Oates, Joyce Carol, ed. *American Gothic Tales.* New York: Plume, 1996.

Oates, Stephen B. *Abraham Lincoln: The Man Behind the Myths.* New York: Harper Perennial, 1984.

———. *With Malice Towards None: The Life of Abraham Lincoln.* New York: Signet Classics, 1977.

Oglesby, Carl. *The JFK Assassination: The Facts and the Theories.* New York: Signet, 1992.

———. *The Yankee and Cowboy War: Conspiracies from Dallas to Watergate.* Kansas City: Sheed Andrews and McNeel, Inc., 1976.

Orwell, George. *A Collection of Essays by George Orwell.* Garden City, NY: Doubleday Anchor Books, 1954.

Padover, Saul K. *Thomas Jefferson on Democracy.* New York: Mentor Books, 1967.

Pepetone, Gregory. "A Fresh Look at the Authentic American Dream." *American Music Teacher.* Vol. 45, No. 4 (Feb./March 1996): 10–13.

Poe, Edgar Allan. *Selected Writings.* New York: Penguin Books, 1967.

———. "The Black Cat." 1843. *American Gothic Tales.* Ed. Joyce Carol Oates. 78–86.

———. "A Descent into the Maelstrom." 1841. *Selected.* 225–42.

Postman, Neil. *Amusing Ourselves to Death: Public Discourse in the Age of Show Business.* New York: Penguin Books, 1984.

Priestley, J. B. *Over the Long High Wall: Some Reflections and Speculations on Life, Death, and Time.* London: Heinemann, 1972.

Remarque, Erich Maria. *All Quiet on the Western Front.* New York: Fawcett Crest, 1956.

Rider–Haggard, H. *Cleopatra.* London: Longmans, Green, and Co., 1905.

Rivele, Stephen J., Christopher Wilkinson, and Oliver Stone. *Nixon: An Oliver Stone Film.* New York: Cinergi Productions Inc., 1995.

RKO 281. Dir. Benjamin Ross. Home Box Office, 2000.

Robin Hood: Prince of Thieves. Dir. Kevin Reynolds. Warner Bros., 1991.

Rosenbaum, Ron. *Explaining Hitler*. New York: HarperPerennial, 1998.

Rowling, J.K. *Harry Potter and the Sorcerer's Stone*. New York: Scholastic Press, 1999.

Ruskin, John. *The Stones of Venice*. 1853. In *Unto This Last: And Other Writings*. Ed. Clive Wilmer. London: Penguin Books, 1997.

Russell, Dick. *The Man Who Knew Too Much*. New York: Carroll & Graf, 1992.

Saint–Saens, Camille. "Danse macabre." *Classics from the Crypt*. New York, 1992.

Schatz, Thomas. *The Genius of the System: Hollywood Filmmaking in the Studio Era*. New York: Henry Holt & Company, 1988.

Schorer, Mark. *William Blake: The Politics of Vision*. New York: Vintage Books, 1959.

Scott, Peter Dale. *Deep Politics and the Death of JFK*. Berkeley: University of California Press, 1993.

Seven Days in May. Dir. John Frankenheimer. Warner Bros. Pictures, 1963.

The Shadow. Dir. Russell Mulcahy. Universal Studios, 1994.

Shakespeare, William. *Hamlet*. 1601. In *William Shakespeare: The Complete Works*. Ed. Stanley Wells and Gary Taylor. Oxford: Clarendon Press, 1986.

———. *Othello*. 1601. In *William Shakespeare: The Complete Works*. Ed. Stanley Wells and Gary Taylor. Oxford: Clarendon Press, 1986.

Shelley, Mary. *Frankenstein*. 1818. New York: Signet Classic, 1965.

The Silence of the Lambs. Dir. Jonathan Demme. Orion Pictures, 1991.

Siodmak, Curt. *Donovan's Brain*. New York: Berkley Medallion Books, 1942.

———. *Wolf Man's Maker*. Maryland: The Scarecrow Press, 2000.

Skal, David J. *The Monster Show: A Cultural History Of Horror*. New York: W. W. Norton, 1993.

The Son of Frankenstein. Dir. Rowland V. Lee. Universal Pictures, 1939.

Sophocles. *Oedipus the King*. Trans. David Grene. *The Complete Greek Tragedies*, vol. 2. Ed. David Grene and Richmond Lattimore. Chicago: University of Chicago Press, 1954. 11–76.

The Spirit of America. Dir. Michael Rhodes. n.d.

Star Wars Trilogy. Dir. George Lucas. Twentieth Century Fox and Lucasfilm Ltd., 1995.

Stevenson, Robert Louis. *Dr. Jekyll and Mr. Hyde*. 1886. New York: Signet, 1978.

Stoker, Bram. *Dracula*. New York, Bantam Books, 1981.

Stone, Oliver, and Zachary Sklar. *JFK: The Book of the Film*. New York: Applause Books, 1992.

Summers, Anthony. *The Arrogance of Power: The Secret World of Richard Nixon*. New York: Viking Penguin, 2000.

Thirteen Days. Dir. Roger Donaldson. New Line Cinema, 2000.

Thomas, Lewis. *Late Night Thoughts on Listening to Mahler's Ninth Symphony*. New York: Bantam, 1983.

Thomas, Tony. *Music for the Movies*. Los Angeles: Silman James, 1997.

Thoreau, Henry David. *Walden and Other Writings by Henry David Thoreau*. New York: Bantam Books, 1962.

———. "Life Without Principle." *Walden and Other Writings by Henry David Thoreau*. New York: Bantam Books, 1962.

Tollin, Anthony. *The Shadow: The Lost Shows*. New Rochelle, NY: Advanced Magazine Publishers, Inc., 1998.

The Tower of London. Dir. Rowland V. Lee. Universal Pictures, 1939.

Twain, Mark. *Huckleberry Finn*. 1885. New York: Signet Classic, 1997.

————. *Pudd'nhead Wilson.* 1894. New York: Signet Classic, 1980.

————. *The War Prayer.* New York: Harper & Row, 1970.

Unbreakable. Dir. M. Night Shyamalan. Touchstone Pictures, 2000.

Van Doren, Charles. *A History of Knowledge: The Pivotal Events, People, and Achievements of World History.* New York: Ballantine Books, 1991.

Vankin, Jonathan and John Whalen. *The Seventy Greatest Conspiracies of All Time: History's Biggest Mysteries, Coverups, and Cabals.* New York: Kensington Publishing Corp., 1995.

Wall Street. Dir. Oliver Stone. Twentieth Century Fox, 1995.

Walpole, Horace. *The Castle of Otranto and Hieroglyphic Tales.* Ed. Robert L. Mack. Vermont: Everyman, 1993.

Watts, Steven. *The Romance of Real Life: Charles Brockden Brown and the Origins of American Culture.* Baltimore: Johns Hopkins University Press, 1994.

Welles, Orson. *The War of the Worlds.* By H.G. Wells. Adapt. Howard Koch. Mercury Theatre on the Air. Rec. 30 Oct. 1938. LP. Evolution, 1969.

Wells, H.G. *War of the Worlds.* 1898. London: Everyman Library, 1993.

West, Thomas G. *Vindicating the Founders: Race, Sex, Class, and Justice in the Origins of America.* New York: Rowman & Littlefield Publishers, Inc., 1997.

Whitmont, Edward C. *The Symbolic Quest: Basic Concepts of Analytical Psychology.* Princeton: Princeton University Press, 1969.

Wilde, Oscar. *The Picture of Dorian Gray.* 1891. New York: Signet Classic, 1995.

Wilson, Colin. *Afterlife: An Investigation.* Garden City, NY: Doubleday & Company, Inc., 1987.

————. *A Criminal History of Mankind.* New York: Carroll & Graf, 1984.

Wise, David and Thomas B. Ross. *The Invisible Government.* New York: Bantam, 1964.

Wolf, Fred Alan. *Parallel Universes.* New York: Simon & Schuster, 1988.

The Wolf Man. Dir. George Waggner. Screenplay by Curt Siodmak. Universal Studios, 1941.

X–Files. By Chris Carter. Perf. David Duchovny and Gillian Anderson. "Grotesque." 2 February 1996.

X–Files. By Chris Carter. Perf. David Duchovny and Gillian Anderson. "Musings of a Cigarette Smoking Man." 17 November 1996.

X–Files. By Chris Carter. Perf. David Duchovny and Gillian Anderson. "Paper Clip." 29 September 1995.

X–Files. By Chris Carter. Perf. Bruce Harwood, Tom Braidwood, Dean Haglung, and Signy Coleman. "Three of a Kind." 2 May 1999.

X–Files. By Chris Carter. Perf. David Duchovny and Gillian Anderson. "Unusual Suspects." 16 September 1997.

X–Men. Dir. Bryan Singer. Twentieth Century Fox, 2000.

Young Frankenstein. Dir. Mel Brooks. Twentieth Century Fox, 1974.

Zinn, Howard. *A People's History of the United States, 1942–Present.* New York: Harper Collins, 1980.

————. *Vietnam: The Logic of Withdrawal.* Boston: Beacon Press, 1967.

Index